The Essence of

KABBALAH

The Essence of
KABBALAH
BRIAN L. LANCASTER

ARCTURUS

ARCTURUS

Arcturus Publishing Limited
26/27 Bickels Yard
151–153 Bermondsey Street
London SE1 3HA

Published in association with
foulsham
W. Foulsham & Co. Ltd,
The Publishing House, Bennetts Close, Cippenham,
Slough, Berkshire SL1 5AP, England

ISBN 0-572-03174-2

This edition printed in 2006
Copyright © 2005 Arcturus Publishing Limited

British Library Cataloguing-in-Publication Data: a catalogue record for this
book is available from the British Library

Printed and bound in Great Britain by William Clowes Ltd, Beccles, Suffolk

*Cover Image: Tree of Life (Stoclet Frieze) by Gustav Klimt (1862-1918), Osterreichisches Galerie,
Vienna, Austria/www.bridgeman.co.uk*

In loving memory of my mother, *Sara Peninah bat Avraham*,
who died 7 Adar 5767, the *yahrzeit* of Moshe Rabbeinu.

. . . and to the feminine in my life.

Contents

Illustrations

Tables

Introduction:
What is Kabbalah?

Defining Kabbalah is not a simple matter. Before we can even proceed to a dictionary, we have the problem of spelling. Does it begin with a *K*, a *C* or a *Q*? And that's just the first letter! This is not a trivial problem, for the plethora of spellings (at least six, and some give two dozen!) is not only a problem of transliteration from the Hebrew original. The diverse spellings reflect the diverse traditions within which Kabbalah has played its part.

Before coming to those diverse traditions, let me clarify the definition that is central to this book. *Kabbalah is Judaism's inner teaching. It primarily addresses the nature of God and the secret meanings of the Torah (the core of God's revelation to humanity). In a secondary sense, Kabbalah explores the deep structure of the mind and of outer reality.* (The meaning of 'Torah' is addressed in Chapter 1. All Hebrew terms are included in the glossary at the end of the book.)

The reason for the diverse traditions surrounding Kabbalah derives from the position of Judaism itself. Judaism is the root monotheistic religion from which are derived the major forces that have shaped much of the modern world. This may seem to be an extreme claim, but when we consider the impact over the ages of Christianity and Islam – both of which sprang from the Judaic core teaching – then the claim may be justifiable. It is not simply that Christianity and Islam have spread monotheism to large parts of the globe. It is also important to recognize the impact of these two religions in shaping modern consciousness. The great philosophical movements that have been responsible for so many of the ways in which we think today arose, or were transmitted, through Muslim and Christian, as well as Jewish, thinkers.

By dint of the widespread influence of the Hebrew Scriptures (the 'Old Testament'), the inner teachings revealing the secrets of those Scriptures have had a broad influence. For example, Jewish teachings on the mysticism of language influenced the earliest phase of the development of Islamic thought. Of especial importance for the diverse forms of Kabbalah in our day was the influence Kabbalah had on Christian thinkers in the early Renaissance. The discovery of a 'new world' of complex ideas about the deeper meanings of Scripture fired the imaginations of these thinkers. Critically, as far as the development of Kabbalah was concerned, this interreligious contact led to the view that the mysticism associated with the Hebrew Scriptures was viable beyond the Jewish matrix within which it had previously been confined. In many ways, this view was a logical continuation of a trend initiated in Christianity's earliest formative period. The teachings which gave rise to Christianity in the early centuries of the Common Era forced an ambivalence towards Judaism: on the one hand, Christian teachings accepted the divine status of the writings that Judaism held as sacred; on the other hand, those same Christian teachings denied that the legal framework of the Torah – the most important of those writings – was binding. In a similar fashion, Renaissance Christian thinkers imbibed the Jewish mystical teachings whilst eschewing the ritual context within which the teachings had been understood in Judaism. This period provided the impetus towards a view that is current to this day, namely, that Kabbalah is not uniquely a preserve of Judaism.

The diverse forms of Kabbalah, with their distinctive spellings, may be traced to these beginnings of the 'Christian Cabala', as it became known. As indicated in my spelling here, the version with a *C* stems from this period. Moreover, the *Q* version may also be traced to this Renaissance connection with Christianity. The form 'Qabalah' is generally used when referring to a version of Kabbalah concerned with magic and the occult. Again, it was the same early Renaissance thinkers who instigated this trend, for they were fascinated with the worldview of magic, which they erroneously thought of as deriving from ancient Egypt. Whilst there clearly are older roots of the occult, the peculiarly 'kabbalistic' form it has taken over recent centuries stems from the Renaissance.

This book is not concerned with *C*s and *Q*s, but with *K*. My interest is with Kabbalah as it has developed, and as it is practised today, *within* Judaism. This is not to imply that I take an exclusivist position. On the contrary, I believe that Kabbalah has much to offer anyone who seeks a viable path of mysticism related to those Scriptures that have helped shape Western consciousness. But I take the view that it is only within its Jewish setting that Kabbalah can be fully understood. Kabbalah is not simply an intellectual, or even 'spiritual', teaching; it constitutes a *way*, a holistic path in life. That holism is broken when it is torn from the religious framework within which it is organically situated. The 'Christian Cabala' is responsible for an unfortunate misperception of kabbalistic teachings, and there is a need to heal the distortions to which that historical chapter gave rise.

Jewish mysticism has a long and complex history, major themes of which I address in Chapters 2 and 3. The phrase I have used above, 'Judaism's inner teaching', is largely synonymous with 'Jewish mysticism'. And, in general, I identify Kabbalah with the broad sweep of Jewish mysticism. However, there are good reasons for maintaining some separation between these terms. Firstly, there is no clear demarcation between mystical Judaism and a supposedly non-mystical religion that goes under the name of 'Judaism'. The essence of Kabbalah concerns its reverence for Judaism's sacred text, the Torah, and the ways in which it attempts to open that text in order to reveal the inner secrets contained therein on account of its divine status. This essence is totally shared with that of Rabbinic Judaism, the *mainstream* path of Judaism that has lasted for at least two thousand years. There is effectively no such thing as 'non-mystical Judaism', and the term 'Judaism's inner teaching' applies across the board. The major kabbalists were all completely infused with the ways of Rabbinic Judaism. Indeed many played central roles in the development of Jewish law, in addition to helping to shape the kabbalistic heritage.

A second differentiation between key terms, this one between 'Kabbalah' and 'Jewish Mysticism', is generally made on account of distinctive characteristics of the former when compared to the earliest phase of Jewish mysticism. Kabbalah is thought of as a specific expression of the more inclusive term 'Jewish Mysticism'. For many scholars, the term 'Kabbalah' refers to a mystical approach, coming to the fore from the twelfth century onwards, which focuses on a specific set of symbols, the *sefirot*, and the *Names of God*. The term 'Kabbalah' also includes meditative, or *concentrative*, practices associated with these symbols. The term *sefirot* is difficult to define (and much of this book is concerned with the task of elucidating their nature), but – put simply – they are the agencies through which God manifests in Creation. They are, at the same time, the principles through which the mystic may come to know the Divine. The infinite, transcendent essence of God is beyond human grasp; the *sefirot* are the vehicles whereby He allows Himself to become known. The term 'Godhead' is often used to refer to these dimensions of the Divine.

Chapters 2 and 3 provide something of a historical overview of Jewish mysticism. In briefly reviewing this history, I have focused on the elements of continuity between Kabbalah today and the mysticism that infused the Hebrew Bible and further evolved over the centuries. This sense of continuity is critical to the view of Kabbalah as a living tradition. Today's Jewish kabbalists see themselves as heirs of a tradition that connects with the word of God, as revealed at Mount

Sinai some 3,500 years ago. A Kabbalah stripped of this sense of continuity is a mysticism largely without heart.

In view of this sense of continuity, many of the principal themes of Kabbalah arise in the context of the historical overview in Chapters 2 and 3. Any reader who may have little interest in purely historical material is warned not to skip these chapters! The themes are explored in more detail in subsequent chapters. Chapter 4, 'Kabbalah and Creation', serves to illustrate the point, for the primary source for all kabbalistic speculation on creation is the opening of *Genesis*, the first book of the Hebrew Bible. Accordingly, in Chapter 2, which concerns the biblical origins of Kabbalah, I briefly discuss the inner meaning of the creation story before presenting a more substantial picture of kabbalistic teachings on creation in Chapter 4. For Judaism, creation as depicted in the opening of *Genesis* is not only a historical event. Rather, the principles of creation are operative at all times. This is asserted daily in the Synagogue Prayer Service, where God is described as 'renewing each day the works of creation'. Moreover, these principles of creation are not only to be found operating in the outer world. A core teaching of Kabbalah is that the human mind reflects the Mind of God and operates according to the principles of creation. The principles may be discerned in the creative processes of the mind, whereby a spark of a thought is born and gestates through stages of mental growth. It is this psychological aspect of creation that makes it so central to kabbalistic teachings. By studying creation, we are not only learning of the ways of God, but also discovering something essential about our own minds. This introduces the critical idea that Kabbalah is not only a tradition of insights into God and Scripture, but teaches about realizing our own potential as well; it is thus a path of transformation.

The Jewish mystical understanding of the Torah is addressed in Chapter 5. The Torah is understood in Judaism as God's blueprint for creation. The stories and injunctions found in the Torah conceal its deeper structure, which reveals everything that can be conveyed about the true nature of God. Kabbalah is a path of connecting with that deeper structure, and Chapter 5 largely concerns the complex ways through which we penetrate beneath the Torah's surface. Like other schools of mysticism, Kabbalah teaches that the whole of life conforms to this pattern: we are confronted with a veil that paradoxically both conceals and reveals the true nature of reality. The mystic is the person who studies and practises in order to grasp that which lies beyond the veil.

Chapter 6 conveys the central role that the Hebrew language plays in Kabbalah. This is the dimension of Kabbalah that sets it apart from other traditions of mysticism. For Judaism, language penetrates to the very core of the divine mystery. Language is the key to everything: it is the agency of God's creativity and it defines the workings of the human mind. Kabbalah is therefore quintessentially a mysticism of language. The Kabbalist uses language to engage consciously with God. Decoding the Hebrew of the Torah is the means to understand God's teaching, and concentrative practices that focus on God's Names align the mystic's mind with the Mind of God.

The ways of meditative concentration are more fully explored in Chapter 7. The everyday practice of Judaism entails study of the Torah, prayer and the performance of actions as commanded by God. Kabbalah brings added dimensions to these forms of practice. Each becomes a means for the Kabbalist to influence the Godhead and bring blessing into the world. Kabbalah sees creation very much as a drama whose script demands participation from the human audience. Kabbalists see their practices as holding the key to that participation.

Finally, in Chapter 8, I consider Kabbalah Today. In some ways, this is the most important chapter, for a Kabbalah that merely recapitulates its past is not truly alive. Kabbalah is a way of knowledge, and, as such, it should be understood within the context of today's world. How does scientific knowledge relate to the insights of Kabbalah? What influence is globalization having on the world of the Kabbalah? In the great formative periods of the Kabbalah, dialogue with other traditions was of considerable importance. During the mediaeval period, for example, Sufism had a significant influence on a number of kabbalistic authors. A parallel to that period may be unfolding today, with the increasing accessibility of Eastern traditions. There can be little doubt that traditions such as Buddhism and Taoism have impacted on Western approaches to spirituality. Kabbalah is not immune to such influences; on the contrary, such influences can help us distil what is central in kabbalistic teachings. A living tradition grows and does not stagnate; it responds to the challenge of diverse inputs into the quest for knowledge; it celebrates the perpetuation of knowledge.

And Chapter 1? Chapter 1 is the beginning, but perhaps it should be the end. Why *this* tradition when the marketplace is full of spiritual delights? What is distinctive about Kabbalah, and why might a sane seeker of truth enter the bizarre ways of Kabbalah? The answer may not be clear from an initial reading of Chapter 1. The suggestions I make as to why Kabbalah constitutes a viable path for today will be informed by the detail of the tradition as covered in the other chapters. And I therefore suggest a re-reading of Chapter 1 at the end.

Hebrew Transliteration

Hebrew letter	name	number	classification in *Sefer Yetsirah*	general transliteration	exact transliteration
א	*alef*	1	mother	Varies – sound of associated vowel	'
בּ,ב	*bet, vet*	2	double	b, v	b
ג	*gimmel*	3	double	g	g
ד	*dalet*	4	double	d	d
ה	*heh*	5	simple	h	h
ו	*vav*	6	simple	v	v
ז	*zayin*	7	simple	z	z
ח	*het*	8	simple	h (pronounced ch, as in loch)	ḥ
ט	*tet*	9	simple	t	t
י	*yod*	10	simple	y if at beginning of word or functioning as consonant; otherwise sound of preceding vowel	y, ı
כּ,כ,ך*	*kaf, khaf*	20	double	k if at beginning of word; otherwise kh (pronounced ch, as in loch)	k, kh
ל	*lamed*	30	simple	l	l
מ,ם*	*mem*	40	mother	m	m
נ, ן*	*nun*	50	simple	n	n
ס	*samekh*	60	simple	s	ş
ע	*ayin*	70	simple	Varies - sound of associated vowel	'
פּ,פ,ף*	*peh, feh*	80	double	p, f	p, f
צ, ץ*	*tsadi*	90	simple	ts	ts
ק	*kuf*	100	simple	k	ḵ
ר	*resh*	200	double	r	r
שׁ, שׂ	*shin, sin*	300	mother	sh, s	sh, s
תּ, ת	*tav (both)*	400	double	t	ṯ

* The last letter given in these cases is a *final letter*. This is the form taken when the letter appears at the end of a word.

The **exact transliteration** is used in cases when the reader may wish to know exactly which letters are intended (e.g., in the case of *gematriot*). Otherwise, the **general transliteration** is used. I generally give the exact transliteration in square brackets.

Chapter 1

Why Kabbalah?

TO SEE THE FACE OF THE KING

Why study Kabbalah? Why would a mature, sane individual become
engaged in the arcane, sometimes bizarre world of the Kabbalah, with its
elaborate systems of ideas, seemingly impenetrable mystical practices,
and complex approaches to the exegesis of the Hebrew Bible? The
answer is simple: Kabbalah is the mystical path for those who seek to
encounter God through an understanding of the secrets that are to be
found within that Bible. Jewish belief holds that God revealed Himself on
Mount Sinai, and the enduring record of that revelation is the Torah, the
first five books of the Bible. Whilst the word *Torah* refers literally to the
five books of Moses, it has a much broader connotation in rabbinic
Judaism and Kabbalah. As the realm of contact between God and
humanity, Torah takes on connotations of the *world soul*, the inner core
of creation and the basis of all Jewish aspirations to know the divine (see
Lancaster 1993).

The kabbalist seeks God through the words of the Torah, and
through the practices that are perpetuated in the oral tradition
associated with the Torah. In a parable given by one of Kabbalah's
primary texts, the *Bahir*, Kabbalah is the path for those who seek to
see the face of the King. Using impeccable logic, the *Bahir* speaks of

those who do not know where the King is. States the *Bahir*: 'First they
should ask the whereabouts of the King's house, and then they should
ask where the King is!' (*Sefer Ha-Bahir* 3).

This parable needs little deciphering (unlike so much of the
imagery employed in the Kabbalah, as we shall discover). The King is
The Holy One, blessed be He, King of Kings – the Divine. The goal of
Kabbalah is to 'see the face of the King'. To anyone with knowledge in
these matters there is no anthropomorphism in this goal. Kabbalah
teaches that the forms we encounter in the everyday world merely
constitute a surface beneath which subtle principles operate. By
'seeing' these concealed levels of activity we begin to become aware of
the real presence lying behind the screen of our own minds. The real
presence, both in the world and in the spark at the root of the mind,
is the Divine, and the kabbalist seeks to know that presence.

In Hebrew, as in English, the term 'face' commonly denotes
'frontage' in general, and therefore implicitly conveys the idea that
something lies behind the face. It is obvious that we 'read' people's
faces for the meaning behind the façade: the subtle allusions given by
slight muscle movements; the pattern of skin folds that reveal the
emotional scaffolding of an individual's life; or the essence that seems
to shine through the eyes. Kabbalah provides the signposts (as well as
the spiritual practices that enable us to notice and read those
signposts) to that which lies behind the surface of things.

To *see the face of the King* is to recognize that 'There is nothing
other than Him' (*Deuteronomy* 4:35). In rabbinic language, God is
both the 'Place of the world' and the 'Master of thoughts' (Midrash,
Genesis Rabbah 68:9; Talmud, *Sanhedrin* 19a) – the face of the King is
to be seen in both the outer and inner worlds. Ultimately, the goal of
Kabbalah is that the individual should come to realize that all pretence
to personal will is illusory. The highest spiritual state is one in which the
ego, or sense of 'I', is recognized as a mere functionary. The 'I' becomes
known as simply a focus of consciousness that accurately perceives its

own nature as nothing more than a channel through which the Divine unfolds. As the authority of 'I' recedes, so the real core of our being, the soul, begins to unfurl its wings and dance in its encounter with the Divine. Kabbalah insists that the soul is a divine spark that seeks to know the ways of God in this world. The Divine is discerned both at the root of the mind and in the world known through the senses.

Why Kabbalah? Because it is a sophisticated system of knowledge that enables us to uncover the depths of the mind and to discern the traces of the divine hand that moves across the stage of history. It is a path to wisdom.

How do we find the 'whereabouts of the King's house'? The beginnings of an answer to this question demand an understanding of the context the *Bahir* provides for its royal parable:

> Why does the Torah begin with the letter bet? In order that it should begin with a blessing [*berakhah*]. . . . There is no 'beginning' other than wisdom, and there is no wisdom except blessing. . . . How do we know that the word *berakhah* derives from the term, *berekh* ('knee')? As it is written (*Isaiah* 45:23), 'For to me every knee [*berekh*] shall bend.' [It refers to] the place where every knee shall bend to Him. To what may these words be related? To those who seek to see the face of the King, but they do not know where the King is. First they ask the whereabouts of the King's house [*bayit*], and then they ask where the King is.

Bet is the second letter of the Hebrew alphabet. Judaism holds that the alphabet is sacred and that deep secrets are to be uncovered both from the letters themselves and from the ways in which they are used in the Torah. Given the superordinate status of the Torah, its first letter is imbued with complex significance. This extract is predicated on numerous rabbinic allusions to the role of the letter *bet* as the opening of the Torah. Here, it is the fact that *bet* forms the initial letter of both *bereshit* (beginning) and *berakhah* (blessing) which becomes the focus for the *Bahir*'s teaching.

In order to explore the allusions in the above extract from the *Bahir*, some explanation of the seminal idea of *Midrash* is necessary. Indeed, most of the key texts of Kabbalah adopt this genre to a considerable extent, and the approach of Kabbalah will remain obscure unless the significance of Midrash is well understood. The term 'Midrash' refers to commentaries on the Hebrew scriptures. The term thus conveys both a body of rabbinic literature and a distinctive approach to scriptural exegesis. The midrashic approach is based on the premise that the divine may be encountered by penetrating into the levels of meaning that constitute the Torah. The Torah establishes the core structure of levels which defines the nature both of mind and of the outer world. In fact, for Judaism the Torah *is* the essence of reality. Study of the Torah is the central religious duty, and is the means for penetrating into the true nature of reality. The key to Torah study is *interpretation*, as conveyed by the term *'derash'* ('explain' or 'interpret'), which is the verbal root of the word 'Midrash'. (The Hebrew language is based on verbal root forms. Frequently, the core meaning of a word is best understood by tracing the verbal root from which the word derives.) Indeed, a cryptic allusion to the centrality of this imperative is found in the Torah. In terms of the overall number of words in the Torah, the exact centre comes between two words in *Leviticus* 10:16: *darosh derash*, meaning '[Moses] intensively investigated'. There is a doubling of the verbal root *drsh*, which, in Hebrew, is the means for conveying intensification of the function indicated by the verb. Here, by doubling the root *drsh* at the literal centre of the Torah, the text conveys the idea that the very existence of Torah is centred on the approach of Midrash – to uncover that which is concealed.

Midrash draws on associations built between Hebrew words, or amongst the letters of the scriptural text, in order to present a meaning that may not be immediately evident from the literal reading of the text. An instructive example is repeated regularly in the Synagogue Prayer Service:

> Rabbi Eleazar said in the name of Rabbi Hanina: The disciples of the wise increase peace in the world, as it says, 'And all your children shall be taught of the Lord, and great shall be the peace of your children' (*Isaiah* 54:13). Read not *banayikh* [your children] but *bonayikh* [your builders].
> (Talmud, *Berakhot* 64a)

This typical piece of rabbinic Midrash is constructed around an apparent redundancy in the scriptural text. The repetition of the word 'children' is unnecessary – the text would have been simpler had it stated 'and great shall be *their* peace'. Given the rabbinic principle that there can be no redundancy in the inspired word of God, Rabbi Hanina informs us that the repetition is intended to convey an additional teaching, namely, that peace is built through the strivings of those who study Torah in all its ramifications. The hook for this central teaching is the punning association between two Hebrew words that are identical in their consonantal form [*bnykh*], that is, 'your children' and 'your builders'.

A Midrash becomes kabbalistic when additional factors come into play. The first of these factors is the experiential dimension. It may be, for example, that the Midrash points towards a state of consciousness achieved through disciplined concentration and/or the use of specific practices. Many forms of kabbalistic Midrash involve a second factor, namely, the use of a distinctive symbol system comprising ten divine emanations, or *sefirot*. (The term '*sefirot*' is plural. The singular is *sefirah*. It is impossible to give a simple translation of this term. For the present, I suggest the English 'number'. However, the reader is advised that I give a more detailed exposition of this term in Chapters 2 and 3.)

Grasping the nature of the *sefirot* is crucial to understanding Kabbalah, and they will feature prominently in the pages ahead. These two factors – the appeal to experience and the inclusion of the *sefirotic* symbol system – largely coelesce, since the *sefirot* carry psychological meaning. Consequently, in Kabbalah, the centrality of mystical experience is always a factor – albeit sometimes concealed – in biblical exegesis. The exegesis may have been inspired through the writer's mystical encounters, and may, in turn, promote the reader's own mystical experience through the distinctive kabbalistic grasp of the biblical text.

For the kabbalist, the Torah cryptically teaches us the nature of these *sefirot* and their interactions. The *sefirot* define the channels through which the impulse originating in the most hidden and transcendent essence of God is given shape and transmitted to the human realm. At the same time, the *sefirot* define the path of mystical ascent towards God. They are envisaged as forming a ladder from earth to heaven, and constitute the steps through which we may develop our spiritual potential.

Later chapters will explore the *sefirot* and their relation to experiential states in more detail. For the present, I wish to return to the above extract from the *Bahir* and its consideration of the letter *bet* with which the Torah opens. In Kabbalah, beginnings are all-important. In asking why the Torah begins with the letter *bet*, the *Bahir* is seeking to convey something of the essence of the Torah. The extract immediately establishes that Torah is identified with wisdom. Indeed the Hebrew root of *Torah* is *yrh* (to teach); Torah is the teaching, and therefore the source of wisdom. From both human and divine perspectives, wisdom is identified with the initial stirrings of an unfolding creative sequence. Wisdom is inextricably bound up with the notion of 'beginning'. From the divine perspective, wisdom contains the seed of creation, the impulse towards a creative plan. From the human perspective, wisdom is the ability to discern the presence of that seed. It is the faculty whereby we might grasp the ramifications of an event or of an idea in its inception, even if these cannot yet be articulated. As we shall note later, sometimes it is *the ability to ask a question*, even though the answer cannot be known, that is indicative of a higher level of mind infused with wisdom. In kabbalistic imagery, wisdom is the unconscious spark of insight that launches a human creative thought. Wisdom (in Hebrew, *Hokhmah*) is the first *sefirah* in the creative emanation from God which becomes active within the immanent realm to which humans have access. It is, accordingly, the highest of the *sefirot* to which humans might aspire in their quest to find God.

Why should the *Bahir* identify the Torah with 'blessing'? In a simple sense this is just one of a plethora of words beginning with the letter *bet*. Clearly, there is something about the idea of 'blessing' that goes to the heart of the teaching that the *Bahir* intends to convey. In Judaism, the notion of blessing is bi-directional, and therefore serves to exemplify the seminal two-way sequence in the *sefirot*. The blessing is both the 'lowering' of God from His transcendent realm that allows Him to engage with the human world, and it is the raising of human consciousness to encounter God on a higher plane. The 'bending of the knee' is not only the human prostration before the Divine, but is also the 'descent' of God into our world in order that we might know Him.

The key that binds the disparate ideas in the *Bahir* extract is the '*House of the King*'. The Hebrew for 'house' is *bayit* [*byt*], identified with the letter *bet* [*byt*]. The 'House of the King', the place where He may be found, is therefore the Torah, which is, as it were, defined by the letter *bet*. Indeed, the *Zohar*, the central text of Kabbalah, draws an explicit connection between God and the Torah: 'The Holy One, blessed be He, is called "Torah" . . . and Torah is nothing but the Holy One, blessed be He' (*Zohar* 2:60a). At the root of this statement is an organismic conception of the Torah, a conception of Torah as a living presence which binds the totality of all that is. Indeed, the Torah is described in the *Zohar* as having 'a head, a body, a heart, a mouth and other organs' (*Tikkune Zohar*, Tikkun 21, 52b). Clearly, this anthropomorphism is not to be taken literally; the meaning becomes evident as the functions of the *sefirot* are decoded from the cryptic allusions in the Torah. Similarly, God is not to be limited by this mystical conception of the Torah. The essence of the Torah plunges into the otherness of the transcendent realm, totally beyond the space-time world that we inhabit. And, in kabbalistic terminology, God is *En Sof* (without end), a term intended to convey the infinitude that is paradoxically both ever-present in the world and yet utterly transcendent.

The midrashic exploration of meanings in Judaism is facilitated by the subsidiary nature of the vowels. In a literal sense the majority of vowels are subsidiary to the consonants in that they are placed below the line of letters. More importantly, sacred writings such as the Torah are 'unpointed', that is, they comprise Hebrew letters devoid of vowels. This introduces a multi-potentiality into the text – a given word could have several meanings. It is this polysemy in the text that is exploited in midrashic exegesis. In the present case, *bayit* (house) is identified with *bet*, the name of the second Hebrew letter. There is much profound symbolism in the Hebrew letters. Kabbalistic allusions frequently depend on aspects of this letter symbolism, which lies at the core of all Jewish mysticism.

The *Bahir*'s teaching is that the first step towards seeing the face of the King is to recognize the Torah as His dwelling place. Once entrance has been gained – that is, when a familiarity with the methods of exegesis has been achieved – one may seek the King directly by mastering the signposts at the secret level of the Torah's meaning.

THE ESSENCE: ISRAEL, TORAH, KABBALAH

The essence of Judaism is to be found in the three terms *Israel*, *Torah* and *Kabbalah*. *Israel* defines a people; not only in relation to the land known by that name, but, as I shall explain, in terms also of the name's historical and spiritual meaning. Clearly, the Torah is the crystallization of the spiritual aspirations of this people. Again, in making this statement I am alluding not only to the outer garment of biblical narrative but also to the inner meaning of a teaching concerned with bringing the divine presence into the life of the people. Finally, what is the place of Kabbalah? The Hebrew root of this word, *kbl*, means 'receive'; a *kabbalah*, *kblh*, is a received tradition. The emphasis on receiving certainly conveys the essence of Judaism. Judaism centres on the revelation at Mount Sinai, by means of which the people *received* the Torah. This is not simply a historical event, for religious Jews believe that the act of studying Torah for its own sake continues to access that spiritual presence which bestows insight into the Torah's true meaning. Revelation is a two-sided contract – God is the giver, and we are the receivers. Kabbalah lies at the heart of this contract. For one truly engaged with the teachings of Judaism, the act of receiving is not merely passive, as if we blindly stand with outstretched hands. On the contrary, we are enmeshed with the Torah, searching out its deepest meanings and striving to live according to its subtle vision of the life of holiness. The more we search, the more our hearts become opened, and the more we can be receptive to the higher teaching.

The opening of the heart is identified with *prophecy*, a state of consciousness to which many kabbalistic practices are directed. The prophetic state is one in which the mystic is open to an influx from a realm beyond the mundane level of the human mind. In the biblical book, *The Song of Songs*, King Solomon writes, 'I am asleep but my heart is awake' (*Song* 5:2). The great Hebrew poet and philosopher Judah Halevi (*c*.1075–1141) comments that this verse alludes to the continuance of prophecy ('my heart is awake') during the period of exile depicted as 'sleep' (*Kuzari* 2:24). For many kabbalists the heart is viewed as an organ of visualization, through which the imagination connects our minds with the sphere of divine influence. I shall explore these kinds of practices in more detail in Chapter 7.

In biblical language, the spiritual function of the heart is obscured by its 'stoniness'. The prophet Ezekiel writes, 'A new heart also will I give you, and a new spirit will I put inside you; and I will take away the heart of stone from your flesh, and I will give you a heart of flesh' (*Ezekiel* 36:26). In Hebrew, the root of the term for prophecy is *neva* [*nb'*], a literal reversal of the word for stone, *even* ['*bn*]. The stoniness must be overcome in order that the heart may achieve its proper spiritual function, that is, as an organ of prophecy.

This idea is connected with a key event in the life of Jacob, the biblical character who is later given the name *Israel*. In *Genesis* 29 we read of the meeting at a well between Jacob and his future wife, Rachel. Kabbalistically, the well represents the waters of the *Shekhinah*, the feminine presence of God, which rise to join in union with the 'waters from above' – those of the male. Imagery concerned with unification, whereby the divisions in both the human psyche and the divine realm of emanation are healed, is central to much kabbalistic thought. The Hebrew for 'well' (*b'er* [*b'r*]) is an anagram of *bara* [*br'*] (to create), alluding to the relation between creativity and the idea of connecting to the source. In the biblical story, Jacob 'rolls away' the stone from the mouth of the well, symbolizing both the future union with his wife and the depth of his encounter with the *Shekhinah*. The stone here depicts a blockage in the channel to the creative source of our lives and to a genuine spiritual encounter; in the imagery of the *Zohar*, it is the 'severe judgement which congeals and freezes water' (*Zohar* 1:152a; 'severe judgement' is *gevurah*, one of the ten *sefirot*). Internally, it is the heart of stone that is to be replaced with a heart of flesh, allowing the divine spirit to be perceived by the heart (Talmud, *Sukkah* 52b).

Why Kabbalah? Because it is the *way of the heart*, a path of encounter that opens the heart-space. The central image of Kabbalah is that of the system of *sefirot*. The whole system is depicted as a *Tree of Life* comprising 32 paths of wisdom, made up of the ten *sefirot* plus the 22 paths that interconnect them. Thirty-two is the numerical value of the Hebrew *lev*, meaning 'heart'. At the same time, *lev* is deeply associated with the Torah, for it is the word formed by connecting its last letter, *lamed* in the word 'Israel' (*Deuteronomy* 34:12), with its first, *bet* (*Genesis* 1:1). This connection is made when its end is linked to its beginning in a never-ending cycle. The Torah is 'a tree of life to those who grasp it' (*Proverbs* 3:18), and it brings nourishment which derives from roots planted in the higher plane of divine wisdom. Learning the ways of the Tree of Life is identified with activating the heart in order that the heart may become a subtle organ of spiritual discernment.

My reference to the numerical value of Hebrew words needs some explanation. Each Hebrew letter is also a number, and therefore every word has a numerical value. This feature of Hebrew is the basis for *gematria*, a hermeneutic device used throughout rabbinic writings and of great importance in Kabbalah. Gematria refers to the idea that words having identical numerical value share some equivalence in their meaning. Thus, for example, 32 is also the numerical value of *kavod* [*kbvd*] ('honour' or 'glory'), suggesting that honour is related to the integrity of one's heart. From a higher perspective, God's *glory* is identified with the integrity of the entire *sefirotic* system, the 32 paths of wisdom.

Historically, the name *Israel* was given to Jacob after he wrestled through the night with a 'man' who turns out to be the angel associated with his adversary, Esau (*Genesis* 32:24–32). In the words of *Genesis,* the name change conveys Jacob's ability to strive 'with God and with men and to prevail'. This powerful narrative intimates the challenge in striving to achieve perfection, another central notion of the Kabbalah. The *Zohar* associates the name *Israel* with completion and with a state of being in which all is balanced and functioning as a whole – again, a function of the heart. The Hebrew structure of the name *Yisrael* [*ysr'l*] alludes to authority and royalty as well as to uprightness before God. In the world of the Kabbalah, Jacob becomes the symbol of the Centre, paralleling the heart's centrality in the body. At the same time, he is also identified as the channel that effects interpenetration of lower and higher levels in the scheme of reality: 'All union between the higher and the lower realms is found in this place which is called 'Israel' . . . And it is the place of faith and perfect union' (*Zohar* 3:96a; the kabbalistic understanding of Jacob is discussed further in Chapter 5).

The essence of Kabbalah is fully conveyed by all that Jacob – and his transformation into Israel – represents. Jacob is identified with truth. The Hebrew for truth is *emet* ['*mt*], a word which comprises the first, middle and final letters of the alphabet. The lesson here is that truth is not merely the absence of falsehood, but the ability to span the whole from beginning to end whilst simultaneously holding firmly to the centre. This idea is succinctly conveyed in a sentence included in the Jewish daily Morning Prayer Service: 'True it is that You [God] are first and You are last; and besides You we have no King who redeems and saves.' The idea of first and last clearly relates to the first and last letters in the word for truth. 'King' relates to the centre, for this is the place from where the authority of kingship is exerted. Indeed, another 'clue' to this idea may be brought from the Hebrew: *melekh* [*mlkh*], meaning 'king', which comprises the central three letters of the alphabet. The point is summed up in the rabbinic maxim which holds that 'God's seal is truth' (Talmud, *Shabbat* 55a; *Yoma* 69b; *Sanhedrin* 64a; Midrash, *Genesis Rabbah* 81:2).

The concern of Kabbalah is with *truth*. It seeks to inculcate an awareness of the true meaning of Torah, understood as its concealed meaning. Indeed, Kabbalah deals with the inner structure of things in general, their true meanings. In the words of the great biblical exegete, Rabbi Moses ben Nachman (1194–1270), known through his initials as *Ramban*, Kabbalah is the 'way of truth'. This is the phrase used by Ramban in his commentary on the Torah when he passes from discussions of the general meaning of the Torah to consider its innermost, kabbalistic meaning. Thus, for example, he writes:

> If you merit and understand the secret of the word
> '*Bereshit*' [the first word of the Torah, 'In the beginning'],
> and why the text does not begin with the sequence of
> words, 'God created in the beginning', you will know that,
> by the way of truth, the scriptural text relates about the
> lower realms but hints towards the higher ones, and that
> the word *Bereshit* alludes to [the *sefirah*] Hokhmah
> ['Wisdom'] which is the very beginning of the beginning . . .
> And therefore the word is crowned by the crown [*Keter*,
> the first *sefirah*] of the letter *bet*.

As I shall discuss in Chapters 2 and 4, the opening chapter of
Genesis reveals the sequence and nature of the *sefirot*. The first verse
intimates the first three *sefirot*, whilst the seven days of creation
described in the rest of the chapter refer to the remaining seven
sefirot. Ramban informs us that the Kabbalah, 'the way of truth',
understands that the word *bereshit* comes first in the Torah because it
alludes to the first two *sefirot*, which actually define the nature of a real
beginning. The term 'crown' traditionally refers to the ornamentation
added on top of certain letters in the sacred scroll of the Torah. Here,
however, Ramban seems to be referring to the 'tail' of the letter *bet*,
which points to the absent first letter, *alef* (see Chapter 4, p. 107).
Ramban is alluding in this context to the meaning of 'crown' as the first
sefirah, *Keter*. As he makes clear, the word *bereshit*, as a whole,
equates to the second *sefirah*, *Hokhmah* (Wisdom).

Only rarely does Ramban's commentary venture into such
kabbalistic areas. Indeed, he explicitly states that it is forbidden to
reveal the secrets of the Torah. Given his use of the phrase 'way of
truth' for the Kabbalah, does it then follow that the greater portion of
his commentary is not 'true'? Clearly, this would be absurd. As with all

biblical commentators in the Jewish tradition, his objective is to direct readers to the correct understanding of the Torah, which reveals truth at diverse levels. There are different *levels* of description and explanation in all areas of enquiry. Consider how we might describe the human body. At one level, we could describe its outer form in detail: the style of hair, general build, and facial expression, for example. At another, if we have the requisite knowledge, we might want to specify the precise arrangement of the DNA code that is the unique determinant of that body. Both descriptions are 'true', but one penetrates to a more profound level than the other. The 'way of truth' in Torah similarly penetrates to a concealed set of core principles, often present in a codified format underlying the appearance of things.

ON KNOWING THE NAME

> There is a further tradition of truth in our hands, namely that the whole Torah is comprised of the Names of The Holy One, blessed be He, for the letters of the words separate themselves into divine Names when divided in a different manner . . . And it would appear that the Torah 'written in black fire on white fire' [Jerusalem Talmud, *Shekalim* 13b] was in this form that we have mentioned, namely that the writing was continuous without breaks into words, and it could be read in the way of the Names . . . In this way, they write the Great Name [in a specific manner] as is practised by the masters of Kabbalah.

This extract from Ramban's introduction to his Torah commentary touches on another of the key ideas of the Kabbalah. He explains that the Oral Tradition, which was received by Moses at Mount Sinai and passed down the generations, conveys an understanding of the Torah directed specifically to knowledge of the

Names of God. In a simple sense, the lack of vowels and the minimal spacing between words in the Torah scroll gives rise to the possibility of divergent readings. In the reading of the text to which Ramban alludes, the entire 600,000 letters of the Torah convey the Names of God. This figure for the number of letters is cited by the *Zohar* (*Zohar Hadash* 74d). It is clearly symbolic, alluding, for example, to the number of souls that were said to be present at the revelation at Mount Sinai. In fact, the actual number of letters is 304,805. Some suggest that the *Zohar* intends that the white spaces between letters should be included in the count. This is not as absurd as it appears, for the spaces themselves convey meaning; hence the tradition that both forms of fire – the black fire and the white fire – are pregnant with potential. However, as Ramban indicates, the idea should not be understood in a simple way, as if it were merely a matter of changing the divisions into words. It is the *primordial* Torah, written in 'black fire on white fire', to which we should aspire in order to understand the role of the Names of God.

The Midrash teaches that the Torah was the blueprint used by God in planning His creation of the world. The Torah is, accordingly, viewed as existing prior to creation. At the root of this teaching is a vision of Torah as a transcendent being, somehow comprising the totality of creation, or the world soul. Clearly, such mystical notions cannot be deciphered by rational logic. Nevertheless, in characteristic fashion, the Midrash addresses a 'logical' problem with the teaching: if the primordial Torah existed before the creation of the world, on what could it have been written?

> On what was the [primordial] Torah written? On [a background] of white fire using black fire, as it is written (*Song* 5:11), 'His locks are wavy and black like a raven'. What does it mean by 'His locks are wavy [*kutsotav taltalim*]'? On each and every jot of the letters [*kots*] there

are heaps and heaps [*tilei tilim*] of legal interpretations.
(Midrash *Tanhuma* (Warsaw) *Bereshit* 1)

What is the fire described here? Clearly, we must overcome any
undue literalism in our explanation, since this fire is itself 'primordial'.
The clue to an understanding of this Midrash lies in the cryptic second
sentence. The similarities amongst several of the Hebrew words are
used to suggest that all features of the 'black' fiery letters are available
for interpretation. The term '*kutsotav*' (hair locks) is interpreted as
relating to features of the Hebrew letters since it shares the same root
(*kvts*) as the term '*kots*' (jot of letters); and the term '*taltalim*' (wavy)
is related to *tilei tilim* ('heaps and heaps' of interpretation) on account
of the shared root *tltl*.

This is not an easy Midrash to grasp in transliteration! I have
included it because it well captures the playful and creative turn in the
rabbinic mind, which is such an important component in Kabbalah. In
the present context, this Midrash serves to illustrate the central idea of
the *multipotentiality* of the text of the Torah. It is this multipotentiality
that is at the core of the teaching about the primordial fire. To express
this in psychological terms, the primordial Torah parallels the
undifferentiated psyche that lies at the core of our being. All the
formed thoughts and images that enter our conscious minds seem to
arise from a 'primordial' core of unconsciousness. Even the sense of 'I'
– the ego that seems to lie at the heart of all our thinking – is,
according to Kabbalah, generated from this inner core of nothingness.
Kabbalah teaches the methods through which that undifferentiated
base to our psychological being may become a channel giving access
to the divine dimension in all things.

It is for this reason that the primordial Torah is identified with the
Names of God. In order to understand this idea, it must first be realized
that the natural driving force of the mind is to give structure to images,
whether they derive from the outside world (as perception) or from the

inner world (as thoughts). It is through this feature of the mind that, for example, the fleeting images on the eyes are translated into meaningful vision. The brain interprets the chaotic neural impulses coming from the senses by imposing order and establishing connections to past memories. Whilst these processes are vital to our everyday functioning in the world, all the principal mystical traditions seem to concur in their view that the processes generate an illusory veil over the true nature of things. In order to achieve our highest potential we must learn to recognize the bias in our perceptions and thoughts. (I have explored these ideas in considerably more depth in my two books on mind and consciousness: see Lancaster 1991, 2004.)

In Kabbalah, the bias in the everyday operation of mind is overcome by focusing on the Names of God. The ineffable four-letter Name (Y-H-V-H) derives from the verbal root *haya* (to be). Grammatically, this Name is a complex form which includes both past and future. One expansion of this Name found in kabbalistic texts is 'He was, He is, He will be,' which yields the numerical value of 72, in turn connecting to another Name of God comprising 72 elements (see Chapter 2, pp. 63-64, and Chapter 6, p. 164 ff). Within these allusions we may focus on two basic ideas: that the Name of God depicts both *being* and the *transcendence of time*. The complex practices deriving from contemplation of the Name lead to an awareness of the undifferentiated core which otherwise remains *unconscious*. In the mystical state, past, present and future seem to fuse as we become aware that there is more to time than appears in normal states of consciousness. Again, I shall present more detail of these practices in later chapters. For the present it is sufficient to note that kabbalists see the four-letter Name as a glyph of the entirety of creation. Central to kabbalistic practice is the phrase, 'I have placed Y-H-V-H before me at all times' (*Psalm* 16:8). This idea is taken in a more literal sense than we might generally expect: whether by visualizing its letters as black fire on white fire, or by complex examination of the associations of its letters, the Name is placed at the forefront of the mind. In this way the Name becomes the superordinate structure in the kabbalist's consciousness, relegating all other thoughts and images to a secondary status.

In attempting to distil the essence of Kabbalah, pride of place must go to the teachings concerning the Names of God. Knowledge of the Names is the path par excellence to the unitive experience of God. Intellectually, understanding the nuances in the various Names of God gives insight into the Divine, for, at this level, a Name is not simply a vague appellation, but conveys the essence of that which is depicted. For this reason, many of the concentrative practices of Kabbalah entail working in distinctive ways with the letters of divine Names.

In this context, it is noteworthy that Rabbi Abraham Abulafia (1240 to after 1291), who left a legacy of detailed practices for attaining the highest states of union with God, specifically referred to his teachings as the 'path of the Names'. Like Ramban before him, Abulafia refers to the Torah as comprising the Names of God. However, whilst Ramban simply alludes briefly to this tradition, Abulafia describes in some detail the practices for exploring the concept meditatively. Essentially, the 'Torah of the Names' takes on real meaning when the kabbalist attains a higher state of consciousness. The practitioner should take individual words and sentences from the Torah and transform them into divine Names. This may be achieved by deconstructing the biblical text into its constituent letters, for 'each and every letter is a name in and of itself' (cited by Idel 1989: 102, from *Perush Havdalah de-Rabbi 'Akiva'*). This is not a simple discursive exercise. Abulafia's methods involve highly complex techniques for working with the letters whilst in a higher state of consciousness. This prophetic state opens a channel for receiving an influx from the Divine and amounts to a state of union with God. Indeed, by means of this practice, the mystic becomes almost Godlike in attaining the ability to 'invent wondrous new innovations' based on creative combinations of letters. In Kabbalah, language is not merely a medium of communication. More fundamentally, the sacred language of Hebrew embraces the very dynamics of divine creation, and is therefore the agent whereby the mystic engages with God.

Why Kabbalah? To put it simply, how can you address someone without knowing their name? Similarly with the Divine: should you wish to 'see the face of the King', then knowledge of the Name is indispensable. There is no need for any intermediary other than this.

THE MASTERY OF SELF

As will become clear in Chapter 3, different aspects of Kabbalah have come to the fore in different ages. In our day, it seems that an interest in psychology has become strong, and it may be that the psychological aspects of Kabbalah will continue to grow in importance. There are undoubtedly many cultural factors that have contributed to the rise of 'self psychology' over the last hundred years. These include the opening of education to a wider segment of society; increased contact with cultures that have differing views of self; more leisure time leading to greater reflectivity; and a growing fluidity over the roles we assume. Richard Tarnas (1991) makes the further point that these cultural changes may themselves be predicated on a deeper *archetypal* shift in our culture, leading to the quest to understand the nature of consciousness itself. In whichever way we try to explain the shift that has occurred, I think there can be little doubt that in our day many are attracted to study Kabbalah for the psychological insights that it conveys.

In some respects the turn towards psychology came earlier within Kabbalah itself than it did within western secular society. Predating Freud by a century and a half, one of the early masters of Hasidism, the Maggid of Mezeritch (1704–42), introduced a concept of the *unconscious*. In the Maggid's thought, the unconscious is both a dimension of the human mind in which thoughts arise prior to their entering the realm of consciousness, and also an aspect of the 'mind' of God Himself. The unconscious is, accordingly, a region of confluence between the mind of man and the Mind of God. It is but a small step from these Hasidic ideas to the contemporary spiritually-oriented psychotherapy in which access to the Divine is viewed as arising through insight into the unconscious.

There is a clear psychological element throughout the history of Jewish mysticism. Indeed, the primary maxim that man is created 'in the image of God' (*Genesis* 1:27) implies that all speculation on the nature of the Divine has implicit reference to the nature of man. Thus, for example, a relationship with human psychology is evident wherever kabbalistic texts discuss thought processes in the Godhead. In the *Zohar*, the stirrings of creation are described in these psychological terms: 'From the midst of thought a desire arose to expand, and it spread from the place where thought is concealed and unknown until it expanded to settle in the larynx.' (*Zohar* 1:74a). The larynx is the source of spoken language and in this passage symbolizes the creative voice of God preparing for the great 'Let there be . . .' of *Genesis*. For our purposes, the key notion in this extract is that God's initial thought, which precedes vocalization, arises in the 'place where thought is concealed'. This 'place' parallels the human unconscious, in which the thinking that occurs is indeed unknown. Whilst the Maggid of Mezeritch may have been the first to write explicitly of a human unconscious, the idea was clearly present in much earlier kabbalistic material. Since the goal of ascending to reach the sphere of this 'unknown thought' (the *sefirah* of Ḥokhmah) was articulated in the earliest kabbalistic texts, the seeds of contemporary spiritual psychotherapy evidently go way back into the annals of kabbalistic lore.

Why Kabbalah? The language of Kabbalah is pregnant with the nascent psychology which exploded into the twentieth century via Sigmund Freud and his many disciples. Kabbalah is a path of insight into the nature of mind, and is a potent vehicle for the transformation of self. It is one of the major sources of western spiritual psychology. As such, it is also potentially dangerous, for its teachings and practices will certainly bring about changes in any serious student. Kabbalah is ruthless in stripping away that which is not real; perhaps for many it is better to be able to hold on to the conventional level of illusion. It is not a simple matter to know the Real . . .

One of the Jewish pioneers of psychoanalysis, Roberto Assagioli, is reported to have stated:

> The base of the spiritual psychology of which I am a supporter . . . is constituted by the biblical affirmations according to which man was made from the image and resembling God. . . . From this basis comes the traditional Jewish teaching of the human psychological constitution consisting of three elements: *nefesh*, *ruach*, and *neshamah*. This represents spiritual elements . . . . My main endeavour has been to give scientific proof of the existence and activity of the spiritual soul (*neshamah*) with the psyche [*ruach*] as an inspiring and unifying factor. (Cited in Kramer 1995: 228)

In kabbalistic thought the three Hebrew terms in this extract constitute levels of the soul. *Nefesh* is the lowest level and might best be captured by the term 'bodymind'. It is the mentality attaching to the vitality of the body – the animal mind. *Ruach* is the mundane human mind, centred on the sense of 'I'. *Neshamah* is the divine soul. It is the guiding light of the mind that directs our strivings to reach a goal dimly intuited. The *neshamah* is a 'portion of God' (kabbalists understand the phrase in the biblical book of *Job*, 'And what is the portion of God from above?' (31:2) as referring to the *neshamah*) and yearns to return to its source. These three levels of the soul are generally depicted in kabbalistic literature as contiguous; they are not three separate souls but part of a larger whole. In particular, the *neshamah* and *ruach* are different levels of the inner being which seeks spiritual nourishment. In our mundane lives, however, we tend to forget the *neshamah*; it may seem that there is only *ruach*, the ego-centred conscious mind.

The importance of bringing the *neshamah* and *ruach* into alignment is detected by the *Zohar* in the word for 'lamp', *ner* [*nr*], in reference to a verse from *Proverbs* (20:27): 'The soul of man is the lamp of God.' The two letters of this word *nr* are the initial letters of *neshamah* and *ruach*. According to the *Zohar*, the word hints at the need to achieve an integration of the two levels of the *neshamah* and *ruach*. The implication is that the lamp can only shine forth when this integration is accomplished:

> The *neshamah* is above and the *ruach* is below and they join together as one, like male and female. When they are united they shine with a supernal light, and in this union they are together called *ner* (lamp). 'The soul of man is the *ner* of God' (*Proverbs* 20:27). What is *ner*? *Neshamah ruach*. (*Zohar* 2:99b)

This emphasis on integration is a primary imperative in Kabbalah. Unification of the levels of the soul is just one dimension of that global process of transformation that is seen by kabbalists as their major task. The challenge is to promote the unification of the entire *sefirotic* structure, symbolized variously in terms of the unification of the divine Name or in terms of the union between the male and female elements within the Godhead. The intention in this regard is exemplified by a prayer said prior to performing one of the *mitsvot* (the precepts enjoined by the Torah): 'For the sake of the unification of The Holy One, blessed be He and his *Shekhinah* with awe and love, in order to unify the name Y-H with V-H in a perfect unity in the name of all Israel, I am prepared and ready to perform this precept . . .'

The name that Assagioli gave to his system of therapy, *psychosynthesis*, suggests that its goals bear comparison with these more cosmological objectives of Kabbalah. As is clear from his words quoted earlier, Assagioli seems to have drawn on the kabbalistic understanding of the divisions of the soul. He posited three realms of the unconscious: a lower unconscious, identified with bodily functions; a middle unconscious dealing with present experiences and their relation to 'I'; and a higher unconscious concerned with intuitive and spiritual functions. Psychosynthesis is directed to the integration of these levels, and especially to forging a synthesis between the personal self and the transpersonal self.

The emphasis on synthesis, and on the psychological means of promoting it, leads to some stimulating parallels between Assagioli's school of therapy and Kabbalah. More than this, Freud's psychoanalytic theory – very much the trigger for all subsequent schools of therapy – displays a number of significant resonances with key themes in rabbinic Judaism and Kabbalah. There is a profound psychological edge to Kabbalah, which gives it especial value in the quest for self-betterment.

HEALING THE WORLD

For all its potential relevance to matters of psychological insight and therapeutic transformation, the real objectives of Kabbalah are considerably larger in scale. The ultimate challenge is that of bringing the dynamics of the Godhead into their proper conformation, thereby promoting *tikkun olam*, the 'healing of the world'. According to Kabbalah, we are players on the biggest stage of all, and its practices of unification are critical for the correct denouement to a drama of cosmological proportions.

The *Sefer Yetsirah*, a highly influential early Jewish mystical text, conveys this point by asserting that the mystic is charged with 'restoring the Creator to His place': 'Ten *sefirot* of nothingness; ten and not nine, ten and not eleven. Understand with wisdom; be wise with understanding. Examine with them and probe from them. Cause a thing to stand on its essence and restore the Creator [lit. the One who gives form] to His place' (*Sefer Yetsirah* 1:4).

As I shall discuss in Chapter 3, the *Sefer Yetsirah* is crucial for our understanding of the term *sefirah*. The *sefirot* are portrayed in this seminal text as ten archetypal numbers which define the parameters of space, time and morality. The first part of the above extract instructs us as to the relationship of the *sefirot* to their transcendent source, described as 'nothingness'. The *Sefer Yetsirah* warns us not to ignore this source, a sin referred to in kabbalistic literature as 'cutting the shoots', for such a wrong view severs the *sefirot* (shoots) from the true source of their existence. Were we to fall prey to this idolatrous ignoring of the transcendent source, we would have counted nine and not ten. On the other hand, it would be equally idolatrous and misguided were we to compromise the absolute transcendence of the source by including it in the count in order to give eleven. This cryptic teaching is one to which I shall return in Chapter 2.

My interest here, however, lies in the latter part of the above extract. What role might be played by humans in the perfecting of the Godhead? The extract continues by instructing us to use the *sefirot* in order to grasp the inner nature of all things – for the *sefirot* are the essential principles on which all things stand. By means of this work, which includes both meditative and intellectual aspects, we do a service to the Divine. The transcendent essence of God is beyond human influence, but the spiritual practices taught by the *Sefer Yetsirah* are viewed as influencing God's relation to the world.

Our task is to discern the inner essences of things, that is, their relation to the *sefirot*. This is the meaning of to 'cause a thing to stand on its essence'. This *in itself* effects the desired connection between the lower and higher worlds. In the scheme of things as presented by the *Sefer Yetsirah*, our ability to discern the essences impacts on the aspect of God involved in forming the world. Different facets of the divine Being come to the fore in different stages of the process of creation. The *Sefer Yetsirah* is concerned with the stage through which the nature of things becomes formed. Indeed, the term '*yetsirah*' means 'formation'. Take the analogy of a potter: following an initial stage during which the essential design of the pot is considered, the clay is formed, or shaped, on the wheel. To what extent can an observer see the initial design reflected in the final form? This is the question that the *Sefer Yetsirah* is asking on a more global scale. To the extent that we are able to detect the operation of the *sefirot* – the initial design – in the diverse forms in which they manifest, we are returning the Former to His place. In this way, we play our part in promoting the harmony of the whole.

These are complex ideas which cannot fully be clarified until we have covered more ground. At this juncture, however, a parallel may be instructive. Let us take the case of a receiving device that must be tuned to receive the signal that is being beamed in its direction. By operating with the *sefirot* as instructed in the *Sefer Yetsirah*, it is as if we are removing the obstacles to the reception of the transmission. In the parallel, the device had been correctly tuned at the outset, but inadvisable human meddling had led to a corruption of its ability to receive the signal. Kabbalah teaches the codes for resetting the device.

The *Zohar* makes this point through an analysis of the verse in *Isaiah* (43:7): '. . . each one who is called by my name; for My glory I created him, I formed him; I have also made him.' The phrase 'for My glory' is interpreted by the *Zohar* to mean that man must effect perfection in the lower realm, for only then will there be perfection above:

> There can be no perfection above without the perfecting influence of humans when they are righteous and act from love. . . . It is for this, for the perfecting influence, that I created him 'for my glory'; that he would perfect it [the glory] with strong pillars and beautify it with improvement

and adornment from below. (*Zohar* 2:155a)

In his monumental work on the *Zohar*, Tishby explains that the 'strong pillars' refer to the unifications effected by human mystical activity within the realm of the *sefirot*. As he writes, 'It is this work that is the real purpose of man's life on earth' (Tishby 1949/1989: 736n120).

Why Kabbalah? It is very simple: we have a job to do. Kabbalah teaches the nature of the task that was entrusted to us, and the means for achieving it. Says Rabbi Tarfon: 'You are not obliged to complete the task; but neither are you free to abstain from it' (Mishnah, *Pirke Avot* 2:21).

Chapter 2

Jewish Mysticism: The Biblical Origins

AN AUTHENTIC TRADITION?

The Hebrew Bible, and most especially the Torah, is the point of reference for all subsequent developments in Jewish mysticism. Kabbalists invariably ground their teachings in the discourse of the Hebrew Bible. Indeed, kabbalistic teachings gain authority largely on account of their perceived place within a biblical tradition that transcends the normal historical process. Situating these teachings within the context of the biblical tradition serves to give them the authority associated with revelation. Rabbinic Judaism holds that all authentic insights into the Torah which were articulated after the original revelation from God at Mount Sinai were themselves included within that revelation. At the outset of the biblical account of the revelation, it is stated: 'God spoke *all* these words . . .' (*Exodus* 20:1). The rabbis explained that the word 'all' here indicates *all* future developments within the *oral* tradition of the Torah. The oral tradition includes the Mishnah, Midrashim and Talmud. Indeed, 'Even the answers to questions that learned scholars are destined to ask their teachers in the future did The Holy One, blessed be He reveal to Moses at that time' (Midrash *Tanhuma* [Buber], *Ki Tissa* 58b). Similarly, authentic expressions of the mystical core of the Torah are viewed as implicit in the word of God spoken at Mount Sinai.

When it comes to the origins of Kabbalah, it is impossible for us to know where truth shades into myth. It is said, for example, that the *Sefer Yetsirah* was taught to Abraham by an angel, which would date its origin to around the eighteenth century BCE. On the other hand, one of the greatest scholars of Jewish mysticism, Gershom Scholem, reasons on the basis of historical evidence that it was composed between the third and sixth centuries CE. Similar problems may be cited in dating the origins of the other two principal texts of the early Kabbalah. The *Bahir* attributes its own authorship to Rabbi Nehunia ben ha-Kahana, who lived in the first century CE, whereas historical evidence would date it to late twelfth-century Provence. Similarly, although historical records attest that the *Zohar* first circulated in thirteenth-century Spain, its authorship is traditionally ascribed to the second-century CE teacher, Rabbi Shimon bar Yohai. The traditional views of the authorship of the *Bahir* and *Zohar* place their composition within the formative rabbinic period in the Land of Israel, where both these sages lived.

There are basically three ways of reconciling these discrepancies. First, the books may have been written at the earlier date, were then passed down amongst secret circles and only emerged for a wider readership later. Second, they may be 'forgeries' in the sense that they were written at the later date, but the earlier authorship was claimed simply to lend them authority. Third, they may be the results of long periods during which their teachings were passed on in oral form only. In this third scenario, the teachings became committed to writing only at the later date, although the key ideas would derive from an oral tradition dating back to the claimed date. The decision to commit such knowledge to writing may have been made only when circumstances required it. The integrity of this oral mystical tradition may have been threatened, for example, by communal strife, or the inroads of diverse cultural influences, or simply through failings of memory.

Whilst it may be difficult to prise apart the above three scenarios, the primary issue concerns the *value* of the teachings. The teachings may be valuable because they are situated within a chain of tradition leading back to the divine revelation, or they may be valuable because their authors were endowed with tremendous depths of spiritual insight. Or these may be two sides of the same coin. At bottom, our interest concerns the extent to which the teachings bring about valuable transformation within the world and within the individual. If, to use a parallel, you want to know whether the vehicle's engine works, you could poke about in the engine compartment for hours, checking all the parts. Alternatively, you could just sit in the driving seat and turn the key . . .

In relation to the Hebrew Bible, two questions need to be answered: First, do we find evidence of continuity between the mystical undercurrents in the Bible and later kabbalistic teachings? Second, how genuine are the claims that kabbalistic writings are essentially *revealing* insights that are intrinsic to the biblical text itself? Were these insights implicit in the Bible's authorship, or are they simply being *imposed* on these biblical texts that happen to be peculiarly open to diverse interpretations? Of course, lying behind these questions is the fundamental issue of the authorship of scriptural works. For Judaism, the very multipotentiality of the text of the Torah is itself viewed as evidence of the divine Hand.

To put it bluntly, if the claim that kabbalistic ideas lie beneath the surface of the Torah is false, then the legitimacy of Kabbalah crashes. We might still find the study of its texts fascinating as historical and intellectual curiosities, but its lifeblood would have been lost. In my approach to the essence of Kabbalah I follow traditional Jewish belief which holds that the Torah comprises the mystical core. At different stages in Jewish history different forms of kabbalistic teachings have been required in order to enable appropriate access to that core. But the essential mystical connection with God, as present in the Hebrew Bible, transcends the historical process.

There are three strands to the kabbalistic tradition. Rabbi Aryeh Kaplan, who did more than anyone in the modern age to make Kabbalah accessible within its authentic Jewish framework, labels these the *theoretical*, the *meditative* and the *magical* (see Kaplan 1982, 1990). It seems to me incontrovertible that essential ideas of each of these strands are indeed present within the Hebrew Bible. I shall consider each in turn.

THEORETICAL KABBALAH

The theoretical Kabbalah is concerned with the inner structure of reality. It is focused on the *sefirot* and their relation to God, to the human soul, and to the angelic beings that inhabit the heavenly hierarchy. The *Zohar*, the primary text of theoretical Kabbalah, interprets biblical events as manifestations of the *sefirot*. For the *Zohar*, the Torah would have little claim to divine status simply as a book of stories and laws. The divine origin of Torah is seen in its concealed treatment of the inner dynamics of the Godhead. From this point of view, and relating to my second question above, the *sefirotic* structure is certainly viewed as being implicit in the Torah and in the Hebrew Bible as a whole.

Figure 2.1 presents the ten *sefirot* in the sequence found in major kabbalistic works. For reasons touched on already in Chapter 1 (p. 42), although there appear to be eleven *sefirot* in the figure, one (*Da'at*) is not actually equivalent in status to the others. The number ten depends on the mutual exclusiveness between the first *sefirah*, *Keter* (crown), and *Da'at* (knowledge). One of these two must be present – hence there will be 'ten not nine', as stated in the *Sefer Yetsirah*; but they are not both present together. The *sefirot* unfold in a creative sequence from top to bottom, as indicated by the arrows. The first in the sequence, *Keter*, is the recondite Will of the *En Sof* (limitless essence of God). As such, it initiates the sequence. However, it does not itself fully enter into the *sefirotic* realm of emanation; once the

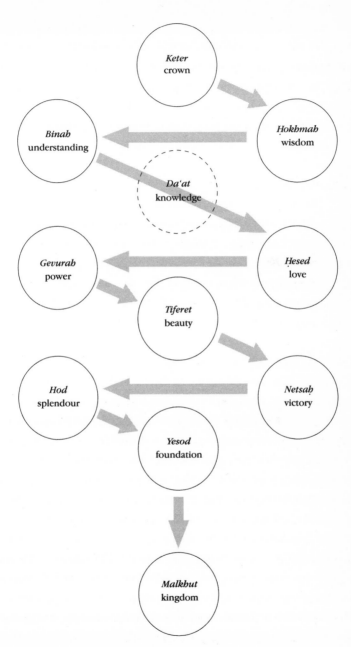

Fig. 2.1. The array of *sefirot* and the sequence of emanation

sequence is initiated by the divine Will, *Keter* withdraws, as it were, back into the infinite perfection of the transcendent realm. It is for this reason that human consciousness can never attain direct contact with *Keter*. Human consciousness simply has no means of access to that sphere. The highest spiritual state is one in which we gain intimate knowledge (*Da'at*) that a transcendent source lies behind all things.

This point is conveyed in the cryptic language of the *Zohar* as follows:

> *Bereshit* ['In the beginning', may be read as] *bet* [the second letter of the alphabet, and the number two] *reshit*, meaning 'two beginnings', because there are two in their enumeration. It is called 'beginning' because this concealed supernal *Keter* is first. However, since it does not enter into our counting, the second is first. On account of this, there are two *reshit*, 'beginnings'. (*Zohar* 1:31b)

By 'enumeration', the *Zohar* is referring to the creative sequence in emanation. The first beginning is *Keter*, but since it immediately withdraws, there is effectively a second beginning in *Hokhmah*. The reference to 'our counting', by contrast, concerns human consciousness, which can never grasp the nature of *Keter*. Therefore, 'the second is first'. In the sequence of emanation, *Da'at* is the confluence of *Hokhmah* (wisdom) and *Binah* (understanding). From the human point of view, *Da'at* is the gateway to the higher intellectual realms of these two *sefirot*.

We find the sequence of 'wisdom, understanding and knowledge' in several biblical sources. In *Exodus* 31:3 it is stated that God filled Betsalel, who is to build the portable Temple ('Tabernacle' or *Mishkan* in Hebrew), 'with the spirit of God, in wisdom, and in understanding, and in knowledge, and in all kinds of workmanship'. The biblical book of *Proverbs* also frequently refers to these three concepts, and we find the specific *sefirotic* sequence in, for example, 24:3-4: 'By *wisdom* a house is built; with *understanding* it is established; and with *knowledge* are its rooms filled . . .'

Can we discern any continuity between the concepts implied by these biblical terms and the complex edifice of meaning placed on them in the Kabbalah? The case of Betsalel is instructive since, in both rabbinic and mystical post-biblical literature, the Temple is regarded as a microcosm, built on the plan of God's original creation. It is therefore appropriate to find the qualities employed in creation mirrored in God's appointed craftsman of the earthly microcosm. Indeed, an allusion to this idea is given in the etymology of the name *Betsalel*, which literally means 'in the shadow of God'. Just as the shadow mirrors the body's moves, so Betsalel reflects the qualities displayed by God as he 'moves' into emanation.

In the Kabbalah, *Ḥokhmah* is viewed as being the initial impulse of design, whereas *Binah* (understanding) is the structuring of that design. The Hebrew *bynh* (pronounced 'binah') is related to *bnh* (to build) and *byn* (between), implying that structure and structural relationships are integral to what *Binah* represents. *Ḥokhmah* might be thought of as the sparking of an idea at the initial stage of a creative process. In order for that spark to lead anywhere, there must be something to catch it and to give it form. This is the role of *Binah*. The design which is formed by *Binah* becomes the basis for the constructive actions of the group of six *sefirot* centred on *Tiferet* (beauty). In the words of *Exodus* 31:3, concerning Betsalel, the role of these six *sefirot* is conveyed by the phrase 'all kinds of workmanship'. *Da'at* is the intermediary through which the design from the higher level is relayed to the six *sefirot* of construction. The *sefirotic* system becomes complete with *Malkhut* (kingdom). For the Kabbalah, the objective of the entire process is that the 'kingdom' and the 'crown' should be in harmony, just as the architect wishes the final building to be a perfect reflection of his initial flash of inspiration at the design stage.

For the present, these descriptions of *sefirot* must remain somewhat abstract. As we proceed, additional ideas and meanings will accrue around the *sefirot*. It is impossible to specify in simple terms the meaning of a given *sefirah*. As the *Sefer Yetsirah* states, the *sefirot* are *beli mah*, '*sefirot* of nothingness'. We grasp at the meaning of a given *sefirah*, yet somehow it seems to slip through our hand. It is only through building a web of associations to the *sefirah* that it may begin to hold its place as a virtual focus at the centre of the web.

The seven lower *sefirot* are cited in a later book of the Hebrew Bible: 'Yours, O God, is the greatness [*Gedulah*], the power [*Gevurah*], the beauty [*Tiferet*], the victory [*Netsah*], and the splendour [*Hod*], for all is in heaven and in earth. Yours, O God, is the kingdom [*Mamlekhah*] . . .' (*1 Chronicles* 29:11). *Gedulah* conveys the meaning of the fourth *sefirah*, *Hesed*. *Hesed* means 'love', and the *sefirah* is equated with the principle of expansion, which is epitomized by selfless love or kindness. Love opens up – or expands – possibilities for oneself and for others. *Gevurah* provides a force to check the expansion of *Hesed*. It is the principle of limitation required in order to control the energy generated from *Hesed*. Power results when we are able to channel energy in precise ways. *Tiferet* arises as the point of balance between the two opposing forces of *Hesed* and *Gevurah*. Beauty is the quality that emerges when all is in balance and functioning as it should. In the overall scheme of *sefirot*, *Tiferet* is the centre of gravity of the whole structure. But it is not merely a passive centre. It has its own function as a force for unification. It divides the entire *sefirotic* structure in two, and functions to unify the upper and lower 'faces' created by this division.

Netsah and *Hod* are lower extensions of the *sefirot* which are vertically above them; they are expressions, that is, of the expansive and limiting principles respectively. A second meaning of the Hebrew word *Netsah* is 'eternity', which perhaps conveys its principle more clearly. This *sefirah* depicts expansion in time, and the 'victory' is the result of long-term perseverance. Related to the noun *Hod* is a word meaning 'echo', and the verbal root means to 'resonate', which gives further insight into the principle represented by this *sefirah*. Resonance gives outer form to the energy within a system. In the case of air entering an organ pipe, for example, the resulting sound is a function of the limitation imposed by the size of the pipe. The term 'splendour' captures the way in which an appropriate application of constraint can enable the potential within the system to shine forth.

The ninth *sefirah* is *Yesod*, which means 'foundation'. In the above extract from *1 Chronicles*, this name is absent. However, later kabbalistic texts detect the principle of operation in the phrase 'all is in heaven and in earth'. 'Heaven' is viewed as referring to the *sefirah Tiferet*, whilst earth is equated with *Malkhut*. *Yesod* is then the channel that functions to align heaven and earth, in which 'all' exists. When the holiness of the heavenly realm shines on earth via this foundation all is as it should be. Using the metaphor of the Tree of Life – a favoured term for the entire *sefirotic* structure – we would say that a strong foundation enables the roots in the earth to reflect accurately the holiness in the branches above. The Hebrew for 'all' is *kol* [*kl*], a union of the letter *kaf*, which completes the first half of the alphabet, with the next letter, *lamed*, which begins the second half. *Kol* (all), alludes to this channel through which the upper and the lower may be united. Symbolically, *Tiferet* yearns to be united with *Malkhut*, but is dependent on the correct functioning of *Yesod* to effect the union.

Finally, in the *Chronicles* verse, 'kingdom' is *Mamlekhah*, which is a direct synonym of the term more favoured in later kabbalistic literature, *Malkhut*. The continuation of the verse is especially instructive: 'Yours, O God, is the kingdom [*Mamlekhah*] and that which raises itself for a head to all.' The last phrase is difficult to translate, but may suggest that some of the complex ideas in later kabbalistic works are already implied in this biblical source. (The King James translation renders the phrase as 'and Thou art exalted as head above all'. Many of the biblical terms and phrases that are especially interesting from a kabbalistic viewpoint are difficult to translate if the mystical intent is not understood. Few translators into English seem to have had such understanding. This phrase serves as a good example, since the King James translation, whilst making sense in general religious terms, is somewhat strained in terms of the actual grammar of the Hebrew original.) Kabbalah suggests that the seeming completion of a creative sequence in *Malkhut* becomes the beginning (cf. 'head' in the *Chronicles* phrase) of a continuing process in a lower world that unfolds from the world of the primary emanation. The concept of multiple worlds is a central teaching of Kabbalah to which I shall return in Chapter 4. For the present, it is sufficient to note this link between the biblical text and the concept of worlds as articulated in later kabbalistic writings.

The claim that kabbalistic ideas are implicit in the mysticism of the Bible is further supported by many numerical and structural features of the biblical text. Numbers that are clearly significant in the Bible have symbolic meanings in Kabbalah that derive from its understanding of the *sefirot*. Thus, for example, where the number seven occurs in the Bible it is understood kabbalistically to refer to the seven lower *sefirot*; the number eight is viewed as indicating transcendence beyond the time-space world of the seven lower *sefirot*; and the number ten is interpreted as referring to the entire *sefirotic* array. Rather than focus on numbers alone, however, I shall elaborate on some of the structural features which seem to indicate that the pattern of *sefirot* portrayed in the Kabbalah is present as an underlying feature of biblical narratives.

In the creation story, for example, the seven days of creation are identified kabbalistically with the seven lower *sefirot*. Not only do the features of each day resonate strongly with the conceptualization of the appropriate *sefirah*, but the structural pattern in the Tree of Life appears to be implicit in the creation narrative. The standard pattern is presented in Figure 2.2. We may note the following parallels between the days and the nature of the *sefirot*. (The reader is referred to *Genesis* 1 and 2.)

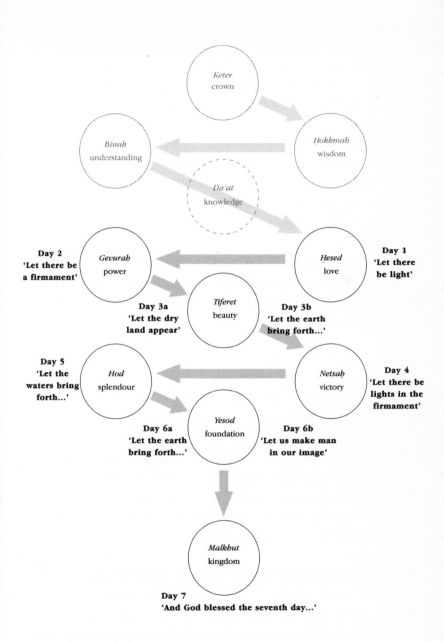

Fig. 2.2. The relation of the seven lower *sefirot* with the days of creation (see *Genesis* 1; 2:1-3)

Day 1: Creation of light. Hesed is the principle of expansion. Light is the example of this principle par excellence, for light cannot but expand to fill any region from its source (with the notable exception of *black holes*).

Day 2: Creation of a 'firmament' to divide the upper and lower waters. *Gevurah* is the principle of limitation. The division brought about by the firmament epitomizes this principle in that it places limits on the expansion of the waters. It delineates realms.

Day 3: A day with two distinct stages. First, the sea and earth are delineated, evidently extending the operation of the previous principle, and, second, the plants of the earth are created. This second stage represents a quantum leap: life is of a different order from what existed in the previous stages. In this sense, life is a new expansion in the creative sequence. These points equate to the nature of *Tiferet*, since *Tiferet* is viewed as comprising elements of both *Gevurah* and Hesed.

Day 4: Creation of 'lights' in the firmament. *Netsah* is a lower expression of Hesed. Since Hesed relates to the general principle of light, it is appropriate that its lower expression is described here in terms of the bodies of light in the sky: the sun, moon and stars.

Day 5: Creation of fish and birds. *Hod* is the lower expression of *Gevurah*, which is associated with generation of the lower and upper 'waters'. On this day, God creates the creatures that populate those realms (the seas and the skies).

Day 6: A day with two distinct stages. First, the animals of the earth emerge, and second, man is created in the image of God. The first stage is the completion of the process initiated on day 3. The second stage indicates another quantum leap. In the worldview of the Bible and of Kabbalah, the human world is of a different order from that of other forms of life. The creation of man is identified with the *sefirah* of *Yesod*, since human consciousness is the vehicle whereby earthly and heavenly realms are united. When humans act righteously, the holiness of heaven is manifest on earth.

Day 7: *Shabbat*, the day of rest. This relates to the *Shekhinah*, the feminine presence of God. The day of 'rest' is a cessation of creative endeavour, in order that we might engage with this sacred presence. *Malkhut* receives the influx from the *sefirot* above. The end of the week is, of course, also the beginning of the next, and the teaching of *Malkhut* is that humankind should recognize the opening for creative dialogue at the spiritual level.

These abbreviated pointers may indicate the extent to which the days of creation embody the *sefirotic* system. Of particular note are the relationships between the days – 1 with 4, 2 with 5, and 3 with 6. These implicitly suggest a structural pattern akin to that of the Tree of Life as given form in kabbalistic works. Indeed, the only simple pattern that would accommodate both the direct sequence from 1 to 7 and the relationships of 1–4, 2–5 and 3–6 is that of the Tree of Life, as presented in Figure 2.1.

Allusions to this structural pattern are also evident in the narrative surrounding the ten plagues that God sent against Egypt (*Exodus* 7–11). In the literal reading of this narrative, these plagues

serve both to 'punish' Pharaoh for his cruelty in refusing to grant
freedom to the Children of Israel, and to persuade him to 'let My
people go'. A deeper reading sees the plagues additionally as a vehicle
for God to demonstrate the structure in a destructive expression of His
presence. In kabbalistic terms the number ten hints that any such
structure relates to the *sefirot*. A close reading of the narrative reveals
a clear threefold structure. Three sets of three plagues are demarcated

Plague	Meeting between Moses & Pharaoh. Is a warning given?	Reason That Pharaoh should recognize...	Human agent for triggering of plague
blood	In morning Moses to meet Pharaoh by river (7:15). Warned	that 'I am God' (7:17)	Aaron – over water (7:19)
frogs	'Go to Pharaoh' (8:1) Warned		Aaron – over water (8.6)
lice	No Warning		Aaron – on earth (8.17)
flies	In morning Moses to meet Pharaoh by river (8:20). Warned	that 'I am God in the midst of the earth (8:22)	None
cattle plague	'Go to Pharaoh' (9:1) Warned		None
boils	No Warning		Moses + Aaron Moses – towards heaven (9.10)
hail	In morning Stand before Pharaoh (9:13) Warned	that there is none like Me in the whole earth (9:14)	Moses – over heaven (9:22–23)
locusts	'Go to Pharaoh' (10:1) Warned		Moses – over earth (10.13)
darkness	No Warning		Moses – over heaven (10.22)
death of firstborn			None

Table 2.1. The threefold structure in the biblical narrative of the
plagues (references are to *Exodus*)

Plague 3: *Kinim* (lice)	*Mem* – 40	*Nun* – 50	*Kaf* – 20	
Plague 6: *Sheḥin* (boils)	*Nun* – 50	*Ḥet* – 8	*Shin* – 300	**358**
Plague 9: *Ḥoshekh* (darkness)	*Kaf* – 20	*Shin* – 300	*Ḥet* – 8	

358

Table 2.2. 'Magic square' of the Hebrew root words for plagues 3, 6 and 9

by three important features in the narrative, as conveyed by Table 2.1. The final plague, being of a different order of magnitude, stands apart from this threefold structure.

The structure can be related to that of the *sefirot*. Given that *Keter* is not to be counted (as noted earlier), the *sefirotic* system comprises three sets of three: *Ḥokhmah*, *Binah* and *Da'at*; *Ḥesed*, *Gevurah* and *Tiferet*; *Netsaḥ*, *Hod* and *Yesod*. However, there is a variety of ways that three groups of three might be arranged. One further feature of the plagues suggests a connection to the typical kabbalistic arrangement. As indicated in Table 2.2, there is a peculiar numerical feature in the Hebrew roots for plagues 3, 6 and 9. When the roots are arranged in a square, the numerical equivalents of the letters give identical sums both vertically and horizontally in the centre. This arithmetic feature only emerges if these three plagues are diagrammatically capable of being related together. If we consider two sets of constraints – first, that the system depicted by the narrative is threefold, and second, that the three last in each set of three (plagues 3, 6 and 9) need to be brought into relationship with each other – a pattern akin to that of the kabbalistic system has to emerge (Figure 2.3).

A more subtle analysis reveals two sequences: the first sequence arises as each plague emanates from God, and a second sequence is given in terms of the execution of the plagues. The first is the sequence shown in figure 2.3. The final column in Table 1, indicating who acted as the agent for triggering the plagues and the realm (water, earth or heaven) involved, suggests a reverse sequence, ascending from lower to higher. That an ascending sequence is involved is reinforced by the fact

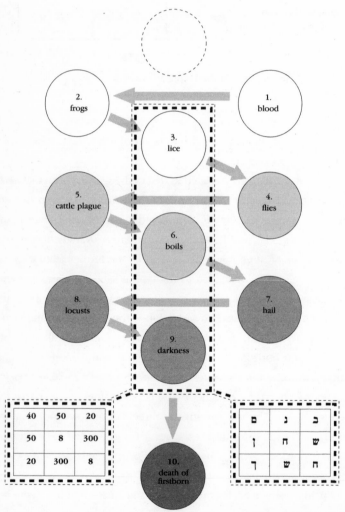

Fig. 2.3. Possible relationship between the sequence of plagues and the *sefirot*

that the Egyptian magicians could emulate the first two plagues only (*Exodus* 7:22; 8:7), suggesting the 'lower' basis of these plagues. Kabbalah accommodates this more complex picture in its notion of 'higher' and 'lower' worlds. The inception of the plagues descends from above to below in the higher world (first sequence), whilst the triggering occurs from below upwards in the lower world (second sequence).

A further point may be gleaned in the arithmetic feature adduced above. The sum is 358, which is the numerical value of the Hebrew *naḥash* (snake). This allusion does seem especially poignant in the context. The snake is a universal symbol of transformation, both for good (as in healing) and for bad (in view of its venom). The whole episode of the plagues concerns a key transformative stage in biblical history, and, of course, the plagues themselves essentially constitute transformations of natural phenomena (water to blood, light to dark, etc.). Moreover, in the *sefirotic* system it is the third member of each triad (*Da'at*, *Tiferet*, *Yesod*) which is typically associated with transformation. In my earlier consideration of the days of creation, for example, it is the days associated with *Tiferet* and *Yesod* that introduce new orders in the scheme of creation (from inanimate to life; from non-human life to human life).

This section has presented detail about the *sefirot* and their relationships. The meaning of each *sefirah* will be further explored in future chapters. The critical idea that has been exemplified through my discussion of the days of creation and the ten plagues is that of the structural plan of the *sefirot*. These aspects of the biblical background to Kabbalah illustrate the consonance between structures encoded in the Torah and the system of *sefirot* as articulated in later kabbalistic works.

MEDITATIVE KABBALAH

God is in His holy Temple; let all the earth keep silence before him.

A prayer of Habakkuk the prophet, according to *Shigyonot*.

O God, I have heard your hearing, and I feared; O God,
revive your work in the midst of the years, in the midst of
the years make known; in wrath remember mercy.
(Hebrew Bible, *Habakkuk* 2:20–3:2)

In the above extract from the prophet Habakkuk, the standard non-
Jewish chapter divisions of the Bible fail to convey the conceptual link
between the first verse and the subsequent two. The first verse is generally
presented as the conclusion to Chapter 2, with 'A prayer of Habakkuk'
opening Chapter 3. When this section is read in the Synagogue, however,
the important link becomes clear, since the reading begins exactly as
above. The earth keeping silence is linked to Habakkuk's prayer.

Silence is the precondition of Habakkuk's prayer. This indicates
the meditative form of the prayer, since silence is universally an
accompaniment of meditation. The major indication of Habakkuk's
meditative intent comes with the word *shigyonot*, however. The
Hebrew root for this word means 'to be absorbed in'. Kaplan draws
on Midrash to suggest that the term is associated with 'the quest for
the spirit of enlightenment and prophecy' (Kaplan 1978: 139).
Becoming fully absorbed, or focused, in the appropriate practice is
the initial stage towards attaining the prophetic state of
consciousness. The successful attainment of this higher state seems
to be intimated by the subsequent phrase: 'O God, I have heard thy
hearing . . .' The phrase indicates the loss of a sense of 'I' as the
subject. Rather there is nothing but God. The human function –
epitomized here by 'hearing' – is nothing other than the action of
God Himself. The individual is but a channel of the divine. Centuries
later, this teaching would become a cornerstone of Islamic mysticism
on account of the saying attributed to Mohammed: 'I [God] become
the hearing with which he hears, the seeing with which he sees, the

feet with which he walks, and the hand with which he touches' (*Hadith*; *Bukhari* 81:38).

The *Zohar* interjects an element here that is associated more generally with mystical states: the reason that Habakkuk 'feared' is that he had experienced death and rebirth. The *Zohar* identifies Habakkuk with the son of the Shunammite woman, who, as recounted in the biblical book of *2 Kings* 4, died whilst a child and was revived by the prophet Elisha. For the *Zohar*, this episode is intimated in Habakkuk's words: the phrase 'revive your work' would be referring directly to Habakkuk himself – he was revived in the midst of his early years.

In Kabbalah, Habakkuk is seen as the paradigmatic biblical mystic. In addition to the above hints about the prophetic state of consciousness discerned in the biblical book named after him, his name is understood as being an allusion to the means though which this prophetic state may be attained. Later, in Chapter 6, I shall discuss the linguistic practices relating to the Names of God that are identified with the path of prophecy. The *Zohar* observes that the name 'Habakkuk' [*ḥbkvk*] is an anagram of the expression 'engraved in him' [*ḥkk bv*]. The word for 'engraved' [*ḥkk*] is employed by the *Sefer Yetsirah* specifically to refer to the initial phase of the mystical practices connected with the Hebrew letters (see Chapter 6, p. 175). Moreover, the Hebrew root *ḥvk* [*ḥbk*] means 'embrace', which is taken to allude to the embrace of Elisha as he revived Habakkuk. In addition, the name 'Habakkuk' is considered to be a codified reference to the sacred 72 Names of God. These Names comprise 72 triple-letter combinations, making a total of 216 letters. This number is the numerical value of the name 'Habakkuk'. These complex associations lead the *Zohar* to state that Elisha revived Habakkuk by mystically using the Hebrew letters:

> Now, when Elisha embraced [Hebrew *ḥbk*] him, he engraved in him [Hebrew of the *Zohar*'s Aramaic = *ḥkk bv*] all those letters of the 72 Names. And the letters of those

> 72 engraved Names are 216 letters. All the letters Elisha
> engraved by means of his breath, in order to revive him by
> the letters of the 72 Names. And he called him 'Habakkuk',
> the name which perfects all sides, and perfects embracings,
> as explained, and perfects the secret of the 216 letters of
> the holy Name. (*Zohar* I:7b)

The implication would seem to be that Habakkuk himself
mastered the mystical practice of using the divine Names, and it was
this that enabled him to reach the prophetic state.

A question posed earlier concerned the extent to which these
kinds of interpretations are implicit in the original biblical text. In this
example, the precision of the allusions, including the phrasing in the
context of Habakkuk's prayer and the many associations with his
name, suggests a deliberate intention by the original author of the
biblical book. In one sense, the integrity of the kabbalistic
interpretations stands irrespective of that intention. Nevertheless, as
remarked earlier, the critical distinction between the perspective of the
outsider, who may be fascinated by kabbalistic 'juggling', and that of
the insider who embraces the Kabbalah as a living system, lies in the
role played by faith. That the Kabbalah simply reveals what had been
intentionally concealed in the Bible can never be fully proved. But it is
a tenet of faith for those who embrace the authentic Jewish tradition.

There are many terms used in the Bible to refer both to
meditative practices and also to the higher states attained through
them. Nevertheless, there is a tendency (exacerbated in the translation)
to present individuals as the passive recipients of an influx of divine
inspiration, as if they were simply chosen by God with no initiative
from the human side. Careful examination of the words used,
however, indicates the active role played by the various biblical
characters themselves in attaining higher states. As in the case of
Habakkuk, they engaged in mystical practices in order to achieve a

state through which God might appear to them. Generally, the correct understanding of the biblical events recognizes a two-way process. Individuals must work on themselves through concentrative and meditative means as a preliminary to being chosen by God for a specific revelation. It is notable in this context that the verb 'to prophesy' in Hebrew is a reflexive form (*hitnabe*), implying that would-be prophets have to do something for themselves in the process of achieving prophetic status. Kaplan (1978: 30) suggests that the prophet 'is focusing spiritual energy into himself'.

The opening of another of the biblical books, that of *Ezekiel*, is viewed in kabbalistic works as a cryptic portrayal of the path to prophecy. Ezekiel is granted a vision of the heavenly realms in which differing orders of angels are seen. Angels are akin to the *sefirot* in that they are considered to be intermediaries between the Will of God and the human realm. Indeed, the Hebrew word *mal'akh* (angel) has as its primary meaning 'a messenger'. This messenger role of angels is a concomitant of the central kabbalistic teaching that there are different worlds. This teaching holds that God's emanation unfolds through four worlds, each of which has its own distinctive quality. These are not worlds separated in space, but realms of reality underpinning our everyday world of experience. Angels fulfil the need for there to be a medium of communication across the worlds. For Kabbalah, even the merest thought which enters the mind seemingly from nowhere is actually an angelic presence. The thought is understood as a communication between the non-physical realm of consciousness and the physical brain. The thought can exist only by dint of the angel traversing the boundary of mind and brain. In this context I should stress that the sentimental and graphic images of angels that adorn Christian religious art actually distract from our ability to understand this aspect of kabbalistic teaching. Essentially, Judaism teaches that nothing happens by chance, and angels are the agents that co-ordinate events behind the scenes of the human realm.

With this in mind, the prophetic state may be understood as one in which the deeper choreography of things is revealed. To continue the psychological tone of the last paragraph, a state of prophetic consciousness is one in which the structuring of the normally unconscious psyche becomes known. The prophet Ezekiel writes: 'And I looked, and, behold, a storm wind came out of the north, a great cloud, and a fire flaring up, and a brightness was about it, and out of the midst of it, as it were the colour of electrum, out of the midst of the fire' (*Ezekiel* 1:4).

To understand this as a description of prophetic consciousness, it is necessary to think of the sentence as describing a sequence of inner experiences. The 'storm wind' is the agitated mind; the 'great cloud' is a depressive obstruction to mystical progress; the 'fire flaring up' is the spontaneous upsurge of imagery in a focused, concentrative state; the 'brightness' is the light that permeates the mind when one transcends the gushing imagery; and, finally, the 'electrum' is the core experience of connection to the divine in a higher state of consciousness. The *Zohar* depicts the stages in this verse as the shells and skins surrounding the kernel of a nut; they constitute the successive layers that one has to penetrate in order to reach the kernel. The kernel itself is identified with the electrum, *hashmal* in Hebrew.

The *hashmal* is a potent focus for much kabbalistic writing. It is experienced through contact with the *sefirah Tiferet*, which becomes the pivotal point in the inner journey towards the upper face of the Tree of Life. The *hashmal* is identified with the ability to contemplate the sacred, supernal letters of the holy Name. It is composed of two component sub-words: *hash*, connected to the Hebrew for 'silence', and *mal*, related to the Hebrew for 'word'. The paradoxical heart of the mystical experience is depicted here as a 'silence of words', a core in which the experience of contact with God is enlivened through the activation of the letters of His Name. At one and the same time it is both linguistic and non-linguistic, for the letters are not those of outer, spoken communication but are employed for an inner transformation of consciousness.

In the biblical vocabulary, transformation is generally conveyed by the more concrete notion of journeying. This is epitomized in the biblical book of *Numbers* where there is a short section, comprising 85 letters, which is set apart from the rest of the book as if with brackets. It reads, 'And it was, when the ark journeyed, that Moses said: Arise, God . . .' (*Numbers* 10:35). The journey of the Children of Israel, guided by God and led by the holy ark, is not simply outer (travelling in the physical desert) but *inner* (journeying to a core experience of the divine). The fact that the section is separated from the rest of the text draws attention to this deeper significance. The very essence of the Torah concerns this inner journey, the path to our spiritual inheritance.

One of the more cryptic of the commentators on the Torah, Jacob ben Asher (known as the *Baal ha-Turim*, 1270?–1340), alludes to a profound connection between this section in the book of *Numbers* and the vision of Ezekiel. The angelic structure conveyed in Ezekiel's vision is understood mystically as comprising a chariot, taken to be the vehicle for exploring spiritual realms. The *Baal ha-Turim* detects codified links between the Hebrew word for 'when [the ark] journeyed' and each of the three terms, *ḥashmal* (electrum), *merkavah* (chariot) and *kise ha-Kavod* (the Throne of Glory). The journey depicted in the Torah's narrative is thereby identified with the inward journey to prophetic consciousness.

The mind can never be stationary; it is of the nature of mind that there will always be dynamic change and movement. When the mind is stilled, through a practice such as meditation, this dynamism of the mind does not *cease*. Rather, the focus is turned away from the superficial ebb and flow of everyday thoughts and towards the deeper bursting forth of the unconscious root of the mind. This is what is implied by the term *ḥashmal*. The root of the mind lies in the *neshamah*, which is our deepest connection to the Mind of God. The ability to open towards that root, as conveyed in kabbalistic teachings about prophecy, entails engaging with paradox. For everything that is taken for granted in a normal state of consciousness becomes disturbed in the *sefirotic* realm:

> [*Hashmal*] goes up and down, for there is no one who can understand it in one place. No eyes or vision can master it. It is and it is not, in one place and then in another place. It goes up and down. In this appearance is hidden that which is hidden and concealed that which is concealed. This is the mystery called *hashmal*. (*Zohar Hadash* 38b, cited in Wolfson 1994: 344)

We even find paradox regarding the gender of the word *hashmal*. The word *hashmal* is a masculine form in Hebrew. However, in *Ezekiel* 8:2 the word recurs, this time as a feminine form, *hashmalah*.

Such paradoxes are indicative of the lower mind attempting to grasp something which can really only be known fully in a higher state. Our everyday world of experience is characterized by distinctions between things – objects are separate; if something is in one place, it cannot be in another; that which is masculine cannot be feminine. Our world of mundane experience is a world of particulars. The higher realm, to which the concept of *hashmal* relates, is undifferentiated; it is holonomic, characterized by unity. Kabbalistic teaching on paradox is akin to the Zen understanding of a *koan*: we must work with it until our mind is able to transcend the normal categories of the mundane world.

MAGICAL KABBALAH

There is no clear boundary between the three branches of Kabbalah. The magical may be defined as that branch concerned with effecting change in the world. However, it is readily apparent that there is considerable overlap with the other two branches, the theoretical and the meditative. It would certainly be an error to think of the teachings of the theoretical Kabbalah concerning the ten *sefirot* as intellectual only. Insight into the *sefirotic* realm is necessary in order that we should play our part in promoting the integration of the *sefirot*. In Chapter 1, I addressed this aspect of the Kabbalah under the heading 'healing the world'. The term 'theurgy' is used to convey this idea that human activity and ritual affects the Godhead. The theurgic objective of rectifying the *sefirotic* realm is presented as being the means for promoting harmony throughout the worlds. In this sense, the theoretical Kabbalah has a 'magical' goal, namely, to change the world. Similarly, there is a necessary overlap between the meditative and magical Kabbalah: it is impossible to engage in so-called 'magical' practices without first attaining the kind of higher state to which the meditative Kabbalah is directed. In a very real sense, the three branches of Kabbalah represent differing emphases drawing from a common root.

The biblical worldview holds that unnatural changes in the world are brought about by divine intervention. Miracles are the business of God, and the human role is to look on in awe. As with prophecy, however, a closer reading implies that human agency plays a role in many of these interventions. An instructive example concerns Jacob and the role he played in ensuring that he would be rewarded with an adequate herd following his twenty years of labour with his uncle, Laban. The story is told in *Genesis* 30. In brief, an agreement was made between the two men that Jacob would receive all the animals that were spotted and speckled. Laban's guile is immediately apparent in the narrative, for it states that he sneaked away any animals that fell into the spotted and speckled category. Jacob then engaged in some activities that seem to have had a magical quality to them. He took staves of poplar, almond and plane trees, and cut the bark such that the staves would have a streaked appearance. He placed these in front of the animals' drinking troughs, with the effect that when the females conceived they gave birth to streaked, speckled and spotted lambs.

As is stated in the next chapter in *Genesis*, this miracle was a consequence of divine intervention. God was ensuring that Jacob received his just reward. Yet Jacob clearly played his part in these events. The *Zohar* states that Jacob's actions were an expression of *Hokhmah* (wisdom). The reference to *Hokhmah* suggests a profound esoteric insight which enabled Jacob to influence the higher spheres, inducing blessings to flow down to lower levels. All worlds are said to be 'watered' by this deed.

According to the Italian kabbalist, Rabbi Yohanan Alemanno (1435–c.1504), Moses similarly 'knew how to direct his thoughts and prayers so as to improve the divine influx' (cited in Idel 1988a: 204). According to this kabbalistic tradition, Moses used prayers, divine Names, words and meditations in order to influence the realm of the *sefirot* with a view to affecting the subsequent emanations from that realm into the world. It was through such means, writes Alemanno, that Moses brought about such miracles as the splitting of the sea and the opening of the mouth of the earth. Whilst the abilities of Moses are clearly in a league of their own, Alemanno presents a view of the whole system of biblical precepts (the *halakhah* as transmitted by rabbinic Judaism) as quasi-magical in nature. The *halakhah* becomes the means for the kabbalist to influence the *sefirotic* realm and thereby to change the course of events in our world.

Inevitably, the boundary between biblical and post-biblical periods becomes blurred. Alemanno articulates a view of biblical magic that is characteristic of the Renaissance perspective of his day. It would be presumptuous indeed to assert that this kind of kabbalistic tradition derives from the biblical period. Nevertheless, in the biblical narrative there are sufficient indications of magical practices that it is possible to envisage some degree of continuity. In addition to Jacob's 'magical husbandry', there is the use of the copper serpent to bring healing from snake bites (*Numbers* 21:5-10) and the examination of the woman suspected of infidelity (*Numbers* 5:11-31). In both these cases, there is evidence of elements of a magical worldview becoming subsumed within the more dominant religious outlook. The genius of Renaissance Kabbalah was that it allowed for the return of a magical perspective within the bounds of the rabbinic tradition.

The single most important feature that unifies the three branches of Kabbalah is the mysticism of the Hebrew language. This feature will concern us throughout the book, and clearly draws on biblical origins. Creation is itself a product of language. This is acknowledged daily in the Jewish Morning Prayer Service with the words 'Blessed is He who speaks [i.e. God] and the world comes into being'. An exoteric reading of the Bible might suggest that the phrase 'And God said, let there be . . .' is simply a convenient way to allude to the divine creative power. This is assuredly not the case according to Kabbalah, however. Language, and specifically the Hebrew language, comprises an esoteric link with the essence of reality. This is why, for example, the creation story includes the assertion that 'whatever Adam called every living creature, that was its name' (*Genesis* 2:19). Interestingly, it is as if God depends on Adam for this function of seeing into the essence of a creature and thereby naming it. The name is presented here not simply as a convenient label but as penetrating to the core reality of any entity. The Hebrew *shem* (name) comprises the identical letters to *sham* (there), implying that the name captures the *thereness* of the entity. The word 'there' brings something into consciousness, makes it real. And, consequently, the power of naming may be thought of as bringing mastery over the created world.

Kabbalah is very much a mysticism of language, for it holds that nothing available to the human realm penetrates to the divine reality to the same extent as does language. As far as the theoretical Kabbalah is concerned, innumerable allusions to the *sefirot* are detected in the Hebrew language and in the narratives of the Torah. The importance of language in relation to the prophetic tradition is exemplified in the case of Habakkuk. Indeed, as will become increasingly clear later, meditative practices generally entail distinctive ways of working with the Hebrew letters and the Names of God. Finally, the magical Kabbalah draws explicitly on what it views as the inherent power in the Hebrew language to influence higher realms in order to effect change in the world. In relation to biblical magical practices, a supernatural role for language is evidenced, for example, in the ritual pertaining to a woman suspected of infidelity (*Numbers* 5). The priest is enjoined to 'blot out' key writings into the potion that the woman is made to drink. The use of language in relation to matters of life and death surfaces in the mediaeval period in one of the most distinctively magical practices in post-biblical Jewish mysticism, the creation of an artificial 'man', or *golem* (see Chapter 8).

The central text that conveys the mystical potency of the Hebrew language is the *Sefer Yetsirah*. This text analyses the Hebrew letters, indicating their correspondences with the different levels of reality in creation. Its essential teaching is that mastery over the core elements of language – the letters – brings the mystic into alignment with the divine Mind. Such mastery entails not only knowledge of the role played by the letters in the process of creation, but also an ability meditatively to imitate God's ways of working with the letters. The *Sefer Yetsirah* may, accordingly, be viewed as the seminal link between biblical and post-biblical expressions of the mystical quest at the heart of Judaism.

Chapter 3

The Rise of Kabbalah

THE PATH OF CREATION

As with the last chapter, my intention is not to present an exhaustive, historical view of Jewish mysticism. In distilling what I conceive to be the essence of Kabbalah, I wish to convey in historical context those themes that I deem to be central to the life of Kabbalah today. These are the themes that are, accordingly, still vibrant for anyone who embraces a kabbalistic vision of the divine and of the potential for transforming oneself into a vessel for transcendent consciousness. Part of the wisdom in Kabbalah concerns the historical process that seems to work beneath the surface of the various epochs of kabbalistic creativity. In this chapter, I convey something of the historical context of the major kabbalistic themes that are revisited in greater depth in the rest of the book.

We do not find the term 'Kabbalah' used in the earliest phases of Jewish mysticism. Nevertheless, the great teachers of Kabbalah from the twelfth century onwards embed their own systems into the context of the first post-biblical stirrings of Jewish mysticism, known as *ma'ase merkavah* (work of the Chariot) and *ma'ase bereshit* (work of Creation). Certainly, the meaning of Kabbalah as a 'received', esoteric tradition applies to these early traditions, for it is stated in the Talmud that 'the work of Creation [may not be expounded] in the presence of two, nor the work of the Chariot in the presence of one, unless he is a sage and understands from his own knowledge' (Talmud *Hagigah* 11b). Implicit in these remarks is the importance of transmitting these traditions through a direct one-to-one encounter, which is a hallmark of the mystical tradition as a whole within Judaism.

In Chapter 2 I alluded to *ma'ase merkavah* in relation to Ezekiel's vision. This was a visionary tradition, in which the 'Chariot' provided the means for journeying in the heavenly realms. Those involved in this quest were known as the 'descenders to the Chariot'. In part this term referred to the characteristic bodily posture adopted: the head was placed between the knees. Additionally, the term seems to reflect a view that the visionary faculty was inferior to the rational intellect. Practitioners of this mystical path were 'descending' into a trance state in which the imaginative faculty was strong. (It is, I believe, no accident that in modern language the *unconscious* is considered as 'lower' than the conscious, it is *sub*conscious. As we shall discover later, the unconscious is a key modern concept for understanding much kabbalistic thinking.) It would seem that Chariot mystics had to learn to harness the visionary faculty without being taken over by it. Such a delicate balancing act – between rigid intellectualism on the one hand and undisciplined fantasy on the other – is a recurring theme in mysticism. As the Talmud indicates (Talmud *Hagigah* 14b), the risks entailed in this balancing act are high: in recounting a story of four who engaged in this form of mysticism, it is related that one became mentally unbalanced, one died, and one lost his religious faith. Only one – Rabbi Akiba – returned unscathed.

Not surprisingly, *ma'ase bereshit* (work of creation) is concerned with the biblical depiction of creation. The central text for this line of mystical speculation is the *Sefer Yetsirah*, which may be thought of as a work critically addressing what lies behind the biblical 'And God said'. How did God use language as an instrument of creation, and how might the mystic emulate His linguistic esotericism?

As we have noted already, the term '*sefirah*' is central to kabbalistic teaching. Texts from the twelfth century onwards use the term explicitly to depict the stages in creation and the differing potencies within God's emanation of His essence. The reason that Kabbalah is deeply interested in the nature of creation lies in this insight concerning the identity between the stages of creation and the forms in which the essence of God becomes enclothed. One may know these forms through an understanding of the stages of creation. In turn, knowledge of the forms by means of which God relates to the world is a key for the mystical goal of attachment to God.

The seminal teaching about emanation and the *sefirot* is conveyed by the opening paragraph of the *Sefer Yetsirah*:

> Through thirty-two mystical paths of wisdom did [the unknowable] engrave *Yah*, the Lord of Hosts, the God of Israel, the Living God, King of the Universe, *El Shaddai*, the Merciful and Gracious, the High and Exalted, the Dweller in Eternity, Whose Name is Holy – He is supernal and holy – and He created His world with three linguistic qualities [*sefarim*]: with text [*sefer*], number [*sefar*] and narrative [*sipur*].
>
> [The Hebrew letter *peh* has two forms, one pronounced 'p' and the other 'f'. Thus, the word *sipur* (narrative) derives from the same root as *sefer* and *sefar*.]

Prior to its analysis of the key Hebrew root, *sfr*, the *Sefer Yetsirah* enumerates ten designations of God. The 32 paths comprise the ten *sefirot* and the twenty-two letters of the Hebrew alphabet. In later kabbalistic works, the twenty-two are understood as the channels that interconnect the *sefirot*. The letters are not conceived as merely linguistic elements in the mundane sense that may apply in other languages. In Jewish thought, the letters are God's agents in the work of creation. For Kabbalah, this means that they become the means for linking one *sefirah* to the next in the unfolding of emanation. The *Sefer Yetsirah* intimates that these thirty-two paths exist primarily in order that we may come to know the divine in all His manifest forms. He, as it were, desires to be known. And it is the mystic's grasp of the *sefirot* that opens the way to the encounter with these diverse forms of the divine, as depicted by His Names.

The *Sefer Yetsirah*'s conception of the *sefirot* is complex and not easily reduced to simple designations of God. In this opening paragraph, the allusions of the Hebrew root are stated in order to portray the qualities of language underpinning reality. In Hebrew, each letter is a textual element (*sefer*), a numerical element (*sefar*), and an element in the construction of narrative (*sipur*). These elements all fuse in the concept of the *sefirot*, and it is this very multiplicity in the essence of the *sefirot* which becomes the key to their understanding. As we shall observe throughout this book, kabbalistic insights are frequently conveyed through gematria, the code which draws on the equation between number and meaning (see Chapter 1, p. 29). Our interest in such equations lies in the specific teaching point being made. Thus, as mentioned earlier, 32 is the gematria of *lev* (heart), and we may discern the important lesson from the *Sefer Yetsirah* that the mystical paths, comprising letters plus *sefirot*, comprise the 'heart of heaven'. Just as the human heart integrates all parts of the body through its circulation of the blood, so the *sefirotic* structure, with its 32 paths, integrates the whole of creation through its interconnectivity across the diverse forms.

Such specific teachings, however, are secondary in importance by comparison with the underlying logic of gematria. The *Sefer Yetsirah*'s reference to the three verbal forms deriving from the common root *sfr* intimates that, in a deep sense, the aspects of language they depict partake of a common core. At the level of reality to which the *sefirot* relate, 'text', 'number' and 'narrative' are inextricably linked. This is the basis for all the linguistic practices in Kabbalah, for the mystic is attempting to elevate his mind to the level of the *sefirotic* reality. The mystical path proceeds from the *relative* world of mundane life to the more *objective* reality of the *sefirot*. The world we know through our senses and reason is characterized by differentiation. In this world, a letter is a constituent of words and nothing more; a number is an independent element of quantity and nothing more; and a narrative is a means of human discourse and nothing more. The *sefirot* depict a higher level which is characterized by the inner harmony of these three elements; a 'more inward' level characterized by deeper meanings. A teaching derived through gematria carries weight, therefore, not simply because it may seem to make a good point, but – more incisively – because it derives from the meaningfulness of the fusion between number, letter and narrative at the higher level of the *sefirot*.

This point is conveyed in a further teaching of the *Sefer Yetsirah*:

> Ten *sefirot* of nothingness. Their measure is ten to which there is no end.

> A depth of beginning, a depth of end; a depth of good, a depth of evil; a depth of above, a depth of below; a depth of east, a depth of west; a depth of north, a depth of south.

> The unified Master – God faithful King – rules over all of them, from His holy dwelling place, until eternity of eternities. (*Sefer Yetsirah* 1:5)

The *sefirot* constitute the inner dimensions of reality. In relation to the mundane level of differentiation we generally recognize four dimensions of space and time. Clearly, these are not the dimensions of which the *Sefer Yetsirah* speaks, for it counts ten dimensions. Again, we must understand that the *Sefer Yetsirah* is interested in a higher world – the world of the *sefirot* – which is characterized by *meaningfulness*. Our connection with that world is through consciousness, and consciousness itemizes one thing at a time. If we want to become aware of the vertical dimension, we first focus on 'above' and then on 'below'. There are therefore eight dimensions of space and time. The additional two again confirm that we are dealing with the dimensions of meaningfulness and not of mundane reality. 'Good' and 'evil' are crucial for defining the 'space' within which meaning unfolds. This is not a matter of dogmatic morality, but simply an acknowledgement of fact. The most fundamental basis of mind entails labelling stimuli as 'positive' or 'negative'; all mental meaning is dependent on this. In Buddhist teaching this is clearly recognized, for in analysing the tiniest processes of the mind, it is asserted that the initial reaction to any stimulus – prior to recognizing its form and meaning – is the judgement as to whether it is agreeable or disagreeable.

In Kabbalah, the good–evil axis is applied to the 'distance' between the *sefirot* and their root in *En Sof*, the limitless essence of the transcendent God. *Keter* is the closest to the root, being the first arising of the impetus to manifestation, and is therefore designated as 'good'. *Malkhut* is the furthest in the ray of emanation from *En Sof*, and is accordingly depicted as 'evil'. The *sefirah* of *Malkhut* is not intrinsically evil. Indeed, it is equated with the feminine presence of God, the *Shekhinah*, which is understood as the pivotal point for all human spiritual progress in coming to know the divine. The notion of evil arises to the extent that *Malkhut* may become separated from its higher source. In later Kabbalah, this idea became crystallized in the idea that the *Shekhinah* is in exile from the higher divine essence. This *divine* exile parallels the exile of the Jewish people as a whole from its own land of Israel, and is a mystical transformation of the rabbinical view that the *Shekhinah* accompanies the Jews in their exile from that land. In this mystical formulation, the *Shekhinah* queen yearns to be re-united with her kingly consort, the divine emanation of *Tiferet*. Many aspects of kabbalistic practice are directed towards fostering this divine marriage and thereby bringing about a reintegration of the entire Godhead.

The *Sefer Yetsirah*'s concept of the moral axis of good and evil ramifies throughout the kabbalistic understanding of human conduct: ultimately that which raises human consciousness towards its divine source is good, whereas those acts and thoughts which increase the separation from the divine root of consciousness are evil. In later chapters, the *Sefer Yetsirah* builds on this axis in defining the meaning of all the letters in relation to the human soul.

In kabbalistic tradition the teachings of the *Sefer Yetsirah* are not simply intended for intellectual analysis alone. They are interpreted as providing cryptic instructions for practices that embed our consciousness in those teachings. Most of these practices relate to the linguistic esotericism that is central to the text as a whole (see Chapter 6). The depiction of the *sefirot* as dimensions is itself a call to engage in a contemplative practice. By means of this practice the mind is trained to explore each dimension to its furthest extent, that is, to a state beyond the words that give us an initial understanding of each dimension. It is worth noting in this context that the word used for depth in each dimension, *omek*, is equivalent by gematria to the Hebrew *devir* (each gives a total of 216). *Devir* is the term used for the Holy of Holies in Solomon's Temple (e.g. 1 *Kings* 6:16). This term derives from the root *dvr*, meaning 'word' (and for this reason is sometimes translated as 'oracle'). The Holy of Holies was the resting place of the Ark of the Covenant, which was the lasting testimony of the revelation of God. The use of the word *devir* in this context expresses the important idea that the deepest teaching (the Torah) takes the form of language but, in depicting the ineffable source of meaning, the language of the Torah transcends the normal bounds of language. It is this connotation of going beyond the normal meaning of words that is relevant to the practice of working with the dimensions enumerated in the *Sefer Yetsirah*.

The practice based on the above paragraph of the *Sefer Yetsirah* entails consciously building up a deep sense of your place in relation to the dimensions. We begin with 'depth of beginning'. You could ask yourself: what first triggered the situation in which you presently find yourself? As the mind arrives at answers (perhaps you are reading this book because a friend thought you would be interested), continue by dismissing the idea that the answer might be definitive and final; there is always a further root (what is it about you that might have led the friend to think you would be interested; where did that quality in you develop from, and so on?). When you can no longer put the answer in words (perhaps some ineffable intimation of a root in your soul), begin to move forwards in time. What seem to be the likely consequences of your immediate situation? Again, continue to go beyond the immediate answers and stretch the bounds of your mental representations. In relation to the depth of good, the question to address concerns that which connects you to the larger whole – to God. And, for evil, what leads to a sense of disconnection? Always, you must stretch the bounds of the answers which pop into the mind. The practice continues with the first of the six directions of space. What is immediately above you? Air . . . the ceiling . . . other rooms . . . the roof . . . birds . . . sky . . . vastness of space . . . the infinite that cannot be formed in the mind . . . It is as if you generate a beam of light from within that is gradually extended further and further whilst maintaining your awareness of the centre, the heart as the source of light . . . And then continue into the remaining directions. You may glimpse your inner core suspended at the heart of a web of infinite interconnections.

Ultimately, the objective is a level of insight into the nature of the *sefirot*. The *sefirot* are themselves infinite and constituted of 'nothingness', yet, paradoxically, comprise the highest form of meaning available, being the expressions of God as symbolized in His Names. The practice is intended to lead you to experience a sense of meaning that can only be described as that of witnessing your own self as a centre within a network of interconnections which plunge into an infinite nothingness. As we have seen, the *sefirot* are the dimensions which define that network of interconnections.

In Chapter 7, I shall describe some kabbalistic practices that underpin the form of prayers in the regular Jewish Synagogue services. It is worth noting in relation to the practice just described, that making conscious connection with the dimensions is a preliminary to recital of the *Shema*, the fundamental declaration of the Unity of God in Jewish liturgy. In Kabbalah, this declaration is focused through immediate personal experience of unification. It is only through consciously unifying the dimensions, as indicated in this *Sefer Yetsirah* text, that one may effectively witness the essential Unity of God. The 'higher' unity and the 'lower' unity are intimately interrelated.

THE HEART OF KABBALAH

The substantive content of mystical thought that has become synonymous with the term 'Kabbalah' down to the present day became systematized during the twelfth and thirteenth centuries. There were two flourishing centres of Jewish mysticism during this period: one in Provence and Spain, and the other in northern Europe. Whilst some of the interests of these two groups were similar, for example, in understanding the potencies through which the Godhead finds expression, and in bringing a mystical meaning to the act of prayer, there were also important differences. The differences may, in part, be accounted for by the intensity of persecution that arrived with the crusades in northern Europe. The writings of these northern European mystics are characterized by a kind of *darkness*. They tend to emphasize renunciation of worldly behaviour: the authors seek a state of equanimity in all things, and assert the value of sacrificing oneself as a 'sanctification of the Name' (of God). In addition, some of the more magical developments of Jewish mysticism were present in this school. For example, Rabbi Eleazar of Worms (known as the *Rokeach* after the title of one of his major works, *c*.1165–*c*.1230), one of the most important of this group of mystics, gives a detailed account of the magical ritual for creating a golem, itself a somewhat isolationist strand in mysticism. I shall discuss the golem ritual in Chapter 8.

A more optimistic outlook seems to have dominated during this period in the southern centre, as evidenced in the two most important texts of the mediaeval Kabbalah, the *Bahir* and the *Zohar*. Both these works are characterized by a creative and speculative outlook. They develop a rich system of symbolization in their depiction of the *sefirot* and the ways of human engagement with the divine. Theirs is a dazzling world of poetic dialogue that draws the reader into a challenging quest to decipher the secrets to which they point.

The *Bahir* first circulated towards the end of the twelfth century in Provence, and the *Zohar* is first documented about a hundred years later in Castile, Spain. The *Bahir* continued the tradition portrayed in the *Sefer Yetsirah* of envisioning the dimensions through which God manifests in the world. Like the *Sefer Yetsirah*, the *Bahir* employs astrological symbolism in its formulation of this 'structural' picture of divine influence. In one parable, for example, God is depicted as having a beautiful fountain from which He distributes water to the twelve tribes of Israel by means of twelve channels. This equates to the standard astrological picture of the sphere of the zodiac as divided into twelve regions, or 'houses', through which 'higher forces' influence the world. Kabbalists note that the four letters in the sacred Name of God (Y-H-V-H) can be permuted in twelve different ways, indicating that the emanation divides into twelve regions of influence. The *Bahir* sees this astrological process as focused in the priestly role described in the book of *Exodus*. Aaron, the priest, wears the sacred Name on his forehead and its influence descends through the twelve stones set into his breastplate, which represent the twelve tribes.

For the *Bahir*, the astrological picture becomes incorporated within a new image, that of a *tree*, which introduces the major image of the tree of *sefirot* that became central for much later kabbalistic speculation. The *Bahir* conceives of a structure comprising twelve diagonal boundaries, which is subsumed within the image of this tree. The tree comprises the 'ten powers of The Holy One, blessed be He, one above the other' (*Bahir* 85). These ten powers are of course the *sefirot*, a term for which the *Bahir* finds a biblical origin in the verse, 'The heavens declare the glory of the Lord' (*Psalms* 19:2). The word 'declare' (*mesaprim*), comes from the root *sfr*, whilst 'glory' (*kavod*) has the numerical value of thirty-two. The verse seems to be esoterically indicating that the *sefirot* define 'the heavens', namely, the structure of thirty-two that constitutes the intermediary region between God and the world.

The *Bahir* identifies the first *sefirah*, 'the highest crown' (*Keter*), with holiness. This holiness becomes the root of the tree, depicted by the letter *shin* (first letter of the word, *shoresh*, 'root'). The root is, as it were, at the top, for this tree draws from the highest in order that it might distribute the divine influx – symbolized as water – to all. Therefore the holiness is next described as a oneness that adheres to all the other *sefirot*. This path of influx is paralleled at the human level, since, according to the *Sefer Yetsirah*, the letter *shin* is associated with the head. The three branches of the *shin* draw from the holiness above in order that the spiritual elixir may become focused in the brain and from there be distributed throughout the body. This association between the letter *shin* and the head is given ritual expression in the head *tefillin*, a leather box containing scrolls worn during Morning

Prayers. Two versions of the letter are embossed on the head *tefillin*, one on the left and one on the right.

The *Bahir* elaborates on the nature of the ten *sefirot*. The first *sefirah*, *Keter*, is the supernal crown, depicted by the first letter, *alef*. The whole purpose of creation is that we should direct our awareness to recognize that 'He is the Unity of Unities, unified in all His Names' (*Bahir* 96). Paradoxically, *Keter* cannot be known conceptually, yet the purpose of Kabbalah is to grasp the unity that underlies all manifestation. The *Bahir* makes this point by quoting a line from a psalm repeated in the daily Morning Prayer service: 'Know that the Lord is God, He made us, and we are to Him' (*Psalm* 100:3). Although the simple meaning of this verse suggests the translation that 'we are His' (i.e. 'to Him'), the key Hebrew word *lo* is written *lamed-alef*, effectively meaning 'to *alef*' (the meaning 'To Him' would be correct were this word written *lamed-vav*; both forms of spelling have the same pronunciation). Mystically, the verse is stressing the imperative for us to direct our awareness to the *alef* – oneness – that underlies all manifestation, by recognizing that what may manifest as two different Names is, at the very core, simply One ('the Lord is God').

In the *Bahir*, the second and third *sefirot* are identified with different aspects of Torah. *Ḥokhmah* is the primordial Torah that God employed at the beginning of Creation. It represents the ground plan of all that is. *Binah* is described as the 'quarry of the Torah', for it is the 'place where The Holy One, blessed be He, quarries all the letters of the Torah and carves them with spirit and with them makes forms' (*Bahir* 96). This cryptic phrase is alluding to the transition from the primordial Torah, in which the letters are as yet unformed, to the Torah comprising letters that convey meaning. The emanation of God associated with *Binah* (Elohim) is described as the One Who brings forms into being, and this is achieved through the intermediary agency of letters, as taught in the *Sefer Yetsirah*.

The fourth *sefirah* (*Ḥesed*) is described as the right hand of God, through which His merits and benevolence pour into the whole world. The fifth (*Gevurah*) is 'God's great fire', the left hand of God. The sixth (*Tiferet*) is the 'Throne of Glory', a term intended to convey God's role as King in relation to His creatures. Just as the ideal king brings a constructive balance between stern judgement and compassion in his dealings with his subjects, so the Throne of Glory depicts God tempering the rigour of *Gevurah* with the merciful presence of *Ḥesed*. Fire is thus balanced with water.

These two elemental qualities of fire and water are conveyed in the Hebrew word *shamayim* (heaven), a word which combines *esh* (fire) and *mayim* (water). Whilst these elements depict antagonistic forces in our world, the Hebrew teaches that at the higher plane intimated by 'heaven' opposites do coexist. The *Bahir* makes this point by applying the biblical verse 'He makes peace in the heights' (*Job* 25:2) to its discussion of heaven. In most kabbalistic works 'heaven' is identified with *Tiferet*. However, the *Bahir* adopts a complex perspective in which the boundaries between the sixth, seventh and eighth *sefirot* (*Tiferet*, *Malkhut* and *Yesod* respectively) are fluid. The seventh is described as 'nothing other than the sixth', and about the eighth the question is asked, 'For what reason is it called the eighth; is it not the seventh?' (*Bahir* 103, 105). It should be noted that the sequence of *sefirot* enumerated in the *Bahir* differs from that given in the *Zohar* and other kabbalistic sources of the period. For the *Zohar*, *Netsaḥ* and *Hod* are the seventh and eighth *sefirot*, whereas their equivalents in the *Bahir* are ninth and tenth. The reason for this difference would seem to be the emphasis the *Bahir* places on the role of *Malkhut* as the centre, the Temple 'which raises them all' (see below).

The key to understanding the fluidity between the three *sefirot* of *Tiferet*, *Malkhut* and *Yesod* may be found in the rabbinic view of the *Shekhinah*. The Rabbis held that the *Shekhinah* withdrew by stages from the intimate relation She had enjoyed both with the higher dimension of God and with the Jewish people in the heyday of the Temple in Jerusalem. Indeed, the Temple is viewed very much as the point of confluence between these three – the Transcendent face of God, the *Shekhinah*, and the Jewish people. This threefold union is the state to which kabbalistic endeavour is directed, and the *Bahir*, accordingly, focuses on the re-establishing of such a union. Whilst there are indeed three separate *sefirot*, each in its own way may be a vehicle for the presence of God – as depicted by the *Shekhinah* – to be restored to Her rightful place. The sixth is the divine throne, depicting the higher aspect of God which must lower Itself – by, as it were, sitting on the throne – in order to engage with the lower beings. In addition to being labelled 'heaven', the seventh is said to be the place of the Holy Temple, the place *par excellence* where 'above' and 'below' are unified. The eighth is the human agent for this unification, namely the *tsadik*, the 'righteous person', who is described as upholding the whole world. The concept of righteousness is that of perfection, since such a righteous person has no sin that would cloud the flow of divine energy. The righteous person is 'beloved and dear above and beloved and dear below' (*Bahir* 105) since he or she is the pure channel through which the desire of 'above' for 'below' and vice versa may be realized. He or she is the 'foundation [*Yesod*] of all souls', since the alignment above and below is the reason that souls come into the world.

In the ideal state, then, these three *sefirot* are intimately aligned, thereby enabling a harmonious link between the human level and that of the divine Being on high. The *Bahir* holds that the key to this link lies with the nature of thought, as becomes clear in the continuation of the above extract dealing with the sixth and seventh *sefirot*:

> Is it the seventh? It is surely nothing other than the sixth.
> But this teaches that here is the Holy Palace [Temple]
> which raises them all [i.e. all the *sefirot*]. It is therefore
> counted as two, and is, accordingly, the seventh. What is it?
> It is thought that has neither end nor object. Similarly, this
> place has neither end nor object.

This emphasis on thought is characteristic of much kabbalistic writing. The seventh *sefirah* is identified with *Shabbat*, the seventh day, and the biblical injunction to 'guard' the *Shabbat* is understood by the *Bahir* to mean refraining from vain thoughts. Thought that has neither end nor object may be understood as the state of pure consciousness to which certain mystical practices are directed. 'Where is the Holy Palace?' asks the *Bahir*, 'It is in thought, and that is *alef*' (*Bahir* 48). Whilst restoration of the holy Temple in Jerusalem is a national concern to be instituted by God, the individual kabbalist can, through concentrative practice, promote the desired alignment with the higher realms. And, ultimately, the state of pure consciousness effects communion not only with the divine throne, but also with the very root of the Tree, the *alef*.

These two themes (amongst many others), namely the dynamic interactions between the *sefirot* and the deep role of thought, are elaborated at greater length in the third great kabbalistic work, the *Zohar*. The quest to bring *Tiferet*, *Yesod* and *Malkhut* into alignment becomes the *Zohar*'s central concern, and is elaborated through various symbols. Pre-eminent amongst these is that of sexuality, whereby the king (*Tiferet*) is reunited with his bride, the Queen *Shekhinah* (*Malkhut*), through the channel of his foundation, or sexual organ (*Yesod*).

The erotic imagery of the *Zohar* constitutes one of the major developments from that used by the *Bahir*. In the latter, the favoured image to depict the need for unification amongst the *sefirot* is that of the king and his 'good, beautiful, fair and perfect daughter':

Is it possible that this king would leave her? You would say
that it is not. Is he able to dwell with her all the time? Again,
you say that it is not possible. What can he do? He places
a window between himself and his daughter and whenever
the daughter needs her father or the father his daughter
they unite together through the window as it says, 'All
glorious is the king's daughter inwardly, her garment is
interwoven with gold' (*Psalm* 45, 14). (*Bahir* 36)

The need for a window is discarded in the eroticism of the *Zohar*. A
typical passage reads:

Come and see! It is written, 'A river goes forth from Eden
to water the garden' (*Genesis* 2:10). This river overflows
its side when Eden unites with it in perfect union through
that path which is known neither above nor below, as
you would say, 'The path which no bird of prey knows'
(*Job* 28:7). They are found in a state of intimate union,
for they are never separated one from the other. Then
fountains and streams go forth and crown the holy son
with all these crowns, and then it is written, 'The crown
with which his mother has crowned him' (*Song of Songs*
3:11). At that moment the son inherits the portion of his
father and mother and he delights in that pleasure and
cossetry. It is taught: When the supernal king sits among
the royal luxuries with his crowns, then it is written:
'When the king was on his couch my spikenard gave forth
its fragrance' (*Song of Songs* 1:12). This is *Yesod*, which
issues blessings to unite the holy king and the queen.
Then blessings are bestowed upon all the worlds and the
upper and the lower realms are blessed. (*Zohar* 3:61b-
62a)

The intimate union between Eden and the river depicts the relationship between *Ḥokhmah* and *Binah*, the 'supernal father and mother' in the language of the *Zohar*. The efflux from this union descends to *Tiferet*, 'the holy son', who is then stimulated to take up his role as king and unite with his queen (*Malkhut*). In this way, the river is able to 'water the garden' – understood as another symbol of *Malkhut*.

This theme of unification, which is central to the entire corpus of the *Zohar*, entails two additional features. Firstly, as indicated at the end of the above passage, the union between king and consort has beneficial effects throughout the created realms. The complex dynamic of intra-divine activity is important because it determines the flow of 'blessings' throughout the worlds. The second feature is the *theurgic* imperative. It is human endeavour that provides the key stimulus for the desired unification within the *sefirotic* realm. The mystic is not some passive reader of the complex drama being retold by the *Zohar*. He or she is a key central player, whose actions will determine the drama's course and outcome. The *Zohar* situates its worldview firmly within the orbit of rabbinic Judaism, and it holds that it is the performance of the prayers and rituals of observant practice that promote the intra-divine marriage. Above all, study of the Torah – the primary injunction of Judaism – brings about the desired union:

> How precious is the Torah before The Holy One, blessed be He, for whoever studies the Torah is beloved above and beloved below. The Holy One, blessed be He, listens attentively to his words and does not forsake him, neither in this world nor in the world to come. And he should labour in Torah by day and by night, as it is written, 'You shall meditate on it day and night' (*Joshua* 1:8) . . . The reason for studying by day is readily understandable; but why by night? It is in order that the holy Name should be perfected by him. (*Zohar* 2:46a)

Those studying Torah are beloved above and below because they bring about the union between above and below. 'Day' refers to *Tiferet*, and night to *Malkhut*. This study therefore brings about the union of these two *sefirot*, as is further intimated in the last line. The four-letter Name depicts the full array of *sefirot*: the *yod* is *Hokhmah* (with the initial point of the *yod* indicating *Keter*); the first *heh* (a letter that indicates the feminine in Hebrew grammar) is *Binah*, the 'supernal mother'; the *vav*, whose number is six, comprises the six *sefirot* centred in *Tiferet*, which emanate from *Binah*; and the final *heh* is *Malkhut*, the *Shekhinah*. In this scheme, the perfecting of the Name means that the initial *yod* and *heh* should be unified with the lower *vav* and *heh*, which is only achievable when the *Shekhinah* is united with the king.

Those engaged in the mystical study of Torah (i.e. study 'by night') are intimately involved in this divine scenario, for the mystical striving in Torah is intended to unite them with the *Shekhinah*:

> Come and see. All those engaged in [the study of] the Torah are bound to the Holy One, blessed be He, and are crowned with the crowns of Torah. They are beloved above and below. . . . How much more so those who are engaged with the Torah at night, for they establish it [Torah]! This is so because they are joined with the *Shekhinah* and they are united as one. (*Zohar* 3:36a)

Kabbalah, and especially the Kabbalah of the *Zohar*, brings a whole new meaning to the notion of intention in the performance of religious injunctions. The mystic's intent is bound up with a complex cosmic drama. It is not enough to regard religious duties as binding simply because God has ruled it so. The deeper reason for Jewish practice, articulated in the *Sefer Yetsirah* as the need to 'restore the Creator to His place', has become highly elaborated into the dynamic *sefirotic* drama, as most richly portrayed in the poetic style of the *Zohar*. Contemplation of this intricate drama becomes the cornerstone of the conscious intent that should be brought into all religious practice.

The second theme I shall briefly introduce here is that of the mystical role of *thought* as portrayed in the *Zohar*. The central teaching which legitimizes the psychological impact of Kabbalah becomes a major pillar of the *Zohar*'s world of symbolism. This is the teaching of correspondence between 'above' and 'below'. All that exists in our world has its counterpart on a higher plane, and the higher and lower forms have an intricate symbolic relationship to each other. There is a 'lower' Temple and a 'higher Temple', a lower court and a higher one, and man is the 'lower world' created on the pattern of the 'upper world'. The *Zohar* portrays the emanation that originates in the most concealed aspect of God as taking the form of different 'faces', or *partsufim*, as it proceeds through the levels of creation. The higher face is termed *Arikh Anpin* (literally, the 'long face') and the lower is *Zeir Anpin* ('short face'). As these terms imply, there is considerable anthropomorphism in the discussion of the *partsufim*. They have 'brains', noses, ears, beards, etc. These anthropomorphisms provide a vehicle for the *Zohar* to explore the most recondite aspects of the Godhead. The principle of correspondence underpins these discussions, for all human systems must be symbolic reflections of the workings at higher levels in the *sefirotic* system.

As was already clear in the teaching of the *Bahir*, thought becomes the ultimate realm of connection between human and divine. Just as any human action has its instigation in thought, so too God's creative actions originate in thought.

> When it arose in thought before the Holy One, blessed be He, to create His world, all the worlds arose in one thought, and by means of this thought were they all

created, as it says, 'In wisdom You made them all' (*Psalm* 104:24). By this thought, which is *Hokhmah* ('wisdom'), were this world and the world above created. . . . All were created in one moment. And He made this world corresponding to the world above, and everything which is above has its counterpart here below, and everything here below has its counterpart in the sea; and yet all constitute a unity. (*Zohar* 2:20a)

The emanative sequence of the *sefirot* begins with God's innermost thought, which is identified with *alef*:

From within the concealed of the concealed, from the beginning of the descent of *En Sof* [*Keter*], radiates a faint light which is unknowable, concealed in recesses like the point of a needle. It is the mystery of the concealment of thought [*Hokhmah*], unknown until a light extends from it into a place of tracings [*Binah*], from where all the letters go forth. (*Zohar* 1:21a)

The human parallel to this depiction of the root of divine thought is the unconscious, in which the initial stirrings of our thoughts lie hidden.

In another of the *Zohar*'s images for the development of thought, *Binah* becomes the larynx, where the budding thought becomes linked with the potential emergence of language. This seems to provide a parallel to the role of language in shaping human unconscious thought into the formed thought that is known in consciousness. The implicit challenge addressed to the reader by the *Zohar* is that of reaching towards the higher recesses of human thought. The correspondence between the human mind and the minds of the two *partsufim* in the Godhead is focused in this notion of the process of thought. The mystic encounters the divine through an opening of the concealed roots of his or her own thought.

The *Zohar* is a highly complex work, with an elaborate array of symbols that extends far beyond these brief illustrations. Moreover, its genius draws on a subtle exegetical technique that derives layer upon layer of insight from the biblical sources lying at its heart. To study its pages is to be drawn into a profound encounter. Whilst it includes allusions to mystical practices, the *Zohar* is not a manual that the aspiring mystic might search for instructions. It is not a recipe book! Its mysticism is of a finer order than this, for it weaves a tapestry of meaning through which the inner nature of the divine becomes a resonant presence. The mystical quest towards union with the divine is promoted by the mystic embracing the symbolic language through which the inner life of God is conveyed. At some point, it is no longer an externalized encounter; the mystic's own inner life becomes entwined with that of the divine.

THE UPWARD PATH

Probably the most influential work specifically on the *sefirot* is *Sha'are Orah* (Gates of Light) by the Spanish Kabbalist, Rabbi Joseph Gikatilla (1248–c.1325). The gates of the title are the *sefirot*, which are described in ascending sequence, beginning with *Malkhut* and finishing with *Keter*. This differs from the approach of the *Zohar*, which invariably portrays the *sefirot* in descending order. This is not a trivial point of distinction, for it would seem to reflect Gikatilla's interest in the upward path, the mystic ascent towards union with the divine. As Gikatilla remarks in his introduction, his interest lies in transmitting to the reader the ways in which God wants us to reach the light emanated through the *sefirot*. It is therefore appropriate in this context to think of the *sefirot* as *gates*, for they are the openings through which we encounter the different emanations of God on the path to enlightenment.

Gikatilla had been a pupil of Abulafia, whose works explore the quest towards union with God more extensively than other early kabbalists. In one of his works, Abulafia cites the reason for giving the upward sequence of *sefirot* as being that 'every branch will return to its root and will be united with it, and every spiritual [entity will return] to its essence and will be linked to it, "and the Tabernacle will become one" (*Exodus* 26:6)' (Weinstein 1994: xxvii). The Tabernacle is understood mystically as a microcosm of the whole created order, in the same way as man similarly is a microcosm. The verse from *Exodus* refers to the way in which the curtains were to be linked together to make the Tabernacle. There were ten curtains and 50 loops and hooks. Kabbalists interpret the ten curtains as alluding to the ten *sefirot*, and the 50 golden hooks as referring to the '50 gates of *Binah*', a classical kabbalistic expression intimating the relationship between the 'supernal mother' (*Binah*) and the lower female (*Malkhut*, the *Shekhinah*). The meaning is that the microcosm is brought fully into alignment with the macrocosm when the *sefirot* are unified, an achievement that depends on human contact with the essence of all the *sefirot*. This contact is achieved through the mystical path of climbing the ladder of the *sefirot*.

Two complementary strands of Jewish mysticism are rooted in the initial statement in the *Sefer Yetsirah* concerning the 32 paths of wisdom. These 32 paths comprise the ten *sefirot* and the 22 letters of the Hebrew alphabet. Given the authority of this text, all kabbalists must recognize the essential place of both the *sefirot* and the letters, as is intended by the *Sefer Yetsirah*. Nevertheless, differences in emphasis are evident amongst different formulations of Kabbalah. Abulafia's approach downplays the role of the *sefirot* by comparison with their absolute centrality for the author of the *Zohar*. Abulafia criticizes the approach of accreting symbols around the *sefirot*, a tendency that is strong in the *Zohar*. Whilst the *Zohar* is practically encyclopaedic in its coverage of the major themes of

Jewish mysticism, its emphasis lies on the many biblical symbols for the *sefirot* and on the role of normative Jewish practice (i.e. prayers and *mitsvot*) in promoting their unification. Abulafia's concern is that the multiplication of symbols may obscure rather than clarify the true nature of the *sefirot*. It is worth noting in passing that much contemporary study of Kabbalah is highly reminiscent of this trend that was criticized by Abulafia seven hundred years ago.

Abulafia's path of Kabbalah places less emphasis on the *sefirot* and more on the role of the letters. His is a distinctive path of language mysticism, in which pride of place is given to working with the Names of God. In Abulafia's scheme, complex practices involving concentrative working with the Hebrew letters and divine Names are directed towards achieving a higher state of consciousness – the 'prophetic state'. He considers that this state will generate a more direct knowledge of the *sefirot* than the drier, intellectual approach which explores *sefirotic* symbolism. The goal of Abulafia's *Path of the Names*, as he called it, is to receive a divine influx which itself derives from the *sefirotic* realm. The desired union is not so much an ascent to a higher realm as a state of exceptional receptivity in which the divine influx transforms the mystic's consciousness. Writing of the physical experience associated with this transformation, Abulafia states:

> . . . you shall feel another spirit awakening within yourself and strengthening you and passing over your entire body and giving you pleasure, and it will seem to you that balm has been poured over you from the crown of your head to your feet, once or many times, and you shall rejoice and feel from it a great pleasure, with gladness and trembling. (Cited in Idel 1988b: 76)

In Abulafia's approach, the *sefirot* become more direct features of experience. This is illustrated, for example, when he notes the equivalence by gematria of the two words *sefirah* and *mahshavah* (thought) – each word has the numerical value of 355. He writes, 'Every thought is a *sefirah* according to the secret of computation and number' (cited in Wolfson 2000: 138). The *sefirot* are the ten separate intellects that function to connect human thought with its divine source:

> This path of Names is of such a profundity that in the profundities of human thought there is no one thing more profound and more excellent than it, and it alone unites human thought with the Divine [Thought], to the extent of human capability, and according to human nature. And it is known that human thought is the cause of his wisdom, and his wisdom is the cause of his understanding, and his understanding is the cause of his mercy, and his mercy is the cause of his reverence to his Creator; and his fear is the cause of his beauty, and his beauty is the cause of his victory, and his victory is the reason of his splendor, and his splendor is the cause of his essence, which is named Bridegroom, and his essence is the cause of his Kingship, named his Bride. (Cited in Idel 1995: 229)

The idea of the *separate intellects* is found in *The Guide of the Perplexed* written by Maimonides (*Rambam*, 1135–1204). Abulafia made a close study of this work, attempting to distil its mystical import. Rambam drew on Aristotle's metaphysics in presenting the separate intellects as the realms through which God's pure intellect overflows in its path towards the human intellect.

Abulafia identifies thought with *Keter*, and views his techniques for working with the divine Names as the means for uniting human thought with its ultimate source. The remainder of the above extract indicates how the divine root then flows through all the *sefirot* which become aligned by means of the power of thought. For Abulafia, the *sefirot* are more explicitly internalized than we find in the *Zohar.*

This internalization of the *sefirot* is complemented by Abulafia's teaching of practices that lie outside the sphere of normative Jewish religious action. As I shall explore in Chapter 6, the linguistic and concentrative practices taught by Abulafia are explicitly intended to bring about an altered state of consciousness. From this perspective they carry a sharper psychological edge than we find in the more theosophical approach of the *Zohar*. Both strands represent major articulations of the roots of Kabbalah that we find in the *Sefer Yetsirah*. Their respective strengths add to the richness of the overall mystical path of Kabbalah.

REVITALIZATION AND POPULARIZATION

The *Zohar* rapidly took on quasi-canonical status within Judaism. To the present day it remains the most important source of mystical lore in Judaism. Its influence was given added weight by the revitalization of kabbalistic thought that occurred in the Israeli town of Sfat in the sixteenth century.

A small group of highly-influential kabbalists had gathered in this town and adopted a pietistic, mystical lifestyle. Many of the group were from families who left Spain following the edict of expulsion in 1492. The mountainous terrain of the region of Sfat was reminiscent of their Spanish past, and the area had an added attraction in that it housed the tomb of the reputed author of the *Zohar*, Rabbi Shimon bar Yohai. Of especial significance for the development of Kabbalah was the coming together of Rabbi Moses Cordovero (1522–70) and Rabbi Isaac Luria (1534–72), universally known as *ha-Ari*, (the Lion). The strength of the former lay in his intellect; his writings give perhaps the clearest systematizations of kabbalistic teachings of all time. Luria's impact, by comparison, lay in his qualities as an inspired visionary. The fact that these two geniuses represented two distinct poles of Kabbalah seems to have been decisive in igniting the community of Sfat. The enormity of Luria's achievement is evident from the fact that, despite living only two years in Sfat before succumbing to a plague, it is *his* teachings that became the principal legacy of the kabbalistic revival of the time.

Lurianic Kabbalah presents a powerful *storyline* which brings the systematisation of kabbalistic teaching to life. Instead of a somewhat rarefied presentation of the *sefirot* as the emanations of the unknowable source, Luria gives us a cosmic melodrama that has the power to draw us intimately into the overall divine scheme. In the process, he provides an accessible language for integrating otherwise highly obscure features of the *Zohar*'s symbolism.

Luria's storyline begins with the *very beginning*. He adopts the key term '*tsimtsum*' (contraction) to convey how the very first dynamic of creation arose. How was it that a motionless totality of divine wholeness and sameness – an absolutely perfect unity – became disturbed, and thereby began a process that eventuates in the creation, as portrayed in the book of *Genesis*?

> When it occurred in His simple Will to create the worlds and to emanate the emanations and to actualize the completeness of His actions and His Names and appellations, for this was the reason for His creation of the worlds . . . then the Infinite contracted Himself into a central point which is truly in the centre of the light, and that light was contracted and withdrew to the sides around the central point. Then an empty place remained with air and empty space. (R. Hayim Vital, *Ets Hayim* I. Luria wrote down none of his teachings. R. Vital was his most influential scribe .)

The teaching of *tsimtsum* is predicated on the notion that the pure Will of *En Sof* desired to be known, not for His own benefit, as it were, but for the good of those creatures that would know Him. This is the purest expression of the will to give that is of the essence of *En Sof*. This potential act of giving requires a self-limitation, for nothing can arise without a dynamic of difference. The contraction of *En Sof* left a vacated space into which shone a single ray of light from the remaining light of *En Sof*. This ray of light carved in the vacated space the form of *Adam Kadmon*, the primordial Adam, which is the archetypal form of all creation.

The second major strand in the Lurianic narrative concerns the further development of this ray of light. Luria taught that the light burst forth from the eyes of *Adam Kadmon*. The initial intent was that the light would be gathered in the *sefirotic* vessels whose purpose would be to channel the light into the further development of creation. The vessels were, however, unable to hold the light and they shattered. The second strand in the narrative is, then, *shevirat ha-kelim*, the 'breaking of the vessels'. Fragments of the vessels, together with some of the light from *Adam Kadmon*'s eyes, fell down in the created hierarchy. This is the primary catastrophe of creation. It is effectively a consequence of the primordial *tsimtsum*, for *tsimtsum* required a force of limitation (contracting the light), which is the progenitor of evil and judgement. Ultimately, there is nothing other than God, and therefore there is no source of 'evil' other than God. The necessity for a limiting of God's light, as portrayed in the teaching of *tsimtsum*, brought the potential for evil. It was the excess of judgement deriving from the primordial *tsimtsum* which became responsible for the inability of the vessels to hold the light.

This catastrophic situation is to be resolved through the third major strand of Lurianic Kabbalah, *tikkun* (rectification). *Tikkun* is the process through which the elements of light may be purified from the shards of evil with which they fell as a consequence of the breaking of the vessels. The human role in this cosmic narrative arrives here in the process of *tikkun*. Humans are the primary beings in the lower realm of the created worlds where the admixture of good and evil has to be finally clarified. It is a human responsibility to effect this clarification in order that the light might be restored to its source. It was the breaking of the vessels that sundered the relationship between the male divine principle (focused in *Tiferet*) and the female principle of the *Shekhinah*. *Tikkun* is the process whereby the union is to be re-established. In Lurianic Kabbalah, the path which promotes this cosmic *tikkun* entails correct practice of the *mitsvot* that define normative Judaism (which has become 'Orthodox Judaism' in our day). In addition, Luria introduced numerous meditative *yihudim* (unifications), designed to promote this rectification of the divine harmony.

The Lurianic narrative began to reach a mass audience only when it was disseminated by the leaders of the modern Hasidic movement. Modern Hasidism begins with Rabbi Israel Ba'al Shem Tov (1700–60), the 'Master of the Good Name', generally known by his acronym, the *Besht*. Amongst the important features of this movement is its use of story-telling as a teaching implement. Despite its highly esoteric details (especially in its treatment of themes from the *Zohar*), the Lurianic 'story' comprises key themes with which the mass of European Jewry could readily identify. Hasidism enabled its adherents to recognize the important role they played in the cosmic drama simply by adhering to the practices of their religion; intense intellectual work was not necessary. Hasidism further introduced a much longed-for emotional dimension into what had seemed to many an overly arid path of intense learning. (In passing, it should be noted that post-Holocaust Hasidism has developed a rather different outlook in which more traditional study is encouraged.)

In many ways eighteenth-century Hasidism represents a democratization of Kabbalah. It is paradoxical, then, that perhaps its most distinctive departure from earlier forms of Jewish mysticism concerns the role of the leader, the *Tsadik* or *Rebbe*. Traditions that developed around the *Tsadik* are distinctively non-democratic. This is evident in both the dynastic passing on of leadership and in the talismanic role that the *Tsadik* came to play. Traditionally, the righteous person, or *Tsadik*, was viewed as a conduit for the channelling of the influx from the *sefirotic* realm into the world. The cult of the *Tsadik* as it developed in Hasidism added to this mystical role a more paternalistic one, whereby the *Tsadik* became responsible for his 'flock'. More than this, the *Tsadik* became the specific intermediary between his Hasidic community and God. The all-too-human aspect of this intermingling of the mystical and social leadership roles led to what was perceived by non-Hasidic Jewish groups as the danger of undue worshipping of the *Tsadik*, a phenomenon that many regard as evident today in the elevation of the leader of Habad-Hasidism, R. Menakhem Mendel Schneerson, to messianic status following his death in 1994.

KABBALAH'S NEW AGE?

In every age there have been new elaborations of the revelation that kabbalists believe lies at the heart of the tradition. Each age brings its own distinctive clothing to the essential core of Jewish mysticism. With the benefit of hindsight it is possible to understand something of the forces which contributed to that clothing. We find that features internal to the Jewish world, as well as influences deriving from surrounding cultures, have played significant roles in shaping the expression of the mystical core as it was played out in a given historical period.

We may identify three principal elements in this shaping process. The first involves a *reactive* propensity within Judaism. New aspects of kabbalistic teachings may have arisen as direct *reactions* to moves within the Jewish community itself. The second element involves *incorporating* material that is generally seen as non-kabbalistic into the kabbalistic system. The non-kabbalistic material that becomes assimilated into kabbalistic thought may involve both Jewish and non-

Jewish aspects. The third element entails *mythologizing* details of the shared Jewish experience. By the term 'myth' in this context I do not imply any lack of truth. The *myth* is the outer garment that perpetuates the core teaching that is continuous with the source of Kabbalah. I shall briefly illustrate each of these three elements.

The *reactive* element is illustrated by the argument that the circulation of the *Zohar* in the thirteenth century was a reaction to the philosophical legacy left by Maimonides. From the philosophical perspective, the primary imperative is recognition of the divine as the transcendent source. In the eyes of some philosophers, the commandments of the Torah (the *mitsvot*) became viewed as having little intrinsic importance beyond that of encouraging this recognition, and generally enhancing human conduct. One obeys the laws simply because God so commands, thereby clearly expressing one's recognition of God and His authority. However, should the force of philosophical argument alone sufficiently compel one to recognize the divine Being, then perhaps the *mitsvot* no longer play a critical role. After all, being a perfect Being, God does not *need* anything from us. The *Zohar* is the great antidote to this line of thinking, for it posits an intrinsic importance to the performance of *mitsvot*. The *mitsvot* in their specific details relate to the entire structure of the *sefirot*. Observance of *Shabbat*, for example, is not simply a way to acknowledge that there is a creator God, but is a specific means to promote the goal of creation by bringing *Malkhut* (the seventh day) into alignment with the rest of the *sefirot*. A commitment to practising the *mitsvot* in their particularities is essential to the role ascribed to man throughout the pages of the *Zohar*:

> The *mitsvot* of the Torah are all limbs of the supernal secret
> [of the *sefirot*]. . . . One who detracts from even one of the
> *mitsvot* of the Torah, it is as if he had lessened the precise
> form of faith, for all the limbs are in the image of the

[supernal] Adam and therefore all ascends in the secret of
unification. (*Zohar* 2:162b)

By insisting that performance of each and every *mitsvah* plays a
specific role in the intricate harmony of the *sefirotic* realm, ultimately
promoting an influx from the higher regions of the Godhead, the
Zohar became an antidote to any moves away from Jewish practice.

The *incorporation* of ideas which were not intrinsically
kabbalistic is exemplified in the teachings of Abulafia. He drew
extensively on Rambam's major reworking of Aristotelian and Islamic
ideas that had resulted in a specifically Jewish philosophy. A central
concept developed by Rambam is that of the non-corporeal *intellects*
which he identifies with the angels who bring God's influence into the
realm of human and worldly affairs. The perfection of the human mind
brings it into alignment with the lowest of these intellects, the *Active
Intellect*. Abulafia identifies these intellects, of which there are ten,
with the *sefirot*. The Torah, equated with the Active Intellect, is the
means for one to 'to actualise one's potential intellect' (cited in Idel
1989: 37). Abulafia's entire path of mysticism is largely predicated on
this principle: his elaborate system of concentrative meditation is
directed towards grasping the secret meaning of the divine Names,
that is, their role both as *sefirot* and as the separate intellects.

Finally, the tendency towards *re-mythologization* of themes is
apparent in Lurianic Kabbalah. The Jewish world in the sixteenth
century had to come to terms with what was undoubtedly its worst
catastrophe in pre-Holocaust Europe – the expulsion from Christian
Spain in 1492. Spain had been the cradle of a revival of Jewish culture
since the tenth century, and the ending of that chapter in torture,
forced conversion and mass expulsion shook Jewish confidence that
any kind of a settled existence in the Diaspora was feasible. It is highly
significant that the subsequent flowering of Kabbalah occurred in the
Land of Israel, in Sfat.

As has been noted by Scholem, we can detect poignant images of the aftermath of the Spanish experience in the Lurianic storyline. Lurianic Kabbalah, as Scholem puts it, constituted a response to the catastrophe. The Lurianic storyline essentially deals with the nature of exile and the role assigned to those who are in exile. The primary move within God, the *tsimtsum*, implies an initial exile, as it were, of God from Himself, for there is a withdrawal of His light. The whole narrative of creation becomes a working-through of the consequences of this primordial exile. The job of *tikkun*, that of seeking out and gathering the fragments of light that fell through the breaking of the vessels, requires the Jewish people to be in exile in order that they might be able to find the sparks in the darkest of places. In this sense, any prolonged 'comfort' in a land of exile, such as Spain, runs counter to the divinely-ordained role of the Jews. The image of the *Shekhinah* accompanying the Jews in their exile, which is central to all rabbinic literature, became considerably elaborated in Luria's insights into the *Zohar*. In this elaboration, a majestic role for the downtrodden was conveyed, and otherwise inexplicable actions of European rulers were rendered intelligible. As Scholem writes: 'The Lurianic Kabbalah is a great "myth of exile and redemption." And it is precisely this bond with the experience of the Jewish people that gave it its enormous power and its enormous influence on the following generations of Jews' (Scholem 1965: 117).

Scholem ends the essay from which this extract is taken by raising the question as to how this process of mythologization might operate in the post-Holocaust world that he was addressing. As he writes, 'What greater opportunity has the Jewish people ever had . . . to fulfil its encounter with its own genius, its true and "perfect nature"?' In addressing essential themes of the Kabbalah over future pages, I shall have this challenge very much in mind. It seems to me that each age poses its own challenge, which entails reformulating the core teaching in ways consonant with the wisdom, as well as the needs, of the age.

The three elements briefly introduced – reaction to internal trends, incorporation of ideas from both within and beyond the Jewish world, and the remythologization of experience – are very much part of the story of Kabbalah in our day. A Kabbalah that looks only backwards, failing to embrace the leading edge of the quest for knowledge in a given age, is, in the final analysis, not true to its heritage.

Chapter 4

Kabbalah and Creation

IT'S BEHIND YOU, STUPID!

> The tail of the *bet* is open to its rear, since, were it not so,
> then a person could not endure. (*Bahir* 11)

The *Bahir* learns many lessons from the shape of the letter *bet*, the first letter of the Torah, which marks the beginning of manifestation. As can be seen in Figure 4.1, the letter is closed around its rear, yet it has a 'tail' which extends beyond the closure; the tail is 'open to its rear'. The 'rear' in this sense is the region towards the preceding letter in the alphabet, the *alef*. As Hebrew is written right to left, the 'rear' means 'to the right'. As already noted in Chapter 3, the letter *alef* indicates the source, *Keter*. The above extract teaches us that it is our root in the transcendent source that enables us to endure. However, it is impossible for us to be cognizant of that root – the letter *bet*, representing our human condition, is closed behind, and from inside the letter we are unable to see, as it were, the tail extending beyond the closure.

This metaphorical tension between openness and closure towards the source extends to a fuller consideration of creation. The 'In the beginning' of *Genesis* begins with the letter *bet* (of *bereshit*) because

front ⟵ ⟶ rear

Fig. 4.1. The letter
bet, indicating the
tail of the letter
that is 'open to its
rear'

Tail of the *bet*

the *alef*, the hidden beginning, 'withdraws' prior to the emergence of
the manifest process of creation. *Keter*, depicted by the *alef*, lies
behind the processes of creation described in the opening of *Genesis*.
However, in view of its absolute transcendence, *Keter* cannot be known
by the human mind. As noted earlier, this is the reasoning behind the
Sefer Yetsirah's cryptic counting of 'ten and not nine; ten and not
eleven'.

In fact, kabbalists point to a more appropriate translation of
bereshit, the first word of the Torah, as being not 'In the beginning', but
'By means of a beginning'. The first verse of *Genesis* is then understood
to convey the idea that the transcendent source, which is so elevated
that it cannot overtly enter into the text, began a process which gave
rise to the aspect of God which 'creates heaven and earth' (*Genesis*
1:1). This latter divine aspect is the 'Elohim' (God) of the biblical text,
and is identified with the *sefirah* of *Binah*. The word 'God' in *Genesis*
1:1 is to be understood as the *object* of the verb 'created', not its
subject. The Torah is initimating: 'By means of a beginning, the
transcendent source created Elohim [God].' As indicated in Ramban's
commentary mentioned in Chapter 1 (p. 31), the word *bereshit* alludes
to the *sefirot* of *Keter* and *Ḥokhmah* which precede the emanation of
Binah. The word *Elohim* is a plural form in Hebrew, a grammatical
point which fits into the kabbalistic scheme since it is understood that
this divine aspect includes within itself, in potential, the additional
aspects of God that emanate as the lower *sefirot*.

The unfolding of the process of creation from its inception to the emanation of *Binah* is described by the *Zohar* as follows:

> When the most concealed of all concealment [*Keter*] sought to be revealed, He made first a single point [*Hokhmah*]; and this arose to become *thought*. He sketched within it all the designs, engraved in it all the openings. He engraved within the concealed holy lamp a singular, hidden pattern – Holy of Holies; a deep structure [*Binah*] emerging from thought. And it was called *Mi* ['who?'], origin of the building [the seven lower *sefirot*]. Existent and non-existent, deep and hidden, called by no name other than *Mi*. *(Zohar* 1:2a)

The name 'Elohim' (*elhim*) is an anagram of the two Hebrew words *mi* and *eleh* (who, these). In the above passage, the *Zohar* draws inspiration from *Isaiah* 40:26: 'Lift up your eyes on high, and see *who* has created *these* that produce by number [*bemispar*] their hosts'. The phrase 'by number' derives from the same Hebrew root as the word *sefirah*, and is therefore understood as intimating the *sefirot*. 'These' refers to the evidence of creation, as expressed through the seven days, corresponding to the seven lower *sefirot*. In the creative sequence of the unfolding of the *sefirot* (see Figure 2.1), the emanation passes from *Binah* to *Hesed*, the first of the seven days of creation (see Figure 2.2). In the symbolic terms which the *Zohar* employs here, the emanation proceeds from *Mi* (*Binah*) to the first of the seven *sefirot* designated by *Eleh* (*Hesed*). To put this idea another way, since the divine name associated with *Binah*, Elohim, includes the two words *mi* and *eleh*, it carries the potential to give rise to the entire array of the remaining *sefirot*. All the 'designs' had been sketched in *Hokhmah*, the concealed thought, but if the emanation had not reached the nurturing impulse from the 'supernal mother', *Binah*, nothing would have come to fruition.

Binah may be known through her fruits, the works of creation, and the closest we may come to understanding the nature of creation is to discern that there is a *Mi*, a Being, who lies behind the fruits. In the creative emanation, the first arising of *Binah* takes the form of *Mi*, an arising of the potential for the expression of the divine Being. This potential is realized when the name 'Elohim' is articulated. Grammatically, of course, *mi* denotes a question. The asking of questions represents the distinctive potential of man; to be sufficiently moved by the beauty and precision of the world to articulate the question 'Who?', 'Who is the one God responsible for all of these?', represents the pinnacle of human understanding.

The word *mi* has the numerical value of 50, and is an anagram of *yam* (*ym*), meaning 'sea'. The number 50 and the idea of the sea are both symbols which are specifically associated with *Binah*: 'Ḥokhmah bestirred its [32] paths and brought a wind to the waters. The waters were gathered to one place [*Binah*] and the 50 gates of *Binah* were opened' (*Zohar* 2:175b). The sea of *Binah* is described as the 'upper waters' to distinguish it from the 'lower waters' of the *Shekhinah* (*Malkhut*). These two feminine poles in the *sefirotic* structure are interconnected through the 50 gates. This number is based on the passage of the emanation from *Binah* to *Malkhut*. Each *sefirah* comprises all the other *sefirot* within itself, giving rise to the holonomic nature of the tree of life. This holonomic principle means that the emanation passes downward effectively through seven times seven stages from the beginning of *Hesed* to the end of *Malkhut*. *Binah* is the one above these 49 levels. In other words, the 'gates' are the stages through which the emanation passes to be completed in *Malkhut*. At the same time, they refer to the stages in the ascending path through which we aspire to the level of understanding associated with the Torah.

The symbol par excellence of this ascent is the biblical Moses. Moses is described in the Talmud as possessing 49 gates of understanding: 'Fifty gates of understanding were created in the world, and all were given to Moses save one, as it says (*Psalm* 8:6), 'You have made him [Moses] lacking but a little from [the status] of God' (Talmud, *Rosh Hashanah* 21b). The *Zohar* conveys the notion that Moses becomes the 'husband' of the *Shekhinah* and ascends to the *sefirah* of *Binah*. Moses is thus the master of all the levels from *Malkhut* to *Binah*.

A cryptic allusion to this idea of Moses' stature is said to be conveyed in the story, related in *Numbers* 20:1-13, of Moses striking the rock to bring forth water. He had been instructed merely to speak to the rock, and was subsequently criticized by God for his action in hitting the rock. Luria points out a subtle relationship between the Hebrew for 'rib' (*tsela*) and the word used in this story for 'rock' (*sela*). As is clear even in transliteration, the two words are very similar in sound – they differ only in their first letters. In view of the role of the 'rib' (or, more accurately, the 'side' of Adam, for *tsela* means 'side') in the biblical story of the creation of Eve (*Genesis* 2:18-25), *tsela* conveys the idea of the root of the female. The *Zohar* states that the *sela* brings forth water through the power of the supernal rock (*Binah*), and that the *tsela* is the 'bride of Moses' (intimating the *Shekhinah*) (*Zohar* 2:64b; *Tikkunei Zohar* 12, 26b). The difference between the two words is numerically thirty (since '*s*' = 60 and '*ts*' = 90), which is the Hebrew letter *lamed*, the initial letter of the word *lashon* ('tongue' and 'language'). The cryptic teaching through these subtle allusions holds that Moses has a relationship with the *Shekhinah* at both higher and lower levels. The higher level is achieved through the mystery of speech, which Moses should have used in relation to the rock of the biblical story. He mistakenly draws the water through striking the rock, indicating the lower relationship. God chastises Moses for the lost opportunity to teach the Children of Israel this lesson concerning the power of speech.

These ideas are certainly somewhat abstruse. Yet the basic idea is re-enacted regularly in the Synagogue service. According to Cordovero, the rituals associated with taking the Torah scroll from the Holy Ark entail effecting the *Malkhut–Binah* relationship. Cordovero identifies *Malkhut* with the table in the centre of the Synagogue at which the scroll is read, and *Binah* with the Ark where it is housed. The Ark is located at the front of the synagogue facing Jerusalem, the Holy City. The reader 'ascends' from *Malkhut* to *Binah* to remove the Torah from its secret place, then brings it back with him to the central point, *Malkhut*, from where its secrets may be disseminated to those listening. As we shall see in Chapter 5, on account of the concealed secrets it contains, the Torah is the mystical core of Judaism. This is the essential principle which leads to both the teaching regarding the role of Moses in relation to the *Shekhinah* and the kabbalistic understanding of the ritual of public reading from the Torah. The act of engaging with the Torah through study in its widest sense is the central precept in Judaism. For the kabbalist, the Torah is the embodiment of the *Shekhinah*, and it is only through Torah study that a full relationship with the *Shekhinah* may be enacted. As we have seen, this relationship is the key to the unification of the *sefirot*, the goal that is viewed as bringing divine influx and harmony to the worlds. Moses brought the Torah from heaven to our earthly realm, and is accordingly the one who has the fullest possible relationship with the *Shekhinah*, the divine presence which is concealed and revealed throughout the body of the Torah.

Returning to the incident of Moses extracting water from the rock, it is significant to note that water generally symbolizes the unconscious. This is an insight recognized by all the great pioneers of depth psychology. The sea, for example, is the source of life (in both the biblical account and in the thinking of contemporary biologists), a fact which directly parallels the role of the unconscious, which is the source of the life of the mind. Movement at the surface of the sea is determined by the currents operating deeper in the ocean, which again parallels what we know of the operation of the mind. The surface layer of the mind is shaped by the forces operating beneath the waves, as it were. For every thought that sparks into the orbit of 'I' at the conscious surface layer of the mind there are levels upon levels of unconscious images operating beneath the surface. If we transcribe the kabbalistic teaching of the fifty gates of understanding into contemporary language, we should emphasize the insights that may be understood by engaging with the unconscious. And it is significant to note that the more spiritually-oriented depth psychologists have recognized that we need to recognize 'higher' and 'lower' realms of the unconscious. According to Jung, the 'higher' is the collective aspect of the unconscious, from where insight may be gained when an individual engages with the archetypes forming our collective heritage. Assagioli includes a 'higher unconscious' or 'superconscious' within his model of the psyche. As with Jung, this higher region is the source of insights and deep intuitions.

The question 'who?' is actually the most transformative question we can ask. Whilst the sense of 'I' appears to be an immediate psychological presence, its real nature is elusive. This is a fundamental insight within Kabbalah that is found in all other mystical traditions. A favoured linguistic observation in kabbalistic writings concerns the Hebrew word *ani*, meaning 'I'. The slightest rearrangement of its letters produces the word *ain*, 'nothing'. (This is the same word as in the term *En Sof*. I have transliterated it here as *ain* to emphasize the anagram of *ani*.) For Kabbalah, the ego is a false god lacking substantiality. It lies at the root of the *yetser ha-ra*, the 'evil inclination' that ensnares the individual into self-serving desires. Kabbalistic work is intended to make real the rearranged form of the word, in order that the individual should gain insight into the emptiness at the core of their being. Where 'I' had been, the higher mystical state reveals nothing other than the divine becomingness that defines the essence of the individual *neshamah*. The root of the ineffable Name of God (Y-H-V-H) itself conveys this key teaching, for it depicts such 'becomingness'. It is, of course, an emptiness that is paradoxically the real fullness.

In addition to the inwardness of the question about self, in Jewish thought there is also an outward dimension. 'Who created these?' we ask about the heaven and the earth. Just as we have to recognize a deeper element of selfhood than the immediate sense of 'I', so too we should recognize the divine 'Self' in answer to the outwardly-directed question. This key recognition of the Oneness of God was the insight of Abraham, who, according to Jewish teaching, was the first to recognize the creator God as a manifestation of the Infinite. Given that the intent behind creation was that the Infinite should become known, Abraham effectively becomes the reason for creation. If there had been no human to recognize the One God, then there would have been no point in creation.

This idea is conveyed exegetically from the following verse: 'These are the generations of the heaven and the earth when they were created [*behibar'am*] in the day that Y-H-V-H Elohim made earth and heaven' (*Genesis* 2:4). The Rabbis point out that the term *behibar'am* is an anagram of *Avraham*, implying that it was for the sake of Abraham that God created the world. It is not without significance that the anagram introduces a change in the sequence of 'heaven' and 'earth'. Abraham's recognition of the unified creator God is the pivotal accomplishment that renders possible the 'return' journey from earth to heaven. Moreover, this is the first occasion in the Torah that the Name 'Y-H-V-H' occurs. This Name expresses the compassionate dimension of the divine, introduced here in recognition of the achievement of Abraham. It should be noted that, in these ideas, the normal conception of time is transcended. The role of Abraham is implicit in the eternal moment of creation.

The *Zohar* introduces a second critical question word in relation to these ideas about the role of Abraham, when it states: '*Mi* ('who') is the end of heaven above; *Mah* ('what') is the end of heaven below' (*Zohar* 1:1b). As noted already, *Mi* is associated with *Binah* (heaven above); the term 'heaven below' is used to indicate *Malkhut*. These two, as already noted in relation to the fifty gates, represent the two extremities which are unified by *Tiferet*, the 'essence of heaven'. In the scheme of the *sefirot*, the role of Abraham is to enable the emanation to proceed beyond *Binah*. In the symbolism of Kabbalah, Abraham is the *sefirah Hesed*. The *Zohar*'s teaching is that once an Abraham – who is cognizant of the true source – exists in the scheme of things, then the intended goal of creation may be achieved. This teaching is conveyed by some further cryptic readings of the first verse of *Genesis*. The Hebrew for 'created' ('In the beginning God created . . .') is *bara (br')*. A rearrangement of these letters produces *ever ('vr*, 'limb'). *Ever* is specifically used to refer to the male sexual organ, identified with *Yesod* in the symbolism of the *Zohar*. (The term 'limb' refers to any functional part of the body.) The role of *Yesod* is to effect the perfect union with the *Shekhinah*, *Malkhut*. It is Abraham who enables this rearrangement to come about, as indicated by the fact that his name is an amalgamation of *ever* and *mah ('vr + mh = 'vrhm)*.

Again, unless we can engage with the *Zohar*'s real objective, these verbal gymnastics may seem like intellectual tricks and little more. The real objective is that we should understand our role in creation. As I mentioned above, it is the ability to ask questions that marks us out as humans. It was Abraham's asking of the question 'what?', that led him to the question 'who?'. As mentioned in Chapter 1, Kabbalah is the path directed to discerning the essential nature of things. Abraham achieved this goal, recognizing that the true essences are discerned in the Hebrew letters. It is for this reason that he is traditionally known as the author of the *Sefer Yetsirah*. Indeed, this book concludes by stating: 'When Abraham our father – may he rest in peace – came, he looked, saw, understood, probed, engraved and carved [the letters]. And he was successful in creation . . . And the Master of All . . . bound the twenty-two letters of the Torah to his tongue and revealed to him His mystery.' Abraham is described as understanding the essential nature of things, and as mastering the profound ways of working with the Hebrew letters that God Himself uses in creation. Abraham thus achieves the highest level of the imitation of God.

Whilst we may not all be capable of Abraham's lofty achievements, these kabbalistic insights into the nature of creation, as given in the *Zohar*, provide clues for our own understanding of the essential principles of spiritual reality. Like the physicist who studies elementary particles in order to glean something of the forces that mould the world, or the biologist who unravels the DNA code in order to understand the life-forms that enrich our planet, the kabbalist places the basic elements of the Torah, its letters, under the microscope in order to know the essential spiritual blueprint of the cosmos.

The tail of the *bet* is open to its rear in order to encourage us to study the secrets of creation that open us to the depths of our own being.

THE MIRROR OF CONSCIOUSNESS

> It has been taught – the book of concealment, the book that is weighed on the balance. It is taught that before there was balance there was no gazing face-to-face. The primordial kings died, their weapons were no longer found and the earth was desolate. (*Zohar* 2:176b; *Sefer de-Tseniuta*)

Thus begins perhaps the most cryptic section of the *Zohar*, the *Book of Concealment*. According to the above extract, the first stirrings of creation constituted an attempt to enable the 'faces' to gaze at one another. What are these faces, and why was there initially a failure to achieve this goal? The answer to the second question is given in the last sentence in the above passage: the goal was blocked by the condition hinted at by the reference to the 'primordial kings'. The kabbalistic tradition holds that ours was not the first cosmos to be created. The earlier, unsuccessful attempts at creating a cosmos are said to be depicted by these primordial kings. According to the *Zohar*, these kings are the ones described in the biblical text as 'the kings that reigned in the land of Edom before a king reigned over the Children of Israel' (*Genesis* 36:31). This biblical statement is followed by a list of eight kings, only the last of whom is described as having a wife. Moreover the biblical text makes it clear that none of these kings was a son of the previous in the list. The *Zohar* is inferring that the absence of balance was evident in the inability of the first seven of these kings to establish an appropriate balance with the feminine.

We have seen already that much imagery in Kabbalah concerns the balance between male and female forms within the Godhead. When we link this notion of balance with the equally central principle of correspondence across different levels in creation, we can begin to understand the *Zohar*'s depiction of the first stirrings of creation. In view of the principle of correspondence, these first stirrings of creation must contain the essence of the intended outcome. If the intended outcome of creation is that what is 'below' should be fully integrated with 'above' – that heaven and earth should be as one – then such integration must be seeded in the inception. If the initial move fails to seed this intended outcome, then the 'architect' will have to start again. The idea that the initial attempts were indeed unable to sustain the intended outcome is conveyed in this image of the primordial kings failing to achieve a rapport with the female, as it were.

The Zohar's description of the 'faces' effectively parallels its treatment of the array of *sefirot*. The intended goal that the 'faces' should be able to 'gaze' at one another in an unclouded vision is congruent with the ideal of achieving a harmonious resolution of any tensions within the *sefirotic* system. In this use of the term 'gaze', reference is being made to the language of the *Song of Songs*, in which the female who seeks the love of her (divine) partner cries: 'My beloved is like a gazelle or a young hart. Behold, he is standing behind our wall, *gazing* through the windows, peering through the lattices' (2:9). The eroticism of this biblical book provides the backdrop for the kabbalistic understanding of the male-female encounter within the Godhead. The 'long face', corresponding to *Keter*, or, otherwise, to the *Hokhmah–Binah–Da'at* triad, wishes to gaze upon the 'short face', comprising the *sefirot* centred on *Tiferet*, which, in turn, is stirred to unite with the *Shekhinah*. The female protagonist in the *Song of Songs* is both the *Shekhinah* and the Jewish people, seeking to take the initiative in promoting the desired union with the higher aspect of God.

As mentioned in Chapter 3, the anthropomorphism in the 'faces' (*partsufim*) intimates the central role of humanity in creation. Although the biblical 'Adam' arrives on Day Six, the 'Adam Kadmon' to whom these 'faces' belong is created at the inception of creation. The whole potential of creation is condensed in the interaction between the 'faces' of the primordial Adam Kadmon. In order that the human Adam can truly be a microcosm, he is created only when the entirety of the rest of creation has been established. The scheme of things dictates that man includes the whole of creation within his being:

> The image [of the *partsufim*] that comprises all images and ... all Names was perfected ... When the various crowns and ornaments become joined with it, it constitutes the perfection of all, for the image of Adam is the image of above and below, both of which are included in it. And since this image includes both the higher and the lower, the Holy Ancient One [Keter] established his own formations [of the 'long face'] as well as those of the 'short face' in this image. (*Zohar* 3:141a-141b. *Idra Rabbah*)

The idea is expressed succinctly in the poem '*Lekha Dodi*', written by the Safedian kabbalist, Shlomo Alkabets (c.1505–1584) in honour of Shabbat. Alkabets writes that man is 'last in making, but in [the divine] thought he was first.'

Given that the whole of creation is comprised within the

archetypal human, then our study of the details of creation amounts to a study of ourselves. For Judaism, the ideal of 'knowing oneself' is contingent on knowing the inner workings of creation. Just as the 'lower face' reflects the 'higher face', so the human mind reflects the divine Mind. Human consciousness is the mirror in which the Divine may, as it were, experience Himself. This core teaching about the role of consciousness is eloquently conveyed in the structure of the letter *alef* (Figure 4.2). The *alef* is comprised of two forms of the letter *yod*, one above pointing downwards and one below, as it were, receiving from its partner. Uniting the two is the diagonal line, which is a stylized form of the sixth letter of the alphabet, *vav*. The shape of the letter *vav* clearly depicts its name, for the Hebrew word *vav* means 'a hook'. Symbolically the *vav*, having the numerical value of six and therefore representing the six *sefirot* centred on *Tiferet*, is the hook that binds the upper and lower realms.

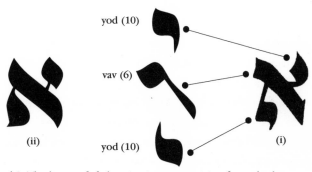

Fig. 4.2. The letter *alef*, showing its composition from the letters *yod* and *vav*. (i) *alef* as it appears in the Torah scroll; (ii) standard printed form

The letter *alef* is, then, the glyph of the central principle of creation, which we find recapitulated at all levels. It is the initial stirring of creation through which the higher face (upper *yod*) desires to gaze at the lower face (lower *yod*); it is the human mind (lower *yod*) that receives its inspiration from the divine Mind above (upper *yod*); it is the impoverished individual who receives sustenance through the charitable giving of a wealthier benefactor. In all these cases, the desired outcome is dependent on the correct functioning of the middle line, the *vav*. The first of the six middle *sefirot* that constitute the *vav* is *Ḥesed*, love, and it is indeed love that is the key to this central principle of creation. That which is above desires to express its love for that which is below by turning towards it and giving, while the lower seeks to unite in love with that which is above it.

This glyph of creation, comprising its three fundamental components – the giving *yod*, the unifying *vav*, and the receiving *yod*, has a numerical value of twenty-six (*yod* = 10, *vav* = 6, *yod* = 10), the gematria of the four-letter Name of God (*yod* = 10, *heh* = 5, *vav* = 6, *heh* = 5). Just as the *alef* conveys the founding principle of creation in its instantiation at the first stirrings of creation, so the four-letter Name depicts the principle as it becomes expressed through the unfolding of creation. In Chapter 3 (p. 90), I noted the way in which the four-letter Name comprises the totality of the *sefirotic* array, from *Keter* to *Malkhut*. When visualized in this vertical format, the Name can equally be viewed as a stylized image of the human form. The *yod* represents the head, the first *heh* represents the shoulders and two arms, the *vav* represents the torso, and the final *heh* extends down into the two legs. In this sense 'man is the measure of all things', that is, the being that spans the totality of creation, and is charged with completing the process initiated by God. 'In the image of God created He him' (*Genesis* 1:27).

The four letters of the ineffable Name are also viewed as representing the four worlds through which creation unfolds. The notion of a plurality of worlds is the vehicle for Kabbalah to convey the idea of fundamentally different domains of being, The worlds are the domains through which the divine ray of creation passes from its origin in the *En Sof* to its final manifestation in our world of spatio-temporal reality. This lowest world, known as *Assiah* (action), is the domain defined by human action, through which the initial divine ray may, ideally, become known. Our actions are determined by thoughts, which transcend the spatio-temporal domain. In the kabbalistic scheme, these non-physical forms are angels, the agencies of a higher domain (see Chapter 2, p. 65). This higher domain is labelled *Yetsirah* (formation). The world of *Yetsirah* is defined by the power of language, for our thoughts are structured by language, and ultimately it is language that determines action. This explains why the kabbalistic work that is pivotally concerned with language is entitled *Sefer Yetsirah*; it is the book that instructs how we should use language to imitate the workings of God (see Chapter 6) and thereby gain mastery over the world of *Yetsirah*.

Above the world of *Yetsirah* is *Beriah* (creation), understood in Kabbalah as the realm of God's throne. The throne symbolizes the domain where new enactments are determined, as with an earthly king whose power to command is symbolized by his throne. In the world of *Beriah*, God, as it were, orchestrates the direction of events and sends the angels to do His bidding. In a less theistic formulation, we might think of this world of *Beriah* as a world of archetypes that determine the course of our lives. The nature of the world of *Beriah* is illustrated by the first chapter of *Genesis*. It is quite clear that this chapter does not convey details of all features of creation. Rather it is intended to convey the principles, the archetypal pattern, of creation. To give but one simple example, the word *bara* (created) is used only of three seminal events: the initial act whereby God brings anything into being (*Genesis* 1:1); the creation of animals (*Genesis* 1:21); and the creation of Adam, the human (*Genesis* 1:27). These are the three quantum leaps in God's work. A further key principle is intimated by the threefold repetition of *bara* in *Genesis* 1:27, the verse concerning Adam ('And God *created* man in His own image, in the image of God *created* He him; male and female *created* He them'). The verse hints that the two earlier uses of *bara* are included in Adam. Adam, as the microcosm, includes the 'heaven and earth' mentioned in verse 1, the animal soul intimated in verse 21, and the freedom of choice that arrives with human consciousness. This chapter is not a 'scientific' treatise on the natural world, but a pointer to the principles on which the world operates and to the moral imperative that a fully realized 'Adam' must embrace.

The highest world, the world above *Beriah*, is *Atsilut* (emanation), the domain in which the essential pattern of the *sefirot* is established. *Atsilut* receives an influx from Adam Kadmon, the primordial form taken by the creative ray in *En Sof*, and shapes it into the *sefirotic* structure, which can then be emanated throughout the worlds. In the process of creation the *sefirotic* pattern becomes recapitulated throughout all the lower worlds.

BRIEF EXCURSUS: LETTERS OF CREATION 1

We started this chapter by examining the letter *bet*, the letter which opens the Torah. Its tail points towards the *alef* to remind us of the oneness and silence from which it derives. The letter *bet* introduces the category of *double letters* in the classification given by the *Sefer Yetsirah*. According to the *Sefer Yetsirah*, there are three categories of letters: 'mothers', 'doubles' and 'simples'. The alphabet is comprised of three mother letters, seven double letters and twelve simple letters. As the name applied to them suggests, the double letters generally take one of two different forms, a hard-sounding form and a soft form. Thus, the letter *bet* can be either a hard 'b' sound or a soft 'v' sound. The two forms are generally differentiated by placing a dot (*dagesh*) inside the letter to make the hard form. The metaphysical teaching associated with the double letters, namely, that created forms are seemingly definite (hard) and yet are really veils to the deeper spiritual reality that sustains them, is hinted at in the grammatical basis of the *dagesh*. The *dagesh*, giving the hard form, is inserted when the definite article is used. The definite article encourages us to think of the entity as substantive (*the* house); the word without the definite article is relatively derivative, and in this sense symbolizes the object's dependency – its soft form. The *Zohar* makes this point by alluding to the creatures that 'run and return like a flash of lightning' (*Ezekiel* 1:14). They run from the higher presence towards the lower world and return from their task in the lower sphere to the higher. 'They run with the *dagesh* and return in the soft form' (e.g. *Tikkunei Zohar*, Tikkun 6:21a).

The *alef* is a mother letter, meaning that it has a distinctive generative potential. I shall explore the teachings concerning mother letters in Chapter 6 (see p. 181ff). Here, my interest lies with the double letters and the meaning they hold for our understanding of creation. Essentially, the import of the double letters is that their dual nature conveys the essential duality of the created realm. Everything that exists conveys the core paradox of reality: An entity is both real

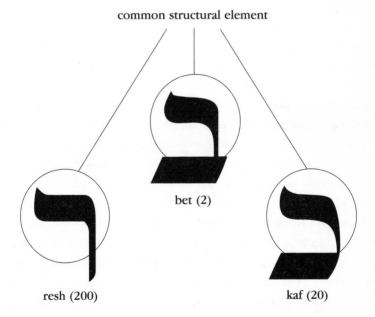

Fig. 4.3. The letter *bet* together with the other letters that have a cognate structure

in itself and yet enjoys only a relative existence since it is dependent on the spiritual essence that sustains it. The *bet* (symbolizing the created world) has a tail to indicate that all is dependent on the concealed *alef* that precedes it.

Two of the other double letters, *kaf* and *resh*, form a cognate set with the *bet* in that all three have an identical upper structure, as can be seen in Figure 4.3. This set further emphasizes the duality of the letters in that their numerical values are two, twenty and two hundred. *Bet-resh-kaf* gives the word *berekh* (knee), from which *berakhah* (blessing) is derived. As we saw in Chapter 1, this etymological link carries deep significance for understanding the meaning of the Torah. The *berakhah* is, at one and the same time, both the descending of the divine into the lower realm (through the giving of Torah) and the act of acknowledgement that we make in recognizing the divine source of all.

A second grouping of the double letters follows the alphabetical sequence. Following the concealed beginning (*alef*) is a sequence of three double letters: *bet*, *gimel*, *dalet*. Again, the teaching is subtly conveyed in the Hebrew language, for these three spell the word *beged* (clothing). The sequence of creation is one in which the concealed beginning becomes clothed in garments that have a dual status – they cover that which is concealed at the same time as hinting towards its presence. In fact, a major theme of the early period of Jewish mysticism focused on the *garment* that covers God's glory. The theme recurs in various later kabbalistic texts, and, in general, the garment is viewed as the form in which a higher spiritual entity appears to a lower being. Thus, reciting the divine Name is said to have the effect of creating a garment, since the recitation elicits the glory of God. The Rokeach sees a metaphor for such a garment in the idea of the bright cloud that conceals and reveals the divine presence:

Kabbalah and Creation

125

For the name is glorified in a bright cloud. Know that the [expression] 'to place His name there' is written in the Torah fifty-two times and there are fifty-two times in the Torah that the [word] cloud is mentioned. That is to say, there is a cloud for each name. . . . It is written, 'Your glorious name'" (*I Chronicles* 29:13), for [the name] is clothed and glorified in splendour. [The expression] 'Your glorious name' is numerically equivalent to 'the four letters' which is the Tetragrammaton [Y-H-W-H]. When Israel mentioned the name in the Temple, then 'His glory filled the whole world, amen and amen' (*Psalm* 72:19). (Wolfson 1994: p. 245)

The two remaining double letters, *peh* and *tav* feature in the word *parokhet* (veil). This word comprises only double letters (*peh-resh-kaf-tav*) and describes the veil in the *Mishkan* (portable Temple) described in *Exodus* 25–7. The veil separated the 'Holy Place' from the 'Holy of Holies'. Its function in this locus is appropriately symbolized by the double letters, for the veil's function is to mediate between the 'two and the one', between the outer holy region which depicts the sacred entering into our lower realm and the inner sanctum which is wholly *other* in its essence. The point is reinforced when we note that the word for the specific location where God states that he will meet with Moses, the *kaporet* – the 'cover' over the ark, is itself an anagram of the word *parokhet*:

And you shall make a cover [*kaporet*] of pure gold; two cubits and a half shall be its length, and a cubit and a half its breadth. And you shall make two *keruvim* of gold, of hammered workmanship shall you make them, in the two ends of the cover. And make one *keruv* on one end, and the other *keruv* on the other end; of the cover shall you make the *keruvim* on its two ends. And the *keruvim* shall stretch out their wings on high, covering the cover with their wings, and their faces shall look one to another; toward the cover shall the faces of the *keruvim* be. And you shall put the cover upon the ark; and in the ark you shall put the Testimony that I shall give you. And there I will meet with you, and I will talk with you from above the cover, from between the two *keruvim* which are upon the ark of the Testimony, of all things which I will give you in commandment to the people of Israel. (*Exodus* 25:17-22)

It is impossible to give a simple translation of the word *keruvim* in this quotation (single *keruv*, plural *keruvim*). It is rendered into English as 'cherub', and the childlike angelic form associated with this term may have some basis in rabbinic sources. However, such images are largely misleading, and it is more appropriate simply to regard the *keruvim* as devices intended to focus our attention to a higher realm. By gematria, they are identified with the 'appearance of glory' (*keruvim* = 278 = *mareh kavod*). It may be significant that the Hebrew root uses the three letters discussed above (*kaf-resh-bet*)

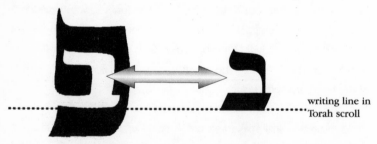

writing line in Torah scroll

Fig. 4.4. The letter *peh*, illustrating the *bet* concealed within its form

Finally, the letter *peh* is distinctively dual in another sense – it contains a second letter within itself, the letter *bet* (Figure 4.4). The importance of this feature is emphasized by the way in which the *peh* is written in the Torah scroll. The bottom line of the *peh* projects below the writing line so that the concealed *bet* is actually in line with all the other letters. The word *peh* means 'mouth' and designates the *Torah she-ba'al peh*, the Oral Torah. The *bet*, as the first letter of the written text, designates the *Torah she-bikhtav*, the Written Torah. Here is perhaps the core teaching of duality. The essential Torah is One with God; there is no separation. However, we are unable to gain direct access to that rarefied level of Oneness without the dual form adopted by the Torah when it descends from its heavenly source into our world. The kabbalist, like his non-mystical Jewish fellow traveller, employs the oral teachings to penetrate through the garment of the written Torah into the pure Being of God.

THE RECAPITULATION OF *TSIMTSUM*

> In its cosmological form *tsimtsum*, through contraction, turns God inside out in order to bring forth the possibility of the finite. In its human form, *tsimtsum* turns the text inside out, revealing its infinite core. (Magid 2002: 177)

Human creativity recapitulates divine creativity. Just as God withdraws His light in order to bring about a dynamic of difference through which His creativity may be expressed, so human creativity demands the generation of an inner space capable of receiving inspiration. The symmetry between the human and the divine minds is conveyed in the above quote: for God, the vacated space is a contraction in which the finite might arise within the infinite; for us, that space is an opening within the finite by means of which we may receive from the infinite. As will become clearer in Chapter 5, in Judaism the vehicle for this reciprocity between God and man is the text of the Torah. Through *tsimtsum* the infinite presence of God is contracted into the letters of the sacred text. The act of reading from the text requires a human *tsimtsum* – a vacating of the ego. That inner space within the depths of the human mind, opened with the attenuation of 'I', is the place of encounter with the infinite – the generative core of the unconscious.

The Lurianic concept of *tsimtsum* is prefigured in the *Zohar* by the image of a 'spark of darkness', the creative instrument used in the initial stirrings of creation:

> 'At the beginning of the will of the King, the spark of darkness engraved a hollow in the supernal luminescence, such that there emerged within the concealed of the concealed, from the head of *En Sof*, a vaporous mass . . . Within the inmost part of the spark emerged an effervescent spring from which colours [the *sefirot*] are derived below. (*Zohar* I:15a)

This spark of darkness emerges from the *En Sof*, suggesting that something of the infinite light of *En Sof* was restricted, giving rise to a creative spark that is dark by comparison with the infinite light. The notion that the divine source of emanation should constitute a relative darkness is perhaps the root of all paradoxes. It implies that we must enter into a darkness in order to receive the light of God. The paradox is succinctly captured in the first paragraph of the *Bahir*, whose title derives from this opening quote: 'And now they do not see the bright light ['*or bahir*] in the clouds' (*Job* 37:21). Continuing with another quote, the *Bahir* notes: 'He has made darkness His hiding place' (*Psalm* 18:12). Judaism demands that we enter the dark complexity of Torah. Torah is the teaching and is understood as light: 'The lamp is the *mitsvah* and the light is Torah' (*Proverbs* 6:23). Kabbalists associate the term '*or* (light) with the word for the mysteries of the Torah (*raz*) since the two words have the same numerical value of 207. Indeed, it is not without kabbalistic significance that the very sound of the word *'orah* (also meaning 'light') comes within the word 'Torah'. Nevertheless, to be immersed in Torah is to enter into a highly complex world of intellectual challenge. Kabbalistic insights are grafted onto the talmudic and midrashic elaborations of the text, and the great kabbalists were invariably experts in the large and convoluted corpus of rabbinic literature.

The spark of darkness 'engraves' the essential designs that will subsequently take form as the *sefirot*. This term 'engrave' is used specifically by the *Sefer Yetsirah* to convey the way in which God begins His work of producing the Hebrew letters (see Chapter 6). The letters themselves take shape through a kind of *tsimtsum*, for engraving produces an *absence*. The spark of darkness, itself a product of a negation of light, sets in train the continuing process of creation by promulgating the *tsimtsum* as a kind of *absence* that permeates the whole of creation. It is through exploration of that absence in himself – the unconscious core of his being – that man is able to play the role assigned to him by the Kabbalah.

Kaplan (1990: 13–14) notes this critical distinction between generating letters through engraving and generating them through writing. The former uses an *absence* to present the letters; the latter uses a presence (e.g. of ink). It is perhaps significant in this context that, in the subtle relationship between the *bet* and the *peh* illustrated in Figure 4.4, the presence of the *bet* is conveyed by an absence. The *bet* stands for the written Torah. The purpose of the writing in ink on the scroll – a presence – is to activate that which is absent: the unconscious. Ultimately, the Torah is a sign of the presence of the absent Author.

It was in post-Lurianic Hasidism that this more psychological approach to *tsimtsum* came to the fore. Luria had viewed *tsimtsum* as an event that effectively distanced the transcendent essence of God from His creation. Through *tsimtsum* the *En Sof* achieves a withdrawal from what will become manifest creation. The Hasidic tradition, by contrast, came to emphasize the role of *tsimtsum* throughout creation.

Tsimtsum gives rise to the paradoxical presence of the hidden God in Torah and in the human sphere. The primordial *tsimtsum* is recapitulated at each level in the emanative process, since each world is filled with God even whilst His infinite essence is unchanging. Far from being a withdrawal, *tsimtsum* came to be viewed as an act whereby God makes Himself available to His creatures. Were it not for *tsimtsum*, the essence of God would be so overpowering that man would be unable to perceive Him.

For Rabbi Nahman of Bratslav (1772–1811), the great-grandson of the Ba'al Shem Tov, the Torah draws us into *tsimtsum* on account of the classic approaches to its study. The study of Torah proceeds through questioning and the approach of dialogical argument (*makhloket*). Asking the right question is always the key towards perceiving the meaning of the text. But it is *makhloket* that epitomizes authentic study of Torah, especially in terms of *halakhic* detail (i.e. understanding the ramifications of the laws given in the Torah for daily conduct). The Talmud records the debates that took place in the major academies of learning over several centuries up to the time of its compilation in the fifth century CE. These debates invariably involved arguments between members of one school of thought and those of another in an attempt to arrive at correct *halakhic* conclusions. The arguments are characterized as being 'for the sake of heaven', and the important principle that applies here is that 'these and these are the words of the living God' (Talmud *Eruvin* 13b; *Gitin* 6b). In other words, both sides of the debate are recorded because all the contributions contain important elements for our journey of encountering the 'living God' through study. Even though the results of one argument may ultimately be rejected as a basis for *halakhic* rulings, we may learn key insights into the Torah through both arguments' exegesis of the text.

It is this principle that Rav Nahman sees as echoing *tsimtsum*, for the paradox at the heart of *tsimtsum* concerns the primary opposites, *yesh* (there is) and *ayin* (there is not). The vacated space is seemingly a place from which God has withdrawn, yet there is no conceivable place that is devoid of the Divine. God *is* and *is not* within the vacated space, a conundrum which is repeated at the heart of *makhloket*, in which each side *is* and *is not* correct.

For Rav Nahman, the vacated space is the real source of human creativity. To ask a generative question is to enter this space, for the question opens the individual to the multiplicity of the Torah, from where an insight to answer the question may be derived. Indeed, as we noted earlier, Kabbalah holds that the ability to ask questions lies at the core of what it is to be human. This idea is supported by a simple gematria: the Hebrew *Adam* and *mah* (what) have the same value (' = 1, *m* = 40, *d* = 4; *m* = 40, *h* = 5). Adam is the question-asking creature, and through asking the question he recapitulates the absence at the dynamic heart of creation. The question acknowledges that which is missing, opening the potential for an answer to arise.

Earlier we saw the association between *mah* (what) and the *Shekhinah*. But there is also a higher aspect to *mah*, epitomized in the kabbalistic 'equation' that *Hokhmah* = *koah mah* ('the power of what', derived by simply inverting the first two letters of *Hokhmah*): 'Thought is Adam Kadmon, the supernal *Mah*; *Mah* is his name. . . . All is *Hokhmah*, the power of *Mah*' (*Tikkunei Zohar* 69:111a). The cryptic core of this idea is derived from the fact that the numerical value of *koah*, 28, is the number of Hebrew letters in the first sentence of the Torah ('In the beginning God created the heaven and the earth'). The 'power' is drawn from the opening of creation. Adam encompasses in his being the totality of creation from the beginning (*Hokhmah*, the higher question) to the end (*Malkhut*, the lower question), and he realizes his potential by entering that mysterious void through which creation began.

Hokhmah epitomizes the co-existence of opposites, for it is the place of 'all'. It is also associated with *ayin* (nothingness), as is demonstrated by reference to *Job* 28:20, which kabbalists understand as intimating that 'Wisdom is found from nothingness'. One of the greatest teachers of the importance of *ayin* was Dov Baer, the Maggid of Mezeritch (1704–72), who was the foremost disciple of the Ba'al Shem Tov. The Maggid interprets this verse from *Job* to mean that the path to acquiring wisdom requires that we consider ourselves as nothing. Only then will God contract Himself as a prerequisite for us to be able to encounter Him. The human *tsimtsum* becomes the precondition for the divine *tsimtsum*.

As we noted in Chapter 3, *tsimtsum* is the primary image of exile – that even God is exiled from Himself, as it were. One final paradox is that *tsimtsum* also becomes the condition for the resolution of exile. The creation narrative comes full circle when we enter that mystery of emptiness through which manifestation became possible, thereby making space for the presence of God to dwell within. The Hebrew verbal root, *galah*, has two meanings: to 'go into exile' and to 'reveal'. Only by going into exile can God reveal Himself, and only through understanding the meaning of exile can we grasp the depths of the revelation. At the heart of this nexus of exile and revelation is the Torah, the mystical text whose letters both contain the contracted God and reveal inner truths to the kabbalist who can annul his 'I':

> He contracted Himself within the letters of the Torah, by means of which He has created the world . . . and the *tsadik*, who studies the Torah for its own sake in holiness, draws the Creator downward, blessed be He, within the letters of the Torah as in the moment of the creation. (Attributed to the Maggid of Mezeritch; cited in Idel 1995: 93)

Chapter 5

The Concealed Torah

A DANCE OF CONCEALING AND REVEALING

> You shall not oppress a stranger; you know the soul of the
> stranger, for you were strangers in the land of Egypt.
> (*Exodus* 23:9)

The above seems to be a straightforward ethical teaching of the
Torah. It comes after a list of commands clearly directed towards
upholding civilized values: you must give true testimony; should you
find your neighbour's property, return it to them; be ready to help
your neighbour; accept no bribes when judging legal cases. The
injunction to remember that the ancestors of the Jewish people were
slaves in Egypt is frequently repeated in the Torah and serves to
emphasize the need to be compassionate to others. The ancestral
memory of the pain of being harshly treated should lead to a
refinement of character that fosters an ideal society.

In Judaism, the approach to the Torah stresses the complexity of
meanings that reside beneath the surface of the text. Without denying
the immediate, contextual meaning, we search out the subtle allusions
that may be concealed in the words. Indeed, this is a primary objective

of Torah study. Kabbalah is focused on the deepest of the levels of meaning – a level that teaches of the dynamics of the divine realm and the secrets of creation. It is characteristic, then, that a verse that means one thing on the surface can be pregnant with a more complex teaching when viewed in a different light. In the hands of the author of the *Zohar,* the verse quoted above takes on a meaning which seems to depart radically from the immediate surface meaning. For the *Zohar*, the verse is not simply describing social responsibility; rather, it addresses the nature of the Torah itself. The 'soul of the stranger' no longer refers to a person of a different group, but is interpreted as referring to the inner meaning of the Torah.

This idea needs some explication. The Torah derives from the heavenly realm, and is divine, yet it has been given to humankind and therefore now resides on earth. In this sense, its 'heavenly' deep meanings are to be found in a realm to which they do not naturally belong. This lower realm is therefore symbolized by referring to it as the 'stranger'. The inner meanings are enclothed and therefore *concealed* within the text. One who is 'full of eyes', that is, an expert in the study of the sacred text, is able to penetrate into the concealed, or 'heavenly', meaning. This revelation of meaning lasts but a moment, for the inner secret is immediately re-concealed in this eternal dance of 'concealing and revealing' that epitomizes the kabbalistic understanding of Torah:

> The Holy One, blessed be He, brings all the secret things
> that He does into the holy Torah, and all is found in the
> Torah. That item which is concealed, the Torah reveals it,
> and then immediately clothes it in another garment, and
> it is hidden there and not revealed. Although the item is
> sealed in a garment, the wise, who are full of eyes, see it
> through the garment. . . . And although it is immediately
> concealed, it is not lost from their eyes. In several places,

the Holy One, blessed be He, gives warnings concerning the stranger, that the holy seed [Jewish people] should pay special attention to them. Afterwards, the concealed subject emerges from its sheath; yet after it has been revealed it immediately returns to its sheath and becomes enclothed there. When He gives warnings concerning the stranger in all these places, the matter emerges from its sheath and is revealed, and He says: 'you know the soul of the stranger'. Then, it immediately enters its sheath, returns to its garment and is hidden, since the verse continues: 'for you were strangers in the land of Egypt'. Scripture thinks that because it became enclothed immediately, no-one will notice it. Through this 'soul of the stranger', the holy soul comes to know the things of this world, and benefits from them. (*Zohar* 2:98b-99a)

In the above passage, the *Zohar* explores a tension between the two biblical phrases 'you know the *soul* of the stranger' and 'for you were strangers in the land of Egypt'. By using the term 'soul' the first phrase seems to be intimating the deeper level of meaning concerning the 'higher' things. However, the second phrase brings such a possibility back down to earth, as it were, since it suggests that the reference was concerned merely with the social level of behaviour. It is as if the second phrase were saying, 'Look, don't read too much into that statement about the *soul* of the stranger; just remember that you were once strangers, and you should therefore treat those who are strangers in your own midst in a decent manner.' The *Zohar* considers that the opening to a higher mystery implicit in the first biblical phrase is immediately re-concealed by the second.

The above passage from the *Zohar* introduces a lengthier discourse concerning the path into the secrets of the Torah. In the discourse, the Torah is depicted as a beautiful woman who calls, and sends messages, to her lover. The lover is, of course, the one who would take this path into the inner mysteries of the Torah. In stages, the woman reveals herself to the lover: first she speaks to him through a curtain, then through a fine veil, and, finally, she 'reveals herself to him face to face, and speaks of all her concealed mysteries and hidden paths which she had kept hidden in her heart from ancient times' (*Zohar* 2:99a).

This central principle of concealing and revealing characterizes the Torah because it is a principle that defines reality itself: 'Throughout the entire Torah we find that the revealed co-exists with the concealed. So it is with the world, both this world and the higher world, everything is concealed and revealed' (*Zohar* 2:230b). There is an inner dimension to things which can never be fully revealed; we have to perceive the concealed structure in subtle ways. As we begin to see something of the inner aspect, we may also begin to realize that there are yet more inward levels still unrevealed. The revealing of one level gives us an insight that there is yet more that remains concealed; at the same time, that which was revealed becomes re-concealed – it is a dance of concealing and revealing, revealing and concealing . . .

Kabbalistic teaching states that, ultimately, the whole of reality is nothing other than a veil over the Names of God. There is always meaning beneath the superficial level of things. Indeed, the Jewish worldview holds that nothing happens by 'chance'; there is always a deeper, spiritual meaning to events. Again, for us, the challenge is to gain insight into this deeper level of meaning. The mystical view of the Torah holds that it is the 'world soul' which comprises the archetypal pattern on which this plurality of meaning is based. As I explained in Chapter 1, at its most inward level the Torah is nothing other than the Names of God. The Torah encompasses the 'stranger' (revealed outer meaning) as well as the 'soul' (concealed inner meaning) and provides the hints whereby we can discern the nature of the 'soul' dimension to things (revelation of the inner meaning).

It is axiomatic to the kabbalist that the Torah is a living organism:

> Come and see. There is a garment that is seen by all. And when fools see a man in clothing that appears to them to be beautiful, they look no further. But more important than the garment is the body, and more important than the body is the soul. Similarly, the Torah has a body, which constitutes the *mitsvot* of the Torah, which are called [in rabbinic literature] the 'bodies of the Torah'. This body is clothed in garments, which are the stories of this world. The fools of the world see only the garments, which are the narratives of the Torah; they know nothing further, for they do not see what is beneath the garments. Those who know more do not gaze upon the garments, but upon the body beneath the garments. But the truly wise, the servants of the supreme King, those who stood at Mount Sinai, look only into the soul, which is the true essence of all, the real Torah. And in the time to come they shall be granted to gaze into the soul of the soul of the Torah. (*Zohar* 3:152a)

This conception of the Torah as an organism is presented in other sources by listing the various organs and structures of the body and their correspondences in the Torah. Moreover, as mentioned in Chapter 1, the view of the Torah as a living presence is emphasized by the kabbalistic identification of the Torah with God Himself. Rabbi Menahem Recanati (late thirteenth–early fourteenth century) notes that there is nothing that is not included within the Torah. Moreover, since 'The Holy One, blessed be He, is nothing that is outside the Torah, and the Torah is nothing that is outside Him, [therefore] this is the reason that the sages of the Kabbalah said that The Holy One, blessed be He, is the Torah' (cited in Idel 2002: 122). Rabbi Judah Hayyat (*c*.1450–*c*.1510) puts it this way: 'The Torah is the image of The Holy One, blessed be He, and from its perspective one can compare the form, which is the soul, to its Creator' (cited in Wolfson 1994: 377). The essential point is well captured by Idel when he writes, 'The Torah is the transparent prism in which the infinite God is seen' (Idel 2002: 124).

The central principle that all is included in the Torah was already conveyed by the *Mishnah* (redacted by the third century CE): 'Ben *Bag Bag* says, "Turn it [Torah] around, turn it around for all is in it . . ." Ben *Heh Heh* says, "According to the effort is the reward"' (Mishnah *Avot* 5:25-26). These two names were evidently made up in order to allude cryptically to the mystical essence of the Torah. The names together have a numerical value of 22, intimating the core idea that, being the agents of creation, the 22 letters of the alphabet encapsulate all of reality. Abulafia comments that the name *Bag Bag* was doubled 'in order to reveal wondrous secrets' (cited in Idel 1989: 79). This doubling of the name conveys the importance of duality in relation to Torah: the Torah, which begins with the second letter, is the glyph of the revealed and concealed dimensions of reality. 'The truth is . . . that the Torah operates on two modes of existence. . . . These are the revealed and concealed aspects; and both are true' (Abulafia, cited in Idel 1989: 77). The Torah itself is given in two forms – the written and the oral. Moreover, the individual who would penetrate to the depths of Torah must repeat their study. Studying a verse once only is inadequate. It is only with repetition that some cryptic allusion may begin to open up beneath the immediate meaning of the text. Indeed, the very word *mishnah* derives from a root meaning to 'repeat'. (This last point is emphasized further by the repetition of 'turn it around' in Ben *Bag Bag*'s aphorism). Finally, *Bag* (*bg*) has the numerical value of five. As well as being a number specifically related to the Torah, which comprises five books, this number connects to the other name, *Heh Heh*, since the letter *heh* is five. *Bag Bag* may be a codified reference to the covenant, as described in the *Sefer Yetsirah*: 'Ten *sefirot* of nothingness are in the number of ten fingers; five opposite five. And the covenant of Oneness is precisely in the middle, in the circumcision (*mila*) of the tongue (*lashon*) and in the circumcision of the male organ' (*Sefer Yetsirah* 1:3).

The commentary of Rabbi Isaac of Acre (late thirteenth–mid-fourteenth century) on this passage asserts that 'all the functioning organs are in pairs except for the mouth and the male organ . . . [which] correspond to one another'. The tongue is related to *Binah* and the male organ to *Yesod*: 'The *sefirah* of *Yesod* binds together the upper *Shekhinah* and the lower one [*Binah* and *Malkhut*], and similarly the tongue is the bond of love through speech between a man and his wife or between two lovers. Therefore lovers kiss one another through their mouths' (cited in Wolfson 1995a: 100–101).

The covenantal relationship with God is specifically connected with a commitment to 'turning the text of Torah around'. The covenant binds us to exploring the depths of the Torah, and the parallel given in the *Sefer Yetsirah* between the 'circumcision of the tongue' and the 'circumcision of the male organ' intimates the approach that should enliven such exploration of the text. The sexual energy that is directed to our biological generative potential is to be additionally directed towards opening the text in order that its inner secrets might be found. The intended meaning is clearer in the Hebrew, for the word '*mila*' means both 'circumcision' and 'word', and *lashon* means both 'tongue' and 'language'.

The 'five opposite five' alludes also to the classic posture of raising the hands during prayer and meditative concentration. As Kaplan (1990: 36) remarks, this posture is used as a means for focusing spiritual energy. He draws a connection between this posture, which entails bringing attention to the potential spiritual influx arising at the mid-point between one's outstretched hands, and the posture of the *keruvim* (angelic presences) in the *Mishkan* and in the first Temple. It was between the two *keruvim*, with their outstretched wings, that God would meet with Moses in the *Mishkan*. For the kabbalist, the focusing of spiritual energy is achieved through entering the inner world of the Torah. To raise the arms is to connect with the unifying function of the Torah, that the 'higher' should be brought into the 'lower' sphere.

The power of the Torah resides in its organismic quality. From a kabbalistic point of view, since the Torah is 'alive', it plays a dynamic role in the encounter between the mystic and the text. It is God dwelling in the Torah that is, as it were, the active party in the encounter. The Torah will open to reveal its inward depths only to one who engages with it in ways deemed appropriate. In the first place, since 'a Torah without *mitsvot* is not the Torah of God' (*Tikkunei Zohar*, Introduction 2a), the seeker must possess the refinement of character brought about by a disciplined attention to God's commands. Study of Torah is not merely an intellectual affair, and, as we shall discuss in Chapter 7, the practical ways of Judaism engrain a fundamental sense of the inner structure of the Torah. Judaism is very much a holistic tradition, in which performance of rituals and familiarity with prayer lay the groundwork for what the intellect will be capable of perceiving.

Within this all-embracing approach to the Torah, the distinctive power of the intellect is brought to bear on the text itself. Every letter, word, and phrase is viewed as being pregnant with a multiplicity of meaning. Indeed, this is tantamount to the hallmark of the text's divine status – the word of God is miraculously a unity that also manifests as a diversity of meaning. The Talmud expounds the basic principle: 'It was taught in the School of Rabbi Yishmael: ['Is not the power of My word like fire, says the Lord], and like a hammer that shatters rock?' (*Jeremiah* 23:29). Just as this hammer produces many sparks, so a single verse has many meanings' (Talmud, *Sanhedrin* 34a). The expansion of the concept is illustrated by Gikatilla's exposition on the same biblical verse:

Our sages said, 'Are not My words like fire? says the Lord.'
Like the forms of the flame of fire that has neither a specific
measure nor specific form, so the scroll of Torah has no
specific form for its verses. Rather, sometimes it is
interpreted one way and sometimes it is interpreted
another way. Thus, in the world of the angels [*yetsirah*] it is
read as referring to one issue, and in the world of the
spheres [*Beriah*] it is read as referring to another issue, and
in the lower world [*Assiah*] it is read as referring to another
issue. So also in the thousands and thousands of worlds
which are included in these three worlds. Each person reads
the Torah according to his capacity and comprehension.
(Cited in Idel 2002: 91; translation slightly modified)

The fluidity in interpreting the Torah is attributable to its distinctive
written form, in which there are neither vowels nor any indication where
one verse ends and the next starts. This openness in the text has led to
the kabbalistic tradition that the entire text can be read as God's Name,
as already noted in Chapter 1. Every word, and even every letter,
potentially opens into a myriad of meanings: 'There is not a single word
in the Torah that does not radiate many lights in every direction,' says
the *Zohar* (3:202a). Ultimately, as was pointed out by Rabbi Moses de
Leon (*c*.1240–1305), since God is identified with the Torah, then the
Torah itself must be infinite, just as God is infinite. At the same time, the
text constitutes a unity, just as God is a Unity. Paradoxically, it is through
encouraging us to engage fully with the multiplicity of meanings within
the Torah that Kabbalah leads us to discern that unity which is concealed
within the rich pattern of ink on parchment.

Kabbalists developed complex techniques for penetrating the
words of Torah, each legitimized by the divinity of the text. The
technique of gematria we have already discussed. There are,
additionally, techniques for discerning diverse meanings by permuting

letters within words or phrases; using special codes to substitute letters (e.g. the *a't b'sh* code, whereby the first letter in the alphabet is transcribed for the last, the second for the second to last, and so on); making new words from the initial, final, or middle letters of words in a phrase of the Torah; and a technique of skipping certain numbers of letters in order to arrive at new words.

Some of these seemingly bizarre procedures may be illustrated by the following extract from Abulafia's exploration of the meaning of the stone tablets of 'testimony' that Moses brought down Mount Sinai. The tablets carried the writing of God, which was miraculously inscribed on both sides (*Exodus* 32:15-16). According to Abulafia, the tablets of stone with their divine writing attest to the organismic quality of the Torah itself. The letters depict the divine dimension – its transcendence – whilst the tablets allude to the natural aspect of the Torah's being. Abulafia demonstrates this as follows:

> The word *luḥot* ('tablets') according to the *a't b'sh* code is *kisei* ('throne'), which is, by gematria, *teva* ('nature'). And in their outer aspect they are 'tablets of stone'. Now the secret meaning of *shtei luḥot* ('two tablets') is that it also alludes to another matter, for by gematria it is *otiot* ('letters'). This is in accordance with their description in the *Sefer Yetsirah*, where it says [of the letters], 'Two stones build two houses'. Now, the numerical value of the phrase *shnei luḥot avanim* ('two tablets of stone') is 891, which is the numerical value of *avnei shayesh tahor* ('pure marble stones') that are within the two tablets of stone. And they are also the *yetser ra ve-yetser tov* ('the evil inclination and the good inclination'). (Abulafia, *Sefer ha-Heshek*; version printed 2002, p. 40)

The beginning of this extract draws on the midrashic idea that the stones were hewn from beneath the Throne of Glory, which is also the realm from where souls derive. For Abulafia, the human soul is the inward aspect of nature, associated with the heart, seat of the intellect. The importance of the heart is alluded to at the end of the extract, for throughout rabbinic literature the heart is viewed as the seat of the 'inclinations': the heart is the organ for choosing between good and evil. In the middle part of the extract, Abulafia establishes the higher dimension of the stones on account of their connection with the letters, which comprise the link with God. Abulafia's overarching interest lies in understanding the status of the Torah, symbolized by the tablets. The outer garments of the Torah place it in the realm of the human heart, the domain of human intellect. The letters themselves transcend this domain, which enables man to reach towards the Active Intellect, the sphere which integrates the human mind with the divine Mind.

The 'pure marble stones', which Abulafia ties in with this analysis of the tablets, are the stones which are understood to pave the floor of the higher, heavenly Temple. They feature in a famous story recorded in the Talmud and already mentioned in Chapter 3:

> Our Rabbis taught: Four entered Paradise, namely, Ben Azzai, Ben Zoma, Aher and Rabbi Akiba. R. Akiba said to them: When you approach the pure marble stones, do not say, 'water, water!' For it is written, 'He that speaks falsehood shall not endure before my eyes' (*Psalm* 101:7). Ben Azzai looked and died. Of him Scripture says, 'Precious in the eyes of the Lord is the death of His saints' (*Psalm* 116:15). Ben Zoma looked and was stricken. Of him Scripture says, 'Have you found honey? Eat as much as is sufficient for you, lest you be overfilled and vomit it' (*Proverbs* 25:16). Aher cut the shoots. Rabbi Akiba departed in peace. (Talmud, *Hagigah* 14b)

It would seem that Abulafia draws our attention to this connection with the marble stones in order to emphasize the role of the Torah in enabling us to reach the heavenly realm.

The injunction not to say, 'water, water!' seems to refer to the danger of mistaking a higher level of the heavenly realm for that of a lower one. The image of 'cutting the shoots' is used to refer to a heretical position. One who 'cuts the shoots' relates to the *sefirot* as if they had fully independent status and fails to acknowledge their root in the *En Sof* (see Lancaster 2004: 273–4).

Among kabbalistic writings at the end of the thirteenth century, this story concerning Paradise came to be associated with the idea of levels in the interpretation of Torah. In Hebrew, *pardes* (*prds*, literally 'orchard', but comes to mean 'Paradise') can be read as an acrostic of the initial letters of four terms that convey these different levels:

> *Pshat* ('simple') – the contextual, or immediate, sense of the words;
>
> *Remez* ('hint') – the allegorical meaning, especially in a philosophical sense;
>
> *Drush* ('interpret') – the homiletic interpretation, as in Midrash;
>
> *Sod* ('secret') – the mystical meaning, as it may relate, for example, to the *sefirot.*

Clearly, the intention of this acrostic is to assert the centrality of Torah and the need to maintain continuity across the levels of meaning. The Jewish mystic is at home on the ladder whose rungs are established in the philosophical and rabbinic approaches to the text. The principle of inclusivity is paramount. The epithet of having gained entrance to Paradise and being capable of emerging intact is reserved for the individual who is learned in all the levels, and who has achieved a state of equanimity.

Mystical practices that transform the mystic's sense of self comprise an important dimension of Kabbalah, as we shall see in Chapters 6 and 7. But it would be an error to view the study of Torah as separate from these practices. Studying Torah through the principles of Kabbalah should not be viewed as 'merely' an intellectual exercise. Kabbalah presents an integrated path in which meditative practices are themselves generally dependent on a knowledge of Torah. At the same time, these practices are uniquely able to enrich the mystic's grasp of the Torah.

The mystical understanding of Torah places it beyond the status of any book, for it is the embodiment of reality, the crystallization of the divine Mind. For this reason, the kabbalistic quest to gain ever more complex insights into the text is also a quest to know the nature of reality. Engaging with the Torah does not only mean plumbing the depths of scripture; it also means perceiving the depths of meaning in both the outer world and the inner world of the psyche. Perhaps this accounts for the impact which the classical Jewish and kabbalistic approaches to the Torah have had in areas as diverse as physics, science fiction, psychology and artificial intelligence. I shall examine the impact of Kabbalah in these contemporary pursuits in Chapter 8. For now, let us simply recall Ben *Bag Bag*'s adage: 'Turn it around, turn it around for all is in it . . .'

JACOB AND JOSEPH

Considerable insight into the detail of the *sefirot* can be gleaned through studying the major biblical characters and the events in their lives. From the religious perspective, it is not simply that a character symbolizes a particular *sefirah*, but rather that the biblical players are part of the unfolding of God's plan, a plan which necessarily recapitulates the sequence of the *sefirot*. This view is intrinsic to the classical Jewish motif that God used the Torah as a plan for creation. The subtle allusions to the characters as *sefirot* are indicative of the entire substructure of the Torah, which teaches of the *sefirot* and divine Names.

In the remainder of this chapter I shall explore some of the deeper ways of reading the biblical stories of Jacob and Joseph, who relate to the *sefirot* of *Tiferet* and *Yesod* respectively. The array of

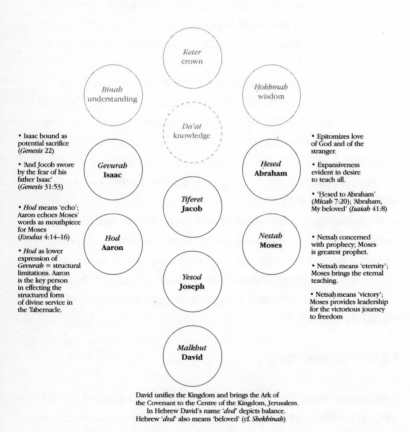

Fig. 5.1. The relation of the seven lower *sefirot* with biblical archetypes (see text for detail of Jacob and Joseph)

sefirot, together with their associated biblical characters, is given in Figure 5.1. It is beyond the scope of this work to enter into detail of each one; a few indicative points are therefore included in the figure. My discussion of Jacob and Joseph will be illustrative of the kabbalistic approach to the more concealed teachings relating to all the biblical figures.

Just as *Ḥesed* gives rise to *Gevurah* which produces *Tiferet*, so Abraham fathers Isaac, whose wife, Rebecca, produces Jacob. Joseph is one of Jacob's twelve sons. Jacob becomes the father of the nation of Israel, and Joseph plays a significant part in the continuation of the nation. Essentially, Jacob depicts the notion of 'centre' and of the spiritual linkage between earthly and heavenly realms, between 'below' and 'above'; the Torah's portrayal of Joseph shows him as both the interpreter of divine messages and as the ideal servant.

The *Zohar* asserts a relationship between the role of Jacob in the *sefirotic* scheme and that of the 'middle bar' in the *Mishkan*. Before quoting the relevant passage, I need to clarify the meaning of the *Mishkan*. In *pshat* (simple) terms, this structure is both a focus for divine worship and also the place where God meets with the representative of His people. It is thus a point of connection from below to above and from above to below. This twofold function already hints at the esoteric meaning of the *Mishkan*, for the Rabbis viewed it as a microcosm which has correspondences with 'above' and 'below'. In the direction 'above' it resonates with the macrocosm, the world of creation; and 'below' it corresponds to the human microcosm. (I have explored this theme in Lancaster 1993: Chapter 3.) In its role of unifying higher and lower realms, the *Mishkan* parallels the Torah itself. Kabbalists have explored in meticulous detail the correspondences between the various structures of the *Mishkan*, described in the book of *Exodus*, and both the make-up of the human body and the pattern of the 'body' of the Torah, that is, the *mitsvot*. In this vein, the author of the *Zohar* builds on the statement, 'And the *Mishkan* will be one' (*Exodus* 26:6), emphasizing that both the human body and the Torah have many parts but that each constitutes a unity. Similarly, the *Mishkan* is made of constituent parts yet shares this key principle of all organisms – that it is a unity. Ultimately, the unity of the *Mishkan* arises because it is the pattern of the entire *sefirotic* system, with Jacob being the principle that establishes its oneness.

The primary meaning of the Hebrew word for 'middle bar', *beriakh*, is a 'bolt', which is significant in this context, for Jacob is viewed as the figure who, as it were, locks in place the structure of the nation. And, of course, *Tiferet* is the central *sefirah*, which establishes the integrity of the whole *sefirotic* structure. The following passage from the *Zohar* makes this point through an analysis of the biblical statement that 'Jacob [was] a simple man dwelling in tents' (*Genesis* 25:27):

> And the middle bar in the midst of the boards shall pass through from end to end' (*Exodus* 26:28). This is Jacob who is holy and perfect, as we have explained concerning the verse, 'And Jacob [was] a simple man, dwelling in tents'. It is not written, 'dwelling in a tent', but 'dwelling in tents', implying *two* tents, for he grasped both this and this. Similarly it is written that 'the middle bar in the midst of the boards shall pass through from end to end' to mean that it grasps this and this [i.e., the two ends]. And we have learnt: what does 'simple man' mean? It is as the Aramaic translation states: *shelim* ('perfect'/'complete'). He is perfect in everything; perfect from both sides, that of the Holy Ancient One [*Keter*] and that of the small face [the *sefirot* centred on *Tiferet*]. He is the completion of the supernal *Hesed* and of the supernal *Gevurah*; the completion of this and this. (*Zohar* 2:175b)

There are two axes intimated in this passage, both of which are integrated through the *sefirah* of *Tiferet*. The first is the vertical axis through which *Keter* is unified with the lower *sefirot*, and the second is the horizontal one, through which Hesed and *Gevurah* are integrated.

Jacob's role as the *sefirah* of integration is conveyed within the biblical description of his dream of a ladder:

> And he came by chance upon the place, and remained there all night because the sun had set; and he took of the stones of the place and arranged them under his head and lay down in that place. And he dreamed, and behold, a ladder set up on the earth and the top of it reaching to heaven; and behold, the angels of God ascending and descending on it (*Genesis* 28:11-12).

The Rokeach detects a concealed meaning in the phrase *va-yishkav ba-makom ha-hu* (and lay down in that place). With a slight change in the way in which the letters are divided into words, it could be read to mean *va-yesh kv ba-makom ha-hu* (and there are 22 [the numerical value of *kv*] in that place), namely, the 22 letters of the Hebrew alphabet. Kabbalistically, there is a relationship between the centre and the whole. Jacob – *Tiferet* – is the centre and the 22 Hebrew letters depict the totality of creation. The 'place' is understood to be Mount Moriah, the site where the Temple would later be built in Jerusalem. Indeed, following his dream, Jacob remarks, 'This is none other than the House of God and this is the gate of heaven' (*Genesis* 28:17).

In rabbinic thought, Temple-building is equated with 'world-building', or creation. As is recorded in the Talmud, 'Rav Judah said in the name of Rav: Betsalel knew how to combine the letters by which the heavens and earth were created' (Talmud, *Berakhot* 55a). Just as God creates through His mastery over the letters, so Betsalel is qualified to build the sacred microcosm on account of his wisdom in relation to the same letters. Betsalel duly builds the prototypical Jewish Temple, the *Mishkan*. Moreover, the place of Jacob's dream is construed as the 'navel' of the world, the place from which the creation of the world began. There is a deeper allusion in the term 'place', for throughout rabbinic literature, the term 'Place' refers to God. God is considered to be the 'Place of the world'. At the same time, the word 'place' (*makom*) and the name 'Jacob' are deemed to be equivalent by a complex gematria (the value of *ya'kov* [Jacob] is 182; add to this 4, representing the four letters of the sacred Name, and you have a total of 186, which is the gematria of *makom* [place]). This calculation may seem somewhat 'stretched'. However, the intention of connecting the name 'Jacob' with the Name Y-H-V-H displays an internal 'kabbalistic logic', bearing in mind the identification of both names with *Tiferet*. It is as if the totality of creation is mystically drawn into the place on which Jacob 'chances' that evening.

The term 'Place' alludes to both God's immanence in the world and His transcendence. This central teaching is captured in the phrase: 'The Holy One, blessed be He, is the place of His world but His world is not His place' (Midrash, *Genesis Rabbah* 68:9). Since there is nothing other than God, the world can only exist *in* God; this defines His immanence. On the other hand, God's essence derives from an altogether other dimension of transcendence. Therefore *His* place is not here, as it were.

This notion that Jacob comprises the totality is detected by Abulafia in his two names. The ladder dream occurs as Jacob is leaving the land of Canaan. Twenty years later, as he is returning to the land, he undergoes the ordeal of wrestling through the night with an angel (see Chapter 1, p. 29), following which his name is changed to Israel. Abulafia notes that Jacob is an anagram of *akbi* (my heel) and Israel is an anagram of *le-roshi* (to my head). Jacob is thus viewed as the image of the whole. In this, he is a recapitulation of the primordial Adam and becomes the perfected microcosmic man from 'heel to head'.

A further allusion is detected in the phrase 'and lay down in that place', which, as we saw above, may be read to mean 'and there are 22 in that place'. The word *hu* (that) is said to refer to *Keter*, whilst the stone which served as Jacob's pillow is identified as the *Shekhinah*, *Malkhut*. The ladder is accordingly that which connects the vertical axis from beginning to end, the ladder of the *sefirot*.

The logic of these allusions is complex. Gikatilla informs us that the word *hu* (here meaning 'that') refers to *Keter*. In addition to meaning 'that', *hu* means 'he' or 'it', and it is for this reason that Gikatilla associates it with *Keter*. We cannot know *Keter*, and therefore can only refer to it as 'It'. In this context, Gikatilla draws attention to the biblical verse describing the *manna*, the nourishment that sustains us during our spiritual journey: 'And the people of Israel saw and said one to another, *man hu* ('what is it?') for they did not know *mah hu* (what it was)' (*Exodus* 16:15). The English 'manna' derives from the Hebrew *man*, but does not adequately convey the point that it is the ability to ask the question that becomes the true sustenance. The name *man hu* is interpreted to mean not simply that they did not recognize it, but rather that the essential nature of the manna concerned the ability to question. The sustenance descends from *Keter* (*Hu*), which is the beginning of any emergence from *En Sof*. The ability to receive this nourishment is dependent both on a recognition that there is an ultimate Other, a transcendent divine essence, and also on the realization that we can never know that essence – we must learn to be satisfied with asking the question.

I have noted already that questions are central to the *sefirotic* structure: 'Who?' applies to *Binah*; 'What?' (*mah*) applies to both *Hokhmah* and *Malkhut*; and now we have this additional equation, that 'What?' (*man*) applies to *Keter*. This is a highly important element in Kabbalah; it is worth repeating the point that asking the question becomes a recapitulation of the primordial contraction (*tsimtsum*).

Asking the question is the only way to make space for the answer to arise. It is significant that the difference in *gematria* between *mah* and *man* is forty-five, the numerical value of *mah* itself. To ask 'what?' is already the dignity of man (the gematria of *adam* = 45); to recognize that there is a higher dimension to things, beyond whatever we might know, and that there is therefore a question that can actually never be answered, is the dignity of the higher man.

The biblical text states that Jacob 'took of the *stones* of the place' to make his head-rest. When he awakes, however, the verse states that 'he took the *stone* that he had arranged under his head, and set it up as a pillar' (*Genesis* 28:18). There is a glaring inconsistency in the text which attracts the attention of every commentator: the stones (plural) before his vision become one stone (singular) afterwards. Traditionally, it is understood that there were initially twelve stones. This exegesis derives from the word *hu*, which has the numerical value of twelve. The phrase *va-yishkav ba-makom ha-hu* (and lay down in that place) could therefore be read as 'and lay down in the place of the twelve'. Jacob is the glyph of the centre which connoted the union of twelve into one:

> These are the twelve holy stones, and they all were made into one stone, as it is written, 'And this stone which I have set up as a pillar' (*Genesis* 28:22). He called them 'stone'. What is the reason? Because all twelve stones are included in one holy supernal stone that is above them [the *Shekhinah*], for it is written, 'And this stone which I have set up as a pillar shall become the House of God [i.e., the Temple, where the *Shekhinah* dwells]' . . . On account of this, all is in the secret of the twelve: the supernal twelve, concealed above, sealed in the holy supernal mystery. They are the secret of the Torah, and they emerge from one small voice . . . There are twelve

> others hidden below, corresponding to them, and they
> emerge from within another voice of that very stone, as it
> is written, 'From there is the shepherd, the stone of
> Israel' (*Genesis* 49:24) . . . This is the *Shekhinah*, who is
> called 'a tried stone' (*Isaiah* 28:16), the stone of Israel.
> (*Zohar* 2:229b-30a)

The immediate reference for the twelve is the tribes of Israel,
deriving from Jacob's twelve sons. This is evident from the biblical
description of the twelve stones on the High Priest's breastplate
(*Exodus* 28; 35). The twelve tribes constitute the nation, and, since the
Temple is the centre of the nation, the 'place of the twelve' is the
Temple. This is prefigured in the arrangement of the *Mishkan*, around
which the twelve tribes were camped, three on each side. The earthly
Mishkan is said to conform to the pattern of a heavenly *Mishkan*,
around which the 'supernal twelve' are ordered. These supernal
twelve are the permutations of the ineffable Name, which comprise
the essence of the Torah, since the Torah is essentially the explication
of the Name. As already mentioned, these twelve relate to the
astrological spheres through which the divine influx is channelled into
the world. Shining through all these allusions is the essential teaching
that the real centre takes on transcendent significance, for it is the
place of communication and unification between that which is 'below'
and that which is 'above'.

The significance of the centre is recapitulated at the level of the
individual. To be open to the higher dimension of the soul it is
necessary to be centred in oneself. Being 'centred', which primarily
means that awareness is focused in the heart, allows for the gates of
deeper consciousness to be opened. Ultimately, the Temple needs to
be built within, in the individual heart, in order that the channel to the
supernal realm might be made conscious. The essence of spiritual
growth is conveyed by the story of Jacob's transformation into Israel,

for the name 'Jacob' signifies the lower self, whilst 'Israel' is the higher self. And transformation does not come about without a struggle. If we choose to embark on the spiritual journey of transformation, at some stage we all must encounter our adversary, as did Jacob when wrestling through that dark night.

The image of the *Mishkan* surrounded by the twelve permutations of the Name is akin to the pattern given in a mandala, whose function is to bring about the centring of awareness necessary for spiritual progress. But it is a mandala in which sound plays the dominant role, for the letters of the Name connote vowel sounds. The four letters of the ineffable Name have a distinctive significance since, in an unpointed Hebrew text (as in the Torah scroll), the letters *yod*, *heh* and *vav* denote the presence of specific vowel sounds – *ee*, *ah* and *oo* (or *o*) respectively (see also Chapter 6, p. 173). The vowel sounds accompany the flow of the breath, for, unlike consonants, they comprise unbounded sound. In Kabbalah, the 'mandala'-like pattern given by the twelve permutations which carve out a centre is not primarily a visual image. Rather, it becomes a 'mandala of the breath', for which the the twelve sound combinations are used in generating a heart-focused, centred state.

The role that Jacob plays as *Tiferet* within the *sefirotic* system is further conveyed in a tradition found throughout midrashic and kabbalistic sources that the image of Jacob is engraved on the Throne of Glory. There is, as it were, a 'lower Jacob' and a 'higher Jacob' (Israel). Again, these ideas are established on the basis of complex allusions in the biblical text. The Rokeach notes that the word *anokhi* (I) may be equated with *kissei* (throne), since they both have the same numerical value (81). He reads the verse spoken by Jacob to Rachel, 'Am I [*anokhi*] in place of God?' (*Genesis* 30:2) as intimating this motif of Jacob as the 'throne beneath God' (the Hebrew translated in Jacob's question as 'in place of' literally means 'beneath'). This, in turn, suggests that the verse, 'And they saw the

God of Israel and under His feet, a paved work of sapphire . . .'
(*Exodus* 24:10) should be read differently: 'They saw God, and Israel
[was] under His feet . . .'. All these feats of exegesis (cited in Wolfson
1995b) are intended to establish that Jacob is identified with the
supernal throne and that he therefore plays a role in the divine
hierarchy. The Rokeach provides a further key when he points out
that, by gematria, the two phrases 'you will see my back' (*Exodus*
33:23) and 'like the image of Jacob that is engraved on the throne'
are equivalent. The verse from *Exodus* records God's words to Moses
and continues by stating that Moses would not be able to see His
face. The implication of the Rokeach's deciphering of the allusions is
that the aspect of God which can be known (i.e. the rear or 'lower'
aspect) is identified with Jacob. Indeed, a similar conclusion is given
in the Talmud:

> R. Aha said in the name of R. Eleazar: From where do we
> know that the Holy One, blessed be He, calls Jacob 'god'?
> Because it says, 'And the God of Israel called him *El* [a
> Name of God]' (*Genesis* 33:20). Should you suppose that
> [what the biblical text means is that] Jacob called the altar
> El, then it should have written, 'And Jacob called it'. Rather,
> it says, 'He called Jacob El'. And who called him so? The
> God of Israel. (Talmud, *Megillah* 18a)

The Midrash is even more explicit, stating in the name of Resh
Lakish that Jacob said to God: 'You are God in relation to the higher
beings and I am god in relation to the lower beings' (Midrash, *Bereshit
Rabbah* 79:8).

This identification between Jacob and an aspect of the divine
emanation raises the question as to what we mean by 'God'. Clearly, in
the normal sense in which we understand the word, Jacob could not
be identified with God! Judaism would reject absolutely any putative

identification between the divine essence and a human. And, certainly, in the thinking of all the major kabbalists, Jacob was a historical figure and therefore fully human. However, Kabbalah is fundamentally concerned with the dynamics through which the unknowable essence of God manifests in the world. The *sefirot* describe the ways in which God may be known through His actions, and the biblical Patriarchs literally embody these ways. Jacob comes to embody the rulership that *Tiferet* asserts in the lower region of the *sefirotic* array. It is for this reason that Jacob is even identified with the four-letter Name (Y-H-V-H), which is the Name ascribed to *Tiferet*. This identification is determined, as already indicated, by adding one for each of the four letters to the numerical value of *ya'kov* (Jacob), which is 182, giving a total of 186. This number is connected with the sacred Name, since it is the sum of the squared value of each of its letters ($10 \times 10 + 5 \times 5 + 6 \times 6 + 5 \times 5 = 186$).

In one sense, there is nothing untoward in asserting Jacob's divine status. Ultimately, there cannot be anything which is not God: given that 'God is the Place of the world', everything exists *in* God. Yet these allusions that Jacob holds divine status as ruler of the lower order in creation have a deeper meaning. Jacob/*Tiferet* is the place through which all are brought into relationship with the higher essence of God. Through his own achievement in meriting the transformation to Israel, Jacob seeds the path through which others can follow. In Jacob/Israel we all can find fulfilment as beings centred in the image of God. We all have the potential to receive nourishment through the integrated heart of creation:

> Jacob . . . arranged his sons around the *Shekhinah* [producing] the perfection of all, and surrounding them were many supernal chariots . . . whereupon the sun became gathered unto the moon and the east was brought near to the west . . . and the moon was illumined and

attained its perfection. And so we learn from tradition that
Jacob did not die. (*Zohar* 1:235b)

The *Shekhinah* is identified with the moon, the archetypal
feminine symbol, and the perfection of the moon (*Malkhut*) is
achieved when it is unified with the sun (*Tiferet*). In order for this to
happen, the channel connecting *Tiferet* and *Malkhut* must function
correctly. And this is dependent on *Yesod*.

Core characteristics of the *sefirah* of *Yesod* may be gleaned
through a close reading of the biblical narrative of Joseph. In brief,
these characteristics revolve around Joseph's status. Joseph proves his
worth in several roles: as the *tsadik* who is in control of his sexuality;
as the interpreter of dreams; as the agent who is responsible for
storing and releasing grain to maintain sustenance; and as the 'director
of events' who endeavours to effect reconciliation between the parties
of the nascent nation.

The first turning point in Joseph's life is signalled when his father
sends him to meet his brothers (*Genesis* 37:12-22). In reply to Jacob,
Joseph answers '*hineni*' ('Here I am'). This is a literary form used in
the Bible to indicate moments of destiny. The Hebrew term *hineh*
means 'here' or 'behold', and has the effect in biblical narratives of
shifting what follows into the present tense. (This effect might be
compared to the flashback style in movies, through which past events
are relived in the present.) An additional point of interest concerns the
shortened construction whereby *hineh* (here am) and *ani* (I) are
linked into one word, *hineni*. This biblical construct is intended to
portray a moment of real presence in which the ego is truncated as an
individual's destiny begins to unfold. The enormity of the events
following Joseph's '*hineni*' is further signalled in verse 15, where
Joseph encounters a 'man', and 'behold, he is wandering in the field'
(following from the point just made, the Hebrew switches here into
the present tense). The oral tradition makes clear that this 'man' is an

angel. The angel pushes Joseph towards his destiny by sending him on to meet his brothers.

The story is familiar, and should be read in the original for the important nuances. Essentially, the brothers throw Joseph into a pit before selling him into slavery. In the original Hebrew, the word for 'pit' is *bor*. It is instructive to note that this same word is repeated, in *Genesis* 41:14, to refer to the 'dungeon' from which Joseph is released at the command of Pharaoh. During the crucial intervening narrative, a different term is used for 'prison', thereby emphasizing that all the events from Joseph's descent into the pit at the hand of his brothers until his eventual release from the dungeon at the hand of Pharaoh constitute a single swing of the pendulum of destiny.

During that swing of the pendulum Joseph achieves his destiny by, firstly, aspiring to the role of perfect servant, secondly, withstanding the sexual temptations offered by Potiphar's wife, and thirdly, coming to understand that the interpretation of dreams comes through God. He is then ready to embark on the next phase in the unfolding text of his life – that of handling the storage and release of grain. Having correctly interpreted Pharoah's dreams by suggesting that there were to be seven years of plenty followed by seven of famine, Joseph is charged by Pharaoh to store grain during the first seven years and to distribute it responsibly during the years of famine. Joseph becomes second only to Pharaoh in the land of Egypt.

What is the unifying theme within these various strands in the narrative of Joseph? A hint may be discerned in the Hebrew for 'grain', *br*, pronounced *bar* ('and let them amass grain beneath the hand of Pharaoh', *Genesis* 41:35). This two-letter word is related not only to *bor*, the term which delineates the beginning and end of the period of Joseph's descent, but also *bara* (create). There is an implicit sexual connotation in these links, which may appear somewhat elliptical until the kabbalistic meaning of the connection between Joseph and *Yesod* is further understood.

Throughout kabbalistic texts, *Yesod* is portrayed as the male sexual organ, and Joseph is the master of all the functions that revolve around sexuality. This is intimated, for example, in Jacob's blessing to Joseph: 'Joseph is a fruitful bough, a fruitful bough beside a well . . . His bow remained firm' (*Genesis* 49:22-4):

> What is meant by 'my bow' [the *rainbow* mentioned in Genesis 9:13]? It is as is written of Joseph, 'His bow remained firm'. Because Joseph is called *tsadik*, such is his bow – it is the covenant of the bow that is included in the *tsadik*, in order to connect this [the male] with this [the female]. (*Zohar* 1:71b)

The reference is both to the covenant established at the time of Noah (which was sealed with the rainbow) and to that of circumcision: the rainbow is symbolically connected with the phallus, for it arches to connect 'heaven' and 'earth'. Paralleling this is the role of *Yesod* which functions to connect *Tiferet* (the male) with *Malkhut* (the female).

Freud was firmly following in the footsteps of kabbalists, whether he knew it or not, in asserting that the primary motivation of the psyche is sexual in origin. *Yesod* is the *sefirah* associated with dreaming and imagination in general. As expressed in a text from the Iyyun circle of kabbalists active in Castile in the second half of the thirteenth century, the ninth sphere, which corresponds to *Yesod*, is 'the king in the power of the imagination' (cited in Wolfson 1994: 316). Joseph's role in storing and releasing 'grain' intimates symbolically that he was able to control the sexual function. As a consequence, he could effect a true channel to God for the purposes of interpreting the works of the imagination.

The actions of Joseph's brothers had threatened the unity of the nation. How could a nation be built of tribes, one of which descended from a brother who had been treated so despicably? It is evident in the long final part of the narrative that Joseph comes to understand that his destiny is not simply to ensure that the family can survive during a time of famine. His role is to work behind the scenes in order to bring his brother, Judah, to the fore as the true leader of the nation. The interested reader will study the biblical text itself for the hints that support this statement. Here, I wish merely to emphasize the function of *Yesod* in the *sefirotic* system. Its function is to effect the union within the Godhead that enables the divine influx to flow throughout the realms of creation. At the level of the nation, Joseph had to work to repair those blocks that had held back the full integration of all the parties; he orchestrated a subtle drama in order that Judah would step forward to achieve his destiny. *Yesod* is the linchpin in ensuring that the entire conformation of players achieves its goal.

Joseph acts as psychopompos on the national level. His function is recapitulated at the psychological level within the individual. We must learn to trust that 'Joseph' function which manoeuvres circumstances to encourage the harmonious alignment of our inner parts. The spiritual and psychological journey towards integration demands an understanding of those aspects of the personality that block moves towards a mature integration. The desired integration can only be fully realized when a channel to the 'higher' is opened, which, in itself, demands the correct operation of the sexual function.

Kabbalah does not seek to deny the importance of the physical expression of sexuality in its proper place. At the same time, a sublimation of the sexual function is at the core of the kabbalist's interest in penetrating the text of the Torah. In this chapter I have indicated some of the ways in which the concealed meaning may be laid bare. In the revealing is a re-concealing, as the Kabbalah insists. It is for this reason, as should be evident to anyone who understands these matters, that:

It is forbidden for a person to look at the rainbow, for it is the appearance of the supernal image; it is forbidden for a man to look at the sign of his covenant [circumcision], for it hints at the *tsadik* of the world; it is forbidden for a person to look at the fingers of the priests when they spread out their hands [in giving the priestly blessing, as prescribed in *Numbers* 6:23-7], for there rests the glory of the supernal King. (*Zohar* 3:84a)

Chapter 6

A Mysticism of Language

THE NAME OF GOD

> The whole world is a book which God, blessed be He, made; and the Torah is the commentary that He made and bound to that book. (Rav Zadok ha-Kohen of Lublin, *Mahshavot Heruts* 44a)

Rav Zadok ha-Kohen of Lublin (1823–1900) expresses here the core of kabbalistic teaching: language penetrates to the heart of reality. Kabbalah is quintessentially a mysticism of language. Practically all kabbalistic teachings arise through analysis of the Hebrew language. Penetrating the language of the Torah is the path to reaching its concealed meanings, and to know the Torah in this way is to know the world. The Torah is not seen as something apart from the world. Indeed, the crucial connection between Torah and the world is explicit in the advice given by Rabbi Ishmael (early second century CE) to a scribe who writes the sacred words on a Torah scroll: 'My son, be meticulous in your work, for it is the work of heaven; should you omit one single letter, or add one too many, you would thereby destroy the whole world' (Talmud, *Eruvin* 13a).

The primary biblical story about language concerns the tower of Babel. Prior to the doomed attempt to build a tower to heaven, 'the whole earth was of one language and words of oneness' (*Genesis* 11:1). The Rokeach demonstrates that the phrase *safa ehat* (one language), is equated by gematria with the phrase *leshon ha-kodesh* (the holy language), namely, Hebrew. Moreover, *safa* (language) has the same numerical value (385) as *Shekhinah*, an equation which is taken to mean that it is specifically through language that we are able to connect with the divine. One of the kabbalistic symbols for *Malkhut* is that of the *mouth*, the organ of outer language, namely, speech. In Jewish practice, it is axiomatic that prayer must entail some movement of the lips; it is not enough simply to speak inwardly. The slight movement of the mouth hints towards the activation of *Malkhut* in the act of prayer. Prayer is a primary path of connection to the *Shekhinah – Malkhut*. The Hebrew for 'mouth', *peh*, has the same consonants as *poh*, meaning 'here'. In simple terms, speech can be effective only when the one to whom you speak is present ('here'). More deeply, the mouth is the organ of intimate connection to another, as in the kiss, which itself is a kabbalistic symbol for the state of cleaving to the *Shekhinah* in mystical rapture.

In addition to prayer, the above verse from *Genesis* that depicts the pre-Babel state intimates a second path of connection to the *Shekhinah*. According to Isaac of Acre (cited in Idel 1992: 69), the 'words of oneness' mentioned in the verse are the 72 forms of the divine Name, comprising 216 letters in total (see also Chapter 2, p. 63) . This Name derives from three verses in the book of *Exodus* (14:19-21):

> 19. And the angel of God, who had been going in front of
>   the camp of Israel, moved and went behind them; and
>   the pillar of cloud went from before them and stood
>   behind them;

20. And it came between the camp of the Egyptians and
    the camp of Israel; and it was the cloud and the
    darkness, yet it gave light by night; and one did not draw
    near the other all the night.

21. And Moses stretched out his hand over the sea; and the
    Lord led the sea with a strong east wind all the night,
    and turned the sea into dry land, and the waters were
    split.

Each of these verses comprises 72 Hebrew letters. In kabbalistic
tradition the 72 triple forms are obtained by placing the middle verse
in reverse order. Thus, the first of the forms comprises the first letter
of verse 19 (*vav*), the last letter of verse 20 (*heh*), and the first letter
of verse 21 (*vav*), giving the name *vahu*. Moses had been instructed
to 'raise your staff and stretch your arm over the sea and split it'
(*Exodus* 14:16). The term *uveka'eihu* (and split it) is an anagram of
baka vahu. The word '*baka*' means 'to split', leading kabbalists to
understand that the meaning concealed within this verse is that
Moses used the divine Name of 72 forms beginning with *vahu*. God
brings about the miracle, but Moses instigates God's intervention
through his use of this Name.

As is well known, the story of the tower of Babel concerns human
arrogance and the desire for idolatry. The quest to reach heaven by
building a tower is answered by God confusing human language and
dispersing the nations. Kabbalah teaches the path to reconnect with
the language of unification that existed prior to the confusion. Again,
this concealed teaching is conveyed through the hints in the text itself.
Following the statement that the 'earth was of one language and words
of oneness', the text continues by informing us that 'they journeyed
from the east [*mi-kedem*] and they found a valley [*bika'h*] in the land
of Shinar' (*Genesis* 11:2). This journey from the east is a journey away

from the 'primordial [*mi-kadma'ah*] root of the world, the place of perfect faith . . . to the place of splitting [*bika'h*], where they lose the higher faith' (*Zohar* 1:74b). This interpretation is based on the etymological relation between *kedem* (east) and *kadma'ah* (primordial), and on the fact that *bika'h* (valley) derives from the root *baka* (split). In this word for 'valley', the *Zohar* detects the essential concept of the dispersal that follows the building of the tower.

Ramban's commentary clarifies the exact nature of the sin of the generation of Babel. As it states in the biblical text, they desired to 'make *for themselves* a name' (*Genesis* 11:4). They wanted a name with which to reach to heaven, but this plan was *for their own purposes*, not for the sake of heaven. By seeking a name that might have magical effects, without acknowledging the higher essence of God, they committed the sin of 'cutting the shoots', as Ramban informs us. Outwardly, the biblical narrative indicates the incorrect motive for wanting to make a name; at the concealed level, it hints at the correct approach of connecting with the Name of God.

The kabbalist attempts to use language to return to the 'primordial root', which is the unknowable essence of all. Kabbalistic practices entail using language in ways that deliberately abandon the normal semantic meaning of words. Specifically using letters and sounds as elements void of meaning brings about the intended connection to that which cannot, by its very nature, be given a finite meaning. Paradoxically, the elements of language themselves become the means for transcending language as a semantic system.

The three verses from *Exodus* convey the crucial context for the kabbalistic use of the Name of 72 combinations. The pillar is paradoxically both the cloud of darkness and a source of light. In terms of the Name, the combinations of letters have no intrinsic meaning ('the cloud and the darkness'), yet they function to connect the adept to the *Shekhinah* ('gave light by night'). 'The more incomprehensible the Names, the greater is their advantage,' writes an anonymous pupil of

Abulafia (cited in Kaplan 1982: 108). The theme of transition constitutes the essence of these three verses. The angel and the pillar transit from the front to the rear; the darkness gives light; and the sea becomes dry land. The verses depict the final turning point in the Exodus from Egypt – the transition from a lower to a higher level of being.

A tradition recorded in the Talmud cryptically alludes to a further understanding of the importance of the Name of seventy-two. This tradition states the size of the tablets of stone given by God to Moses (Talmud, *Bava Batra* 14a). Each tablet was six handbreadths long, six wide and three deep. In these measurements kabbalists find a hint to the Name of seventy-two combinations: the individual measurements yield a product of 108 for one tablet (6 x 6 x 3), and therefore 216 for the two tablets (108 x 2). As noted above, 216 is the total number of letters in the 72 combinations. The theme is further emphasized by the fact that 216 is the numerical value of *devir*, the Holy of Holies in Solomon's Temple, resting place of the holy tablets (see Chapter 3, p. 79). These numerical calculations underpin a kabbalistic teaching that the Name of 216 was placed in the Ark of the *Mishkan*. The Name occupies the space of nothingness that accompanies the tablets in the Ark.

Clearly, all these allusions give focus to the intention that accompanies the kabbalistic practice of working with the Name. The Name is the medium of transformation. The mystic is endeavouring to transit from our post-Babel state to the pre-Babel language of oneness. He is intent on journeying from a lower to a higher level of being; from a confined state of consciousness to an expanded state. And he is striving to engage with that nothingness from which the divine influx may descend to enliven his soul.

Abulafia teaches the technique for this practice. Prior to performing the linguistic practice itself, one must achieve a state of purification. Wearing clean clothes and lighting candles is recommended. But the purification is, of course, primarily inward: there needs to be firm control over one's thoughts. It is necessary to meditate in a secluded place and to 'unify the heart' (see Chapter 7 for more detail about practices of unification involving the heart). When a focused state of mind has been achieved, one begins to work with language. The first practice Abulafia describes entails examining ordinary words for all possible permutations of their letters and other associations. Such linguistic activity is claimed to be the path to understanding the secrets of the Torah. This form of 'language working' is a preliminary to chanting combinations of the Name itself. Initially, the 'language working' is conducted outwardly with ink on a 'tablet'; subsequently, a more inward focus is deployed. The mystic cultivates an attitude that might be described as one of respectful play towards the linguistic elements. As Abulafia illustrates, the word *Adam*, for example, becomes *amad*, *dama*, *da'am* and *mada'*. Skill in this and the other associative techniques (using gematria, initial letters, codes, and so on) becomes an essential prerequisite for chanting the divine Name.

Abulafia informs us that the goal of this practice is to receive the divine influx, an event which is described partly in physical terms: it is felt as a 'warming of the heart', a 'trembling of the body', or as the feeling of being anointed with oil. Beyond the bodily experience of this awakened state, it is the influx of new knowledge that is the desired aim. The mystic's quest is for knowledge that derives from a source beyond that of the human intellect:

> Begin to combine a few letters with many. Reverse them and revolve them rapidly, until your heart is warmed through the revolutions. Pay attention to their movements and to what you bring into being through their revolutions. And when you feel that your heart has been greatly warmed through the combinations, and when you have derived understanding from them – new ideas that were never disclosed through human tradition and that you could not have known through intellectual analysis – then

you are prepared to receive the divine influx. The influx will
then emanate upon you, and will stimulate you to many
words, one after the other. (Abulafia, *Hayei ha-Olam ha-Ba*
2001 edition: p.67)

According to Rabbi Judah Albotini (d. 1519), who drew heavily on
the Abulafian practices in his own manual of Hebrew language
mysticism, the practitioner 'releases thought from the prison of the
natural realm and raises it to the divine realm' (cited in Blumenthal
1982: 43). The practice 'stimulates the soul, increases its warmth, and
speeds its movement, bringing it from potency to actuality'.

For Abulafia, the associative dimension is the very core of language.
Indeed, he notes that the gematria of *tseruf* ('combination', the term he
uses generally to include the associative connections that are built
between letters and across words) is identical with *lashon* (language) –
each totalling 386. In a very real psychological sense this view is correct:
the essence of language depends on our ability to build associations
between words and across meanings. The distinctive kabbalistic feature
lies in the diverse rules of combination and permutation which are
legitimated by the assumed divinity of the language. Moreover, Abulafia
holds that the esoteric significance of language extends throughout all
languages. Again, a connection based on gematria supports this
assertion: the phrase *tseruf ha-otiot* (the combination of letters) has the
same numerical value (1,214) as *shiv'im leshonot* (seventy languages).
The number seventy is used symbolically to depict multiplicity (there
are, for example, said to be 'seventy faces of the Torah'). In relation to
language, a genealogy of the descendants of the sons of Noah is given in
Genesis 10, immediately preceding the story of the tower of Babel. This
chapter gives a total of seventy descendants, which is taken to mean that
the dispersion gave rise to seventy nations, each with its own language.
For Abulafia, then, the gematria equating the arcane linguistic alchemy
with the symbolic number of worldly languages intimates that the

esoteric basis of language extends throughout all the languages of the world. Nevertheless, Hebrew is the 'Mother of all Languages', the language chosen by God in view of its profound affinity to the inner nature of things. Hebrew is the primordial language alluded to in *Genesis*'s depiction of the pre-Babel world, when 'the whole earth was of one language and words of oneness'. Hebrew is therefore the key for returning to that pre-Babel level of being.

The 'words of oneness' characterizing that pre-Babel state are identified with the Name of God for the simple reason that God is One and His Name is identified with the nature of His Being. The path towards the higher state of consciousness associated with the pre-Babel 'words of oneness' begins with the standard rabbinic approach to the biblical text. Even without any meditative or concentrative technique, the playful and fluid *midrashic* exploration of meaning sensitizes the mind to the oneness within language. The very basis of Midrash is predicated on this oneness that underlies all the words of Scripture. It is legitimate to play with the diversity of meanings of a specific word of the Torah, for example, because it is held that the sacred language penetrates to the inner Being of God. Just as the various forms through which God interacts with the world (the *sefirot*) are all rooted in the ultimate Oneness of His Being, so too the diverse forms to which a word of the Torah may give rise through Midrash are rooted in the oneness of the true intent of the Author. The Psalmist's statement, 'The head of your word is truth' (*Psalm* 110:160), is understood by the Rabbis and kabbalists to mean that the inner meaning – the primary intention – in God's word is a truth which becomes concealed in the very words which endeavour to express it. The ultimate truth is the Oneness of God, and the kabbalist dives into the multiple forms inherent in the words in order to connect with that Oneness.

Midrash is, then, the exoteric way of working with language which lays the mental groundwork for language mysticism. The Abulafian path introduces the additional concentrative elements associated with Jewish meditation. In the first stage of letter permutation, mentioned above, there are complex rules of letter transposition – as we have seen, these may include gematria and the use of diverse codes, for example. When the mystic advances to chanting the divine Names, there are specific rules for regulating the breath, for linking the sounds with head movements, and for locating specific sounds within the body. As should be appreciated, this is by no means a simple practice.

Figure 6.1 uses the first six triplicities to illustrate the Abulafian techniques for chanting the combinations comprising the Name of

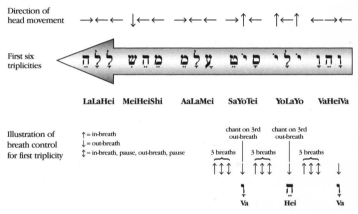

Fig. 6.1. Technique for chanting the first six of the 72 combinations of the Name

seventy-two. The sounds are to be chanted with a perfect intent and with an 'upright, pleasant and sweet melody'. Each letter is chanted with the sound of its 'natural' vowel (the first vowel in the letter's name). The chanting is performed with breaths that are elongated, and each sound is accompanied by a head movement depicting the form of the vowel. The 'o' sound, for example, is indicated in Hebrew by a vowel point above the letter. Its movement in Abulafia's system therefore entails moving the head upwards, beginning from a neutral position, until it is facing vertically up. These movements are also seeded in the heart, meaning that the practitioner has to visualize the movement. It will be clear that this practice requires an advanced ability to maintain focus. The various aspects of the practice bring all the individual's faculties into alignment.

A yet more complex approach taught by Abulafia places the letters of the Name of 72 in circles in groups of nine letters. One 'cycle' of the Name thus uses 24 circles (216 = 9 x 24). These nine letters are visualized internally according to a tripartite division into head, middle and end. The nine comprise the 'head of the head', 'middle of the head', 'end of the head', 'head of the middle', and so on. Thus, for example, in the first cycle the letter *heh* is visualized in the middle of the head:

> Envision the middle of the head as if you were contemplating and seeing in the middle of your brain, with its central points within your thought. And you should see upon it [i.e. on the centre of the brain] the letter *heh*, engraved so as to guard the existence of the points of your brain. (Abulafia, *Hayei ha-Olam ha-Ba* 2001: p. 81)

The whole complex system eventuates in the Name being fixed unshakeably in the mind and body of the adept. As mentioned above, from its biblical context, the Name of 72 is identified with *transition* in general. Here, Abulafia is teaching the ways to use the Name as an agent for changing the mystic's whole body into a vehicle for the divine influx.

A statement of the essential keys to the ways of Kabbalah would undoubtedly include reference to the Names of God and the *sefirot*. In their own distinctive ways, each of these twin pillars of Kabbalah concerns our ability to penetrate the surface of things and to detect the presences that govern reality. Each is approached through copious elaborations of the concealed teachings of the Torah; and both require of the kabbalist a commitment to practice. In Chapter 7, I shall discuss the path of practice associated with the *sefirot*, which very much centres on prayer and performance of *mitsvot*. The path of the Name, by comparison, includes practices which lie beyond the normative conduct of Judaism. Nevertheless, such practices as that of chanting combinations of letters of the Name build on the foundation given by the traditional rabbinic framework.

The two aspects of this core of kabbalistic teaching are to some extent integrated in the traditional *sefirotic* assignations of the major Names of God found in the Torah. Figure 6.2 gives these assignations. Each Name conveys a particular guise through which God interacts with the human world. As I have indicated above in Chapter 3 (p. 90), the sacred four-letter Name is superordinate in that it depicts the entire system. Whilst it is associated with the specific *sefirah* of *Tiferet*, its four letters additionally depict the emanation from *Keter* to *Malkhut*. As I noted when discussing Jacob in Chapter 5, the centre is in resonant rapport with the totality. Mystically, the centre is the point of access to the whole.

In an unpointed Hebrew text, the three letters, *yod*, *heh* and *vav* designate vowel sounds. This is a crucial insight into the Name, for 'the vowels bring life to the consonants' (*Bahir* 83). In one sense, the Name cannot be pronounced because it is simply the sounds of becoming-ness, with neither beginning nor end. The beginning and end of linguistic sound are signalled by consonants. In the symbolism of the *Bahir*, the consonants are squares, yet the vowels are circles. The circle symbolizes an unbroken whole, appropriately identified here with the sounds of vowels without consonants to contain them. The Name depicts a process through which the intra-divine polarity is ever moving towards its consummation.

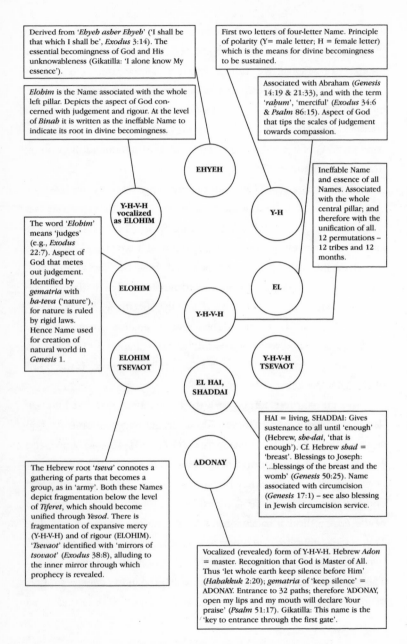

Derived from '*Ehyeh asher Ehyeh*' ('I shall be that which I shall be', *Exodus* 3:14). The essential becomingness of God and His unknowableness (Gikatilla: 'I alone know My essence').

First two letters of four-letter Name. Principle of polarity (Y= male letter; H = female letter) which is the means for divine becomingness to be sustained.

Elohim is the Name associated with the whole left pillar. Depicts the aspect of God concerned with judgement and rigour. At the level of *Binah* it is written as the ineffable Name to indicate its root in divine becomingness.

Associated with Abraham (*Genesis* 14:19 & 21:33), and with the term '*rahum*', 'merciful' (*Exodus* 34:6 & *Psalm* 86:15). Aspect of God that tips the scales of judgement towards compassion.

Ineffable Name and essence of all Names. Associated with the whole central pillar; and therefore with the unification of all. 12 permutations – 12 tribes and 12 months.

The word '*Elohim*' means 'judges' (e.g., *Exodus* 22:7). Aspect of God that metes out judgement. Identified by *gematria* with *ha-teva* ('nature'), for nature is ruled by rigid laws. Hence Name used for creation of natural world in *Genesis* 1.

EHYEH

Y-H-V-H vocalized as ELOHIM

Y-H

ELOHIM

EL

Y-H-V-H

ELOHIM TSEVAOT

Y-H-V-H TSEVAOT

EL HAI, SHADDAI

ADONAY

HAI = living, SHADDAI: Gives sustenance to all until 'enough' (Hebrew, *she-dai*, 'that is enough'). Cf. Hebrew *shad* = 'breast'. Blessings to Joseph: '...blessings of the breast and the womb' (*Genesis* 50:25). Name associated with circumcision (*Genesis* 17:1) – see also blessing in Jewish circumcision service.

The Hebrew root '*tseva*' connotes a gathering of parts that becomes a group, as in 'army'. Both these Names depict fragmentation below the level of *Tiferet*, which should become unified through *Yesod*. There is fragmentation of expansive mercy (Y-H-V-H) and of rigour (ELOHIM). '*Tsevaot*' identified with 'mirrors of tsovaot' (*Exodus* 38:8), alluding to the inner mirror through which prophecy is revealed.

Vocalized (revealed) form of Y-H-V-H. Hebrew *Adon* = master. Recognition that God is Master of All. Thus 'let whole earth keep silence before Him' (*Habakkuk* 2:20); *gematria* of 'keep silence' = ADONAY. Entrance to 32 paths; therefore 'ADONAY, open my lips and my mouth will declare Your praise' (*Psalm* 51:17). Gikatilla: This name is the 'key to entrance through the first gate'.

Fig. 6.2. Names of God and the *sefirot*

The Name Y-H-V-H is substituted by A-D-O-N-A-Y in study and worship. The intent of this substitution concerns the union of *Tiferet* and *Malkhut*. The substitution lies at the heart of the concealing-revealing dynamic explored in Chapter 5. The four-letter Name is the essence of the Written Torah, whereas it is spoken as A-D-O-N-A-Y, a Name hinting at the Oral Torah. The concealed Y-H-V-H can only be expressed as the revealed A-D-O-N-A-Y, a term indicating recognition of the Divine as Master of All. Moreover, the worshipper facilitates the union between *Tiferet* and *Malkhut* by being inwardly mindful of the Name Y-H-V-H associated with *Tiferet* at the same time as pronouncing the Name of *Malkhut*, A-D-O-N-A-Y. This same union is promoted by the ubiquitous *Amen* uttered in response to a blessing. The numerical value of the Hebrew *'amn* is 91, which equates with the sum of the two Names Y-H-V-H and A-D-O-N-A-Y (26 + 65 = 91). Rabbinic Judaism holds that the individual should make 100 blessings each day. Esoterically, the blessings provide the opportunity to develop a mindfulness of the unification of the two Names that should permeate the whole of the individual's day.

LETTERS OF CREATION 2

The primary source for all kabbalistic language practices is the *Sefer Yetsirah*. This work explains how God used the Hebrew letters in His work of creation. The mystic's desire to draw close to God is realized through imitating God's own ways of working:

> 22 foundation letters. He [God] *engraved* them, *carved* them, *weighed* them, *permuted* them, *combined* them, and *formed* with them all that was formed and all that would be formed in the future . . . He engraved them with voice, carved them with breath, fixed them in the mouth in five places . . . He placed them in a wheel, like a wall with 231 gates. The wheel revolves forwards and backwards . . . How? He weighed them and

> permuted them: *Alef* with them all and all of them with *alef*,
> *bet* with them all and all of them with *bet*. They continue in
> cycles and exist in 231 gates. Thus, all that is formed and all
> that is spoken derive from one Name. (*Sefer Yetsirah* 2:2-5)

In addition to recording God's arcane methods of working with
the Hebrew letters, the *Sefer Yetsirah* is instructing the reader on the
methods that should be used in order to imitate God's ways. The
Hebrew of the paragraph could be translated either as 'He engraved
them . . .' or as 'Engrave them. . .'. Kabbalists hold that both meanings
are intended. The mystic is enjoined to emulate the ways in which God
worked with the letters.

The sequence of six processes given in the beginning of this extract
(which I have emphasized by italicizing the verbs) is used in a visualization
practice. Preparation for visualization requires closing or half-closing the
eyes. Normally, when we close the eyes we automatically turn the visual
sense off inwardly as well. For this kind of a practice, however, we must
remain acutely aware of the visual sense even whilst being closed to
outward seeing. It is as if we are seeing the screen made by the insides of
the eyelids. *Engraving* means outlining the letter in the mind's eye; as the
outline is built up, we hold a clear intent to operate with a specific letter.
Carving entails establishing the letter as a powerful presence in visual
consciousness; energy is focused on the letter until it blazes like fire on the
inner screen of the mind. The intent behind *weighing* is that of allowing
the letter's qualities to impress themselves upon us; a receptive state must
be cultivated, in which we might, for example, find meaning in the letter's
shape, its constituent parts, its relations with other letters, and so on. This
is followed by *permuting* the letter with other letters; perhaps, having
focused on the letter's constituent lines, other letters using those lines
arise in the mind. Letters are then *combined*, enabling them to enter into
relationships one with another. The final stage concerns the meaning of
those combinations; what kind of a presence is *formed* when those

specific letters come together? It is not simply a matter of knowing the word (and, in fact, not all combinations produce words), but rather we are attempting to discern the nature of the entity depicted by the specific combination of letters. What tensions arise between the letters, or do they share a more harmonious relation?

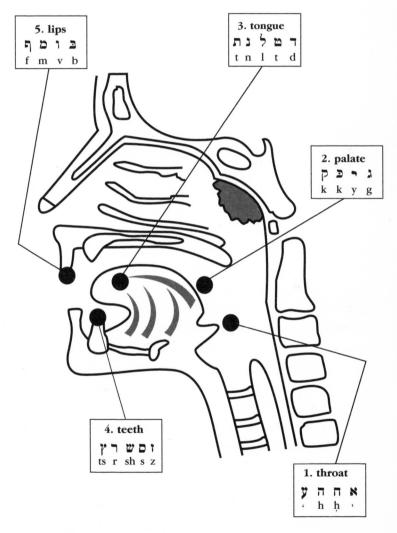

Fig. 6.3. Locations for sounding the Hebrew letters

The *Sefer Yetsirah*'s phrase concerning the 'five places' in which the letters are fixed refers to the locations in which the letters' sounds are produced. The five locations are the *throat, palate, tongue, teeth*, and *lips* (see Figure 6.3). These locations also relate to the five primary vowel sounds in Hebrew – *a, ei, o, ee, oo*, thereby providing the basis for a chanting meditation (see Kaplan 1990: 102-8). The essence of the meditation involves becoming aware of the site of origin for each letter. Of course, at the same time that you are engaging with the origin of the letter within your own anatomy, you should be cognizant of its ultimate origin in the divine Being.

The final section in the above extract from the *Sefer Yetsirah* focuses on the method of combining individual letters. The creative fluidity in language as a whole is seeded by the 'wheel' used by God in forming letter combinations. This wheel brings letters into combination, generating words, and therefore – according to the worldview of the *Sefer Yetsirah* – bringing forms into being. The motif of the wheel recurs in the *Bahir* in relation to the ramifications of meaning in scriptural words: 'What is a "word"? As is written, "[Apples of gold in settings of silver is] A word fitly [Hebrew *of'nav*] spoken" (*Proverbs* 25:11). Do not read "fitly" [*of'nav*] but "its wheel" [*ofanav*], as in "My presence will go" (*Exodus* 33:14)' (*Bahir* 33; I have discussed the psychological importance of this passage in Lancaster 2004: 240–6).

The path to the 'apples of gold', a term indicating the concealed truth of the scriptural text, requires accessing the wheel of meanings to which any given word relates. The *Bahir* subtly conveys this instruction via the very *midrashic* technique it encourages. The vowel-less form of Hebrew scriptural texts means that the word translated in most English Bibles as 'fitly' could be articulated differently, giving the word meaning 'its wheel'. In accommodating both meanings, we may say that the reading of a scriptural text becomes 'fitting' to the extent that its words are elaborated by the 'wheel' of their associations and subtleties of meaning.

The perspective of the *Bahir* is complementary to that of the *Sefer Yetsirah*. The *Sefer Yetsirah* is concerned with God's activation of the wheel of letters in His work of forming all that exisits. The *Bahir* is viewing things more from the perspective of the mystic who aspires to grasp the nature of creation through the study of Scripture. The mystic uses the very potency that God injected into the language in the first place in order to unveil the divine presence in Scripture.

Mathematically, there are 231 two-letter combinations (without doubling letters and without reversals) from the Hebrew alphabet of twenty-two letters. Abulafia points out that the name *Israel* could be read *yesh ra'el* (both are spelled *ysr'l*), meaning 'there are 231'. The implication of this equation is that the path to the higher state connoted by the name 'Israel' requires that the mystic studies and practises these 231 combinations. The kabbalist aspires to the highest possible alignment with God by exploring these 'gates' in a concentrated meditative state. A further gematria is critical for Abulafia's understanding of the goal of this practice: both *Israel* and *yesh ra'el* have the same numerical value (541) as *sekhel ha-po'el* (the Active Intellect). The Active Intellect is also identified with the Torah. In the mediaeval map of spiritual realms, the Active Intellect is the sphere of union between the human and divine minds. Abulafia is using these various formulas to indicate that immersion in the Torah, including a total knowledge of the ways of letter combinations, is the path to that union.

According to Abulafia, the 'wheel of the letters' is under the jurisdiction of the angel *Metatron*. This angel is identified by the Talmud with the angel mentioned in *Exodus* 23:20: 'Behold, I send an angel before you to guard you in the way and to bring you to the Place which I have prepared.' The next verse states, 'My Name is in him.' The Talmud sees in this verse an allusion to the name *Shaddai*, which has the same numerical value (314) as the name *Metatron* (Talmud, *Sanhedrin* 38b). The simple meaning is that Metatron will be the guide for the journey to the Promised Land. At a deeper level, the reference to 'Place' alludes to the journey towards closeness to God, which entails a mystical grasp of the wheel of letters. The *Zohar Hadash* (*Yitro*, 39d) connects Metatron with the 'one wheel on the earth' in Ezekiel's vision (*Ezekiel* 1:15). The *Zohar* proceeds to describe how the letters of the ineffable Name are engraved in a flame that emerges from the angel. These are the letters at the core of kabbalistic practices. Ultimately, each of the 22 Hebrew letters is viewed as a Name in its own right. Thus, by engaging in mystical concentration with the wheel of the letters, the kabbalist aspires to encounter Metatron, guardian of the way to union with God.

In the above extract from the *Bahir*, the reference to *Exodus* 33:14 is poignant in this context. The full dialogue between Moses and God in the *Exodus* passage goes as follows:

> And Moses said to the Lord, See, You say to me, bring up this people; and You have not let me know whom You will send with me. Yet You have said, I know you by name, and you have also found grace in my sight.
>
> Now therefore, if I have found grace in Your sight, make known to me Your way, that I may know You and that I may find grace in Your eyes; see that this nation is Your people.
>
> And He said, My presence will go with you, and I will give you rest. (*Exodus* 33:12-14)

Etymologically, the allusion in the *Bahir* to the phrase 'my presence will go' is simple enough, since the Hebrew words for 'presence' and 'wheel' have letters in common. But the author of the *Bahir* seems to be alluding to a deeper tradition. The passage from *Exodus* describes God's intention to reveal His presence to Moses. This event represents the pinnacle of all individual human–divine encounters portrayed in the Hebrew Bible. As the biblical commentators emphasize, the reference is to God in His very essence. According to Ramban's commentary on this passage, the Torah is intimating that God agreed to Moses' request that He reveal to him the details of His Name. The deeper meaning of the *Bahir* extract appears to be that the wheel of letters and language provides the key to grasping and using the Name. The mystic who aspires to an encounter with 'the King' must be at one with the fluid ways of the Hebrew language, as well as possessing an intimate knowledge of the practices by means of which God's Name is fully internalized.

THE FUNDAMENTALS OF SOUND

As already indicated in Chapter 4, the *Sefer Yetsirah* classifies the Hebrew letters as 'mothers', 'doubles' and 'simples'. The mother letters are *alef, mem* and *shin*. The term 'mother' is used to convey the generative potential of these letters. There are a number of ways of understanding the role of these letters as progenitors. Firstly, they produce the three 'elements' of air, water and fire. *Alef* is dominant in the word *avir* (air), *mem* is dominant in the word *mayim* (water) and *shin* is dominant in *eish* (fire). These elements go on to produce other realms (heaven from fire, earth from water). Secondly, the letters play key roles in generating the 32 paths of wisdom, comprising the ten *sefirot* and 22 letters. *Alef* is the first letter and, as the *Bahir* states, 'alef brings about the existence of all the letters' (48). The *Bahir* identifies the letter *shin* with the roots of the *sefirotic* tree since it resembles a root in shape. (The resemblance is clear when the *shin* is inverted. However, the root of the tree of *sefirot* is above, in *Keter*. For this reason it is appropriate to think of the *shin* in its standard orientation as the root of the tree.) Indeed, the letter *shin* is prominent in the word *shoresh*, which is Hebrew for 'root'. *Mem* is the exact centre of the full Hebrew alphabet when 'final' letters are included. As mentioned already in relation to *Tiferet*, the centre has a crucial link with the whole. Accordingly, the source, centre and root of the whole structure are defined by these three letters – *alef*, *mem* and *shin*, respectively. A third connotation of their 'mother' status may be discerned in relation to the physical nature of their sounds. *Alef* has no sound. The sound of *mem* is a pure humming, which corresponds to the simplest sinusoidal wave. And the sound of *shin* is 'sh . . .', the most complex sound since it is the sound of white noise, in which all frequencies are combined.

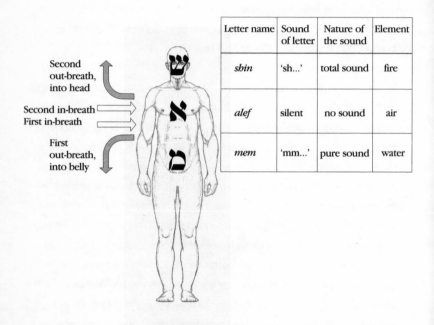

Letter name	Sound of letter	Nature of the sound	Element
shin	'sh...'	total sound	fire
alef	silent	no sound	air
mem	'mm...'	pure sound	water

Second out-breath, into head

Second in-breath
First in-breath

First out-breath, into belly

Fig. 6.4. Meditation on 'mother' letters

This last point finds expression in the *Sefer Yetsirah*'s statement, '*Mem* hums, *shin* hisses, and *alef* is the one breath that reconciles between them' (Kaplan 1990: 95). A relatively simple practice derives from this teaching. As indicated in Figure 6.4, the three mother letters are associated with bodily locations: *alef*, the chest; *mem*, the belly; and *shin*, the head. The very shapes of the letters seem highly appropriate: *alef* resonates with the hearts and lungs; the *mem* is the shape of the lower bodily cavity, its rounded top resembling the diaphragm; and the *shin* connects with the two versions of this letter on the *tefillin* box attached to the head during Morning Prayers. The *alef* represents the giving and receiving of breath, which may be understood as our connection with the deep rhythm of the cosmos – the divine breath that enlivens God's use of language in maintaining creation. The *mem* represents the flow of water. And the *shin*, with its strokes that reach upwards, represents flames of fire.

The practice begins by spending some time internalizing all these connections. (Most people find that awareness of air in the chest, water in the belly and fire in the head arises quite readily.) We continue by cycling between the letters, focusing on the heart as we become aware of the intake of air (some kabbalists refer to the heart as the 'organ of breath'); we breathe out, as it were downwards, making a slight humming sound as our awareness shifts to the water of *mem*. Our awareness then returns to the heart for a second in-breath; the second out-breath is, as it were, pushed upwards through the head, making the hissing sound associated with the fire of *shin*. With practice, the many associations of these letters become sharply focused in our awareness, and a sense of truly balancing the elements, both inwardly and outwardly, may be achieved.

Breath is the essence of the human soul: 'And the Lord God formed Adam, dust from the ground, and breathed into his nostrils a breath of life; and Adam became a living soul' (*Genesis* 2:7). For Judaism, the most authoritative translation of the Torah is the Aramaic *Targum* written by Onkelos, a second-century CE convert to Judaism. In this work, the phrase 'living soul' is rendered 'speaking soul'. Onkelos indicates that the real divine gift is the ability to form the sounds of speech and to use language to forge a relationship with God.

We have seen already in Chapter 5 that language is a key component of the covenant with God. The Talmud emphasizes that it is specifically the oral dimension of the Torah which forms the core of this covenant (Talmud, *Gittin* 60b). This is the covenant associated with *Malkhut*, entrance to the 32 paths of wisdom. Gikatilla teaches that there are actually three covenants (*Sha'are Orah* 46). In addition to this covenant of the Oral Torah in *Malkhut*, there are covenants associated with *Binah* and with *Yesod*. *Binah* represents the divine source of language descending to become the Written Torah, which is identified with *Tiferet*. The covenant associated with *Yesod* is the covenant of the rainbow and of the flesh (see p. 159 above). The kabbalistic goal is to unify all these elements, as symbolized in the sacred four-letter Name. The *yod* (numerical value ten) is identified with the ten fingers outstretched towards heaven, drawing from the level of *Binah*. The first *heh* (five) represents the five locations by means of which linguistic sounds are generated (Figure 6.3). The *vav* and final *heh* (together making eleven), which are identified with the Written Torah and the Oral Torah respectively, depict the ten toes and the male organ. This glyph complements the more general equation between Adam and the Name, derived by using the numerical value of the full spelling of God's Name ($yvd = 20, h' = 6, vv = 12, h' = 6$, giving a total of 45, which is the numerical value of *'Adm*). For Kabbalah, these esoteric linkages between Adam and the Name of God constitute the real meaning of the statement that man is made in the image of God. It is through the esoteric understanding of the oral covenant that we may achieve our full status by living in that image.

Chapter 7

Prayer and
Concentrative Practice

THE GATE OF PRAYER

In Figure 6.2, I quoted *Psalm* 51:17 in relation to the Name of God associated with *Malkhut*: 'Adonay, open my lips and my mouth will declare Your praise.' This verse is recited prior to the silent Standing Prayer (*amidah*), which constitutes the spiritual high point of all Jewish prayer services. Jewish teaching is unequivocal: as we utter these words of the Psalmist, we should cultivate the awareness that we are stepping forward into the presence of the Master of All and commencing an intimate dialogue. This comprises the essence of prayer.

How do we distinguish between the prayers of a committed worshipper who does not consciously cultivate a kabbalistic approach and prayer that is explicitly kabbalistic? In no other sphere of Jewish life is there such proximity between kabbalistic and non-kabbalistic practice. This is because prayer without *kavannah* (inner concentration) hardly counts as prayer. Prayer is known as the 'service of the heart' (Talmud, *Ta'anit* 2a and elsewhere), implying that an inner awareness lies at the essence of prayer. Prayer is a core aspect of the 'Duties of the Heart' enunciated by Bahya ibn Pekuda (second half of the eleventh century), for whom it entails a complete surrendering of self to God. Rambam further established the key approach to prayer for Judaism: 'Every prayer that is uttered without *kavannah* is no prayer . . . What is *kavannah*? One should turn attention [lit. 'heart'] away from all [mundane] thought, and regard oneself as if one were standing in the presence of the *Shekhinah*' (*Mishneh Torah, Hilkhot Tefillah* 4:15-16).

These characteristics – surrendering the 'I'; controlling attention from wandering after mundane thoughts; contemplating the presence of God – define the approach to prayer in 'non-mystical' Judaism. And yet these characteristics are clearly features of all theistic mysticism. The dividing line between what is, and what is not, kabbalistic is, then, not to be found in these core characteristics of prayer. Moreover, the words uttered by kabbalists in prayer do not differ from those spoken by their Orthodox, but non-kabbalistic, co-religionists. The words of prayer were established by the 'Men of the Great Assembly', an institution understood to have been headed by the biblical Ezra. This Assembly bridges the end of the period of biblical prophecy and the rise of rabbinic Judaism, which would date it around 300 BCE.

Whilst the very nature of prayer demands some fluidity – in that there must be place for one's own words and supplications – it is the fixed format of prayers that becomes the subject of most kabbalistic interest. It is assumed that the sacred source that inspired the Men of the Great Assembly invests the prayers with the classic depths of kabbalistic meaning. A prayer becomes kabbalistic when its words are understood in relation to the hallmarks of all kabbalistic inquiry – the Names of God and the *sefirot*. Such understanding may involve the kinds of subtle codes, including gematria and so on, which infuse much of kabbalistic writings. For the kabbalist, *kavannah* means a state of concentration on the concealed ideas to which the words of prayer allude. Thus, as I shall illustrate, whilst articulating in the Synagogue the same words of prayer as those who may not be mystically inclined, kabbalists have a whole world of distinctive imagery on which to focus inwardly. Their prayers may be enlivened by visions of dynamic interactions between the *sefirot*; by complex permutations of the letters of God's Name; or by conceptual associations based in gematriot.

In order to illustrate the conceptual associations within prayer I shall return to the idea of the *Throne of Glory*, which, as noted in earlier chapters, depicts the pivotal sphere in God's involvement with the world and with humanity. In early mystical works, reference is made not simply to one throne, but to *seven thrones*, one of which is found in each of the seven heavens. The tradition of the seven heavens is found in early rabbinic and mystical literature, and, in similar fashion to the notion of a tree of *sefirot*, concerns both the levels through which God's influence extends downwards and the stages by which the mystic can ascend towards God. The *Sefer Hasidim*, a work thought to have been composed by R. Judah the Hasid (*c*.1150–1217), teacher of the Rokeach, notes the precise number of times the term 'throne' appears in the Shabbat prayer service. The term occurs seven times, which is taken as alluding to the seven thrones. As the seventh day, Shabbat is the day uniquely appropriate to contemplation of the seven heavenly realms. The book informs us that the numerical total of all seven occurrences of the term 'throne', in their various forms of spelling, is 611, the gematria of the word 'Torah' (cited in Wolfson 1994: 250). I have already noted the codified relationship between the tablets given by God and the Throne (see p. 154). The connection with the Torah completes this seminal triad of ideas. According to *Sefer Hasidim*, the Torah is read on Shabbat precisely because of this relationship, further evidenced by the fact that the Torah reading is divided into seven sections. In rabbinic tradition, both the Throne and the Torah preceded the beginning of creation on Day One, but their pre-eminence can be acknowledged only on the seventh day.

The point of these statements is to bring the worshipper to a mystical encounter with the inner, or heavenly, realms. The object of the prayers is to *enthrone* the *Shekhinah*, both as the presence that resides in the Torah and as the female consort to the King on the Throne. Judah the Hasid's mysticism holds that all the words of prayer fixed by the Men of the Great Assembly similarly contain complex allusions to the nature of God and His heavenly realms. The letters and words of the prayers comprise a whole world of harmonic numerical relationships with which worshippers engage through their vocalization of the prayers. Although much of his work has unfortunately been lost, Judah provides us with important keys through which a state of *kavannah* can be cultivated that includes conscious connection with the inner world of the Godhead.

The central associations between the *sefirot* and the Names of God frequently inform kabbalistic commentaries on prayer. The essential declaration of faith repeated daily in the Morning and Evening Prayer Services, the *Shema,* serves to illustrate this point clearly. In reading the *Shema* we articulate the essential unity of God, as is evident in the first verse: 'Hear, Israel, Y-H-V-H is ELO-HANU (our God), Y-H-V-H is One' (*Deuteronomy* 6:4). The *Shema* brings together the two concepts of unification and love. The continuation of the passage from *Deuteronomy* states: 'And you shall love the Lord your God with all your heart, with all your soul and with all your might.' The connection between love and unification should be clear – love is the expression of closeness that leads to ultimate union. In the Hebrew, the point is made through gematria: both *'ahavah* (love) and *'ehad* (one) have the numerical value of thirteen (and the two together therefore add up to twenty-six, the value of the Name Y-H-V-H). The kabbalistic *kavannah* for the *Shema* focuses on unification of the entire *sefirotic* system, as depicted by the Names of God. One tradition conveyed in the *Zohar,* for example, connects the first mention of Y-H-V-H with *Hokhmah*, the Name ELO-HANU with *Binah*, and the second mention of Y-H-V-H with the six *sefirot* centred on *Tiferet*. The six are bound in the will to be united with the consort, *Malkhut*. This will towards unification is expressed through *Tiferet*.

The word *'eḥad* is itself considered to depict the unification of the entire array of *sefirot*. An early kabbalistic source cited by Idel identifies the first letter of *'eḥad*, *alef,* with *Keter*, the second letter, *ḥet*, with the eight *sefirot* from *Ḥokhmah* to *Yesod*, and the final letter, *dalet*, with *Malkhut* (Idel 1988a: 55). These are not random connections, but are grounded in firmly established kabbalistic symbolism. I have referred to the relation between *alef* and *Keter* in Chapter 3 (p. 84) – essentially *alef* is the unsounded source of all the letters, just as *Keter* is the unknowable source of creation. The letter *ḥet* is not only the initial letter of *Ḥokhmah*, but also the number eight, alluding to the eight *sefirot*. Finally, in view of its connection with the word *dal*, poverty, the letter *dalet* is associated with *Malkhut*. Concerning the letter *dalet* the *Bahir* states, 'There are ten kings in one place, all of whom are rich. One of them, although his riches are great, is poor by comparison with the others' (*Bahir* 19). The 'ten kings' are the *sefirot*, and the one which is relatively poor is *Malkhut*. Its poverty comes about because it is the final *sefirah* in the system. All the other *sefirot* give to those below them; *Malkhut* can only receive. This itself is a teaching worth pondering. Poverty is associated with a state of being unable to give – not simply because one has nothing to give (after all, *Malkhut* receives from all the other *sefirot*), but because it is the act of giving that confers the status of being rich. According to Jewish law, we are required to give one-tenth of our income to the poor. Clearly, the figure of one-tenth derives from the status of *Malkhut* in the kabbalistic system. Moreover, even one who is poor is enjoined to donate a tenth of whatever income they have. Again, the act of giving brings dignity to the giver, and these rabbinic laws are founded on a vision which holds that such dignity brings its own rewards.

Ultimately, in order to be transformed from a state of poverty to one of richness, *Malkhut* is dependent on human intent. Through our concentrated intent to effect unification amongst the *sefirotic* array, *Malkhut* is raised to a higher level. Indeed, the goal of all these practices of unification is to bind the *sefirot* to their root in *En Sof*:

'One' – to unify everything from there upwards as one; to raise the will to bind everything in a single bond; in fear and love to raise the will higher and higher as far as *En Sof*. And not to let the will stray from all the levels and limbs, but to let the will ascend with them all to make them join to each other, so that all shall be one bond with *En Sof*. This is the practice of unification of Rav Hamnuna the Elder, who learnt it from his father, who had it from his master, and so on, until it came from the mouth of Elijah.

He said further that to concentrate the whole idea of unification in the term 'one' is a more perfect way; and it is for this reason that we lengthen our pronunciation of the word 'one' – in order to draw the will from above to below and below to above, that all should be one . . . 'One' refers to the mystery of above and below and the four directions of the world. This is the way of unification: above, below, and the four directions of the world. These are the mystery of the supernal Chariot [the four *sefirot* of *Hesed, Gevurah, Tiferet, Malkhut*] in order to bring all to one bond, in a single unification to *En Sof*. (*Zohar* 2:216b)

Rav Hamnuna is referring here to the word 'one' in the first line of the *Shema*. There is a custom to elongate pronunciation of the final 'd' sound of "*ehad*" when reciting the *Shema*. In kabbalistic terms, this elongated pronunciation allows us to focus on *Malkhut* ('d' for '*dal*') with the intent that it should be raised through its union with *Tiferet* and ultimately restored to its root in *En Sof*. The letter *dalet* is the number four, alluding to the four compass directions. In the Morning Service this spatial connection is emphasized when, just prior to the *Shema*, the liturgy makes reference to the 'four corners of the earth'. At this point in the service men gather the four threads at the corners of the *tallit* (prayer shawl) and hold them to the heart. This is the posture in which to 'unify [God] with love'.

In Chapter 3 (p. 80) I described an exercise from the *Sefer Yetsirah* that is based on the understanding of the *sefirot* as the dimensions of time, space and the moral order. I noted there that the objective was to witness the self as the centre of a network of interconnections which plunge into an infinite nothingness. This meditative exercise promotes a state of psychological unification, and is, accordingly, highly relevant to the *Shema*. With practice, at the time of reciting the *Shema* the worshipper can connect with the state of consciousness brought about by the meditation. In addition to the psychological emphasis on unification, the *Shema* alludes to unification of the limbs of the body. This allusion is drawn from the total number of words in the *Shema*, 248, which is said to be the number of 'limbs' in the human body. The term 'limbs' is variously thought of as 'bones' or 'sinews'. Symbolically, it is referring to the structural make-up of the body. The number 248 is also the gematria of *Avraham* (Abraham), the *sefirah* of love, the second focus of the *Shema*. As with all kabbalistic practices, the desired effects at the level of the higher worlds and the Godhead are promoted through analogous psychological and physical states. Based on the central principle of correspondence above and below, unification of the *sefirot* is predicated on unification of self – at both psychological and bodily levels.

Ultimately, unification of self means transcending any experience of self as being an autonomous entity, for the unification is achieved only through *devekut*, cleaving to God. The Maggid of Mezeritch states: 'One must regard oneself as nothing and forget oneself totally, directing one's prayer on behalf of the *Shekhinah*. Then one can transcend time, aspiring to the world of [pure] thought where all is equal – life and death, ocean and dry land' (*Maggid Devarav le-Ya'akov* 186). The realm of pure thought is a realm where normal thought is annihilated, together with the ego which illusorily believes that it controls those thoughts. Rabbi Ezra of

Gerona (d. 1238 or 1245) explains the tradition recorded in the Talmud that, prior to prayer, the ancient sages would spend an hour in meditation: They 'elevated their thought to its source . . . and through the cleaving of thought [to the divine], the words were blessed and increased, receiving a [divine] influx from the annihilation of thought' (cited in Matt 1995: 82, translation slightly adapted). This divine influx is compared to water from a pool spreading in all directions. Ezra's contemporary, Rabbi Azriel of Gerona, writes of the word *barukh* (blessed) which surrounds the recitation of the *Shema* in the liturgy: '*Barukh* is comprised of every power, from the source of life, from life, and from the light of life. It is blessing, it blesses, and is blessed, like the source of a pool that is blessed' (cited in Tishby 1949/1989: 948). Azriel is drawing here on an important etymological link: the Hebrew *berakhah*, 'blessing' is practically identical with *berekhah*, meaning 'pool'. The descent of divine influx is like the flow of sustaining water from a pool high in the mountains.

From the kabbalistic perspective, the goals of prayer are essentially theurgic. Whilst there is always space for personal petitions, the fundamental motive in prayer is that of *tikkun*: that the structure of the Godhead be rectified through unification and the *sefirot* be raised to their root in *En Sof*. Only through this *tikkun* can we bring about the desired influx back down the tree of *sefirot* and into the world. We are nourished when the Godhead is restored to its inner harmony, and prayer is a primary means by which we promote that harmony.

It will be obvious that much practice is needed in order to be able to recite prayers with the required kabbalistic level of intention. It is characteristic of the kabbalistic approach to prayer that a complex of detailed ideas is brought to their recitation. We have seen in the case of the *Shema*, for example, that worshippers should engage in some or all of the following:

- they should be firmly grounded in the sense of the body's oneness;

- they should cultivate a state of consciousness that is fully centred;
- whilst focusing on the levels of meaning in the liturgical words, they should be aware of the dynamics of the *sefirot*, together with their links to specific divine Names.

Other prayers are similarly associated with interactions between the *sefirot* and divine Names. To be effective, these complex connections must be established outside the time of prayer. Study of the *sefirot* and their various associations brings a familiarity which can underpin the words of prayer. Similarly, meditative exercises of the kind mentioned above sensitize us to the state of consciousness which is conducive to the cosmic influences that prayer may achieve. Prayer is the gate of the *Shekhinah*, and through this gate the world may be healed.

VISUALIZATIONS

One of the central rabbinic texts is the code of Jewish Law known as the *Shulhan Arukh*, composed by the Safedian kabbalist, Rabbi Josef Karo (1488–1575). This work opens with the words of the Psalmist: 'I have placed Y-H-V-H before me at all times' (*Psalm* 16:8), a verse that holds a distinctive kabbalistic meaning. The verse is taken to be an instruction for us to visualize the four-letter Name ('the Lord'). We place this Name before us by visualizing it literally. Isaac of Acre informs us that we should keep the letters of this Name constantly in mind as if they were in front of us. The letters should be visualized in the mind's eye, whilst the thoughts of the heart are directed towards the *En Sof*, the infinite. This is the path of *devekut*, cleaving to God. Three centuries later, Luria describes this technique as the way to purify the soul.

I described the technique of visualizing letters in Chapter 6 (p. 176). As indicated there, we should attempt to bring a fiery quality to the imaged letters. When we visualize these letters of the four-letter Name, we attempt to capture the whiteness at the hottest part of the flame: 'You may picture the Ineffable Name like the white flame of the candle, in absolute whiteness' (anonymous source, cited by Idel 1988b: 34).

The value of visualization is twofold. Firstly, from a psychological point of view, the practice of visualization brings a level of control to the mind. To be able to hold an image of the sacred letters in the mind's eye 'at all times' is, in itself, a major feat. All concentrative practices inculcate the mental discipline of detaching from extraneous thoughts. Most people are not used to visualizing in this disciplined fashion, and simply switching to a non-habitual mode of the mind can give rise to an increased level of mental control. The second value in visualization derives from the object visualized. Kabbalah holds that an intrinsic holiness and power resides in the divine Name, and holding it before our eyes in this way is understood to impart to us some of its power.

An important aspect of the psychological dimension is indicated by a subtle ambiguity of the language in the verse from Psalms. The Hebrew original for 'I have placed' is *shiviti*. This word is related to the verb *shavah*, meaning 'to be equal', from which is derived the kabbalistically-important term *hishtavut* (equanimity). Equanimity is the partner of visualization, for it indicates a high level of mental discipline. Just as visualization entails learning to hold the image firm in the face of any tendencies for it to be disrupted by distracting thoughts, so too the state of equanimity demands a firmness in the face of any triggers to emotional distraction. The cultivation of equanimity is seen as a critical stage on the kabbalistic path to achieving prophetic consciousness. Isaac of Acre makes this point when further discussing the verse from Psalms:

> He who reaches the secret of *devekut* [adhering to the
> divine] will merit the secret of equanimity; and when he

has received the secret of equanimity, then he will know
the secret of concentrative meditation; and once he has
knowledge of concentration, he will merit the spirit of
divine inspiration; and from this he will merit prophecy,
and he will prophesy and foretell the future. (cited in Idel
1988c: 112)

For Isaac of Acre, placing the Name in the mind's eye at all times is
the 'secret of true cleaving' to God. The connection in the Hebrew
between 'placing' and 'equanimity' means that this visualization provides
a focus and a 'rock' that is conducive to inner stability amidst the ebb and
flow of worldly events. Equanimity is the essential prerequisite for the
higher state of consciousness understood by the term 'prophecy'.

The central importance of visualization for the kabbalistic path is
said to be indicated in the Hebrew *Adam* (human). *Adam* is related to
adameh, 'I shall imagine', or 'visualize'. Human beings are distinct
from animals through the gift of imagination, and it is this ability that
must be harnessed if we are to advance on the spiritual path.

In addition to the divine Name, the tree of *sefirot* becomes a focus
for visualization in kabbalistic instruction. By visualizing, or otherwise
imagining, the *sefirot*, the mystic is able to ascend into their realm. This
is a teaching which is easily misunderstood, for it may be construed as
implying that the *sefirot* constitute only an imaginary reality. Crucially,
the faculty of imagination is distinguished from that of fantasy. Our
everyday sense of reality, together with the worlds we create in
daydreams, are the product of fantasy. Kabbalah teaches that we can
know the true reality, namely, the *sefirot* and their root in the *En Sof*,
only when we detach from the force of fantasy, and use imagination to
build a grasp of reality based on the teachings in the Torah.

The ability to visualize the *sefirot* is firmly connected with our
intellectual grasp of their nature. In Chapter 2, I explained that we build
up a sense of the meaning of a *sefirah* through its many associations

given in kabbalistic and rabbinic sources. Visualization of *Malkhut*, for example, may be aided by a firm grasp of the meaning of the *Shekhinah*, or of the role of the mouth (*peh*) in prayer and by establishing an awareness of *presence* (see the discussion in Chapter 6, p. 164). In addition to general associations of the *sefirot*, there are codified systems for visualization. One such system involves the letters, which constitute the twenty-two paths that connect the *sefirot*. A second system uses specific colours assigned to each *sefirah* (see Figure 7.1). The colours are considered to be coverings of the *sefirot*, and, as such, may be used to gain access to the quality associated with each. The true essence of each *sefirah*, however, remains unknowable and cannot be limited through being visualized. As the *Sefer Yetsirah* asserts, the *sefirot* are *belimah*, that is, 'of nothingness'.

This last point expresses a general principle in kabbalistic meditation. The intention is invariably to progress from form to formless, from that which can be visualized to that which transcends the grasp of human imagination. A similar conclusion may be drawn from a kabbalistic meditation on light. Following a description of the various forms of light that may be witnessed in the meditation, we finally read of the 'perfect glory of the concealed light that cannot be seen; it has neither form nor image, measure nor magnitude, extent nor bounds, neither limit nor ground nor number, and is infinite in every way' (ascribed to Azriel of Gerona; cited in Wolfson 1994: 302). In becoming aware of this hidden light, the meditator has established a conscious connection with the *En Sof*, with the result that his will is unified with the Will of God. This unification results in the opening of the channels for the divine influx to descend: '. . . he draws down the influx that crowns the secret of things and essences . . .'

Prior to the stage of experiencing the hidden light of *En Sof*, this meditation identifies the lights of the *sefirot*:

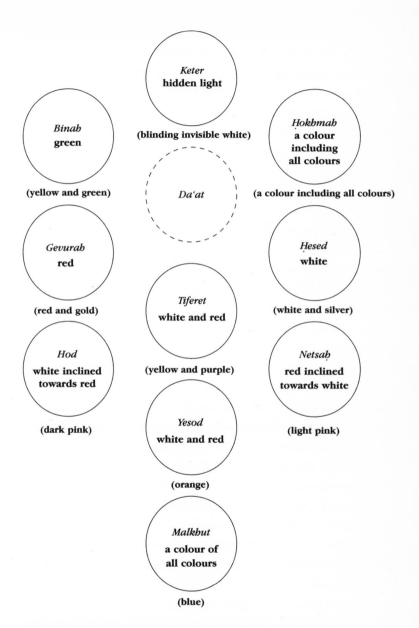

Fig. 7.1. Colours associated with the *sefirot* according to Azriel of Gerona. Cordovero's system is given in brackets beneath each *sefirah*

> Imagine that you are light and all about you is light, from
> every direction and every side, and in the midst of the light
> a stream of light, and upon it a glowing light [*Gevurah*], and
> opposite is a throne and upon that a good light [*Hesed*] . . .
> Turn to the right and you will find pure light [*Netsah*], and
> to the left and you will find an aura which is the radiant light
> [*Hod*]. And between them and above them is the light of
> the glory [*Tiferet*], and around it the light of life [*Yesod*]. And
> above it is the crown of light [*Keter*] that crowns the
> objects of thought, illumines the paths of ideas, and
> brightens the splendour of visions.

Working with light is an important feature of kabbalistic practice.
The ability to detect subtle nuances in different qualities of light can be
nurtured in a more basic approach that entails contemplating the
flame of a candle or oil lamp. The *Zohar* notes that we may become
aware of five shades of colour when contemplating a flame: white, red,
yellow, black and blue. The white and yellow are seen in the rising part
of the flame, whilst the black and blue are at the base adjacent to the
wick. Red is seen occasionally in the blue, due to contamination in the
wick. Throughout kabbalistic symbolism, blue depicts the *Shekhinah*.
The blue light is, in the words of the *Zohar*, a 'throne' for the white,
but may be flecked with the red of *Gevurah* if there is spiritual
contamination in the system. The white light alludes to *Tiferet*, and its
contact with the blue depicts the union of *Tiferet* and *Malkhut*. In
addition to the identifiable colours, there is a 'concealed light which
surrounds the white'. This higher light is described as the 'supernal
mystery' (*Zohar* 1:51a). It is the aura that may be seen around the
flame, and alludes to *Binah*.

Visionary abilities lie at the heart of the prophetic state, which, as
we have seen, is the goal of much kabbalistic practice. Ultimately, these
abilities have to be harnessed in uniting the human mind with its

source in the Divine. In the mediaeval formulation of Abulafia and other kabbalists, the specifically human function of mind is transcended by engaging with the Active Intellect. The resulting infusion of images into the human mind is the gift associated with the prophetic imagination. The power of the human imagination, as practised through visualization and other techniques, becomes the springboard to a receptive state though which the higher influx enters the mind. In one of Abulafia's formulations, 'the Name . . . will begin to move within him . . . and begin to cause him to pass from potentiality to actuality' (Abulafia, *Sefer Gan* Nu'al. 1999 edition: p41).

This fusion of the human intellect with the divine Mind is conveyed in an anonymous work associated with Abulafia's teachings. The text delves into the biblical verse in which God says, 'See now that I, even I, am He' (*Deuteronomy* 32:39). According to the author, the secret of this verse is 'the circle of prophecy', such that the human and the divine comprise two halves of a complete circle (cited in Idel 1988a: 64). The repetition of 'I' in the verse is taken to be referring to the union of the human 'I' with the divine Essence – the eternal 'I'. This interpretation is clearer in the original Hebrew, for the phrase from *Deuteronomy* comprises only the pronouns 'I, I, He' (Hebrew *Ani Ani Hu*). By gematria this phrase equates to the phrase 'the circle of prophecy' (in this gematria an additional unit is added for each word, giving each phrase a total of 137), intimating that the prophetic state is one in which the human 'I' is indeed united with the divine 'I'.

According to a much older rabbinic axiom, the prophetic state enables one to visualize an aspect of the Divine in human form: 'Rabbi Yudan says, great is the power of the prophets who are able to compare the likeness of the Almighty on high with the form of man'. This statement appears in several rabbinic sources (e.g. see Midrash, *Numbers Rabbah* 19:4). Some caution is required in interpreting this statement, for it comes close to idolatry. The essence of God can never be captured in visual, or any other, form. Nevertheless, one of the biblical texts brought in the Midrash to support R. Yudan's statement carries the clear implication that what is to be envisioned is indeed an aspect of God ('Almighty'; *Gevurah* in the Hebrew). This biblical support is drawn from Ezekiel's vision: 'And on the semblance of a throne was a semblance as the appearance of a man above it' (*Ezekiel* 1:26). Ezekiel was evidently seeing in a vision an aspect of God in human form.

The essential teaching of Kabbalah is that God manifests through the *sefirot*. One of the palpable images for the system of the *sefirot* is that of the human form. *Keter* sits above the head; *Hokhmah* and *Binah* comprise the two sides of the brain; *Hesed* and *Gevurah* are the two arms; *Tiferet* is the torso; *Netsah* and *Hod*, the two thighs; and *Yesod*, the male organ. *Malkhut* depicts the female who is united in love with the rest of the array. As already noted in Chapter 4 (p. 120), this anthropomorphism extends to the four-letter Name as an expression of the totality of the *sefirot*: the *yod* is the head, the first *heh* is the shoulders and arms, the *vav* is the torso, and the final *heh* depicts the legs. Of course, this anthropomorphism should be understood merely as a means for humans to grasp the nature of the Divine – we can know only that which has some resonance with our essential nature. God has no form; yet finite structure is required for human understanding. R. Yudan's statement is, then, intended to convey the idea that we are able to enter the 'circle of prophecy' by effecting this link between the infinite and the finite. In Kabbalah, the *sefirotic* tree constitutes this link between the infinite and the finite, with the latter specifically having human form. Indeed, this is the correct meaning of the biblical teaching that Adam is created in the image of God.

One of the most important of the biblical commentators, Rabbi Abraham ibn Ezra (1089-1164) writes about the prophetic state attained by the biblical prophet, Daniel, stating that 'he who hears is a man and he who speaks is a man'. In relation to this comment, a pupil of Abulafia writes:

> Know that the complete secret of prophecy consists for
> the prophet in that he suddenly sees the shape of his self
> standing before him and he forgets his self and it is
> disengaged from him and he sees the shape of his self
> before him talking to him and predicting the future. (Cited
> in Scholem 1946: 142)

This writer goes on to describe his own experience of seeing his self standing before him. This occurred whilst he was engaged in writing 'kabbalistic secrets', presumably following one of Abulafia's techniques of letter combinations.

It will be obvious that, for these mystics, witnessing one's self externalized is not a purely psychological event. Isaac of Acre explains that the experience results from immersion in the spiritual world. As worldly aspects are transcended, so the spirit of God comes to dwell in the individual's soul. It is this divine spirit, manifesting in the externalized self, which is the locus of prophetic encounter. The extent to which we might understand these mystical phenomena in psychological terms is a matter that I shall consider in Chapter 8. For the moment, let me conclude this section with the graphic words of another of Abulafia's pupils. The pupil describes the various stages of ascent associated with the Path of the Names taught by Abulafia. The ultimate stage, demanding a final push of spiritual energy, is one in which:

> . . . that which is within will manifest itself without, and
> through the power of sheer imagination will take on the
> form of a polished mirror. And this is 'the flame of the
> circling sword' [*Genesis* 3:24], the rear revolving and
> becoming the fore. Whereupon one sees that his inmost
> being is something outside of himself. (Cited in Scholem
> 1946: 155)

KABBALAH AND *HALAKHAH*

Daily observances in Judaism revolve around *Halakhah*. This word derives from the Hebrew root *halakh* (walk) and conveys the rabbinic maxim that the daily path of one's life should be structured according to the word of God, as recorded in the Torah. In Chapter 2 (p. 70) I noted that, in Kabbalah, the *halakhah* becomes a quasi-magical system, inasmuch as the various rituals that form the *halakhic* path are viewed as having influences on the *sefirot*. Promoting harmony amongst the *sefirot* through the correct performance of *halakhic* ritual and conduct is considered to bring blessings to the one following the *halakhic* dictate, as well as to the world as a whole.

Given the kabbalistic view of the Torah as comprising diverse levels of meaning, it clearly follows that the *mitsvot* (commandments) – which comprise much of the text of the Torah – must adhere to this principle. From this perspective, the *mitsvot*, which are the basis of the *halakhah*, are seen as having both overt and concealed levels of meaning. Performance of these *mitsvot* with the appropriate *kavannah* – by which is meant a focus on the intended *sefirotic* effects of the *mitsvah* – then becomes the third limb of kabbalistic practice. The other two are prayer and concentrative meditation, or visualization. These three forms of practice complement the overarching interest in the study of Torah, the divine Names, and the intellectual quest to grasp the meaning of the *sefirot*.

Illustrative of the kabbalistic view of the *mitsvot* is the understanding of charity in relation to *Malkhut*, discussed earlier in this chapter (p. 189). In the *sefirotic* system the function of *Malkhut* is that of receiving. By giving to charity, one promotes the role of *Tiferet* as the sphere that is able to give to *Malkhut*, thereby promoting unification of the *sefirotic* system. Of course, there are perfectly good moral and social reasons for charitable behaviour. These constitute the outer dimension of the *mitsvah*; but in the kabbalistic vision, one is able to achieve considerably more through the effects on the *sefirot*. One is not simply giving to the needy; rather, by promoting the harmony of the *sefirotic* system, one is correcting the channels through which sustenance flows from the *En Sof*. By effecting the intended conformation of the *sefirot*, one is actually establishing the Name of God: 'Who is it that makes the holy Name every day? Let us say that it is the one who gives charity to the poor' (*Zohar* 3:113b).

By penetrating into an understanding of the dynamics of the Godhead, the kabbalistic approach to the *mitsvot* leads to a less sentimental vision than that associated with non-mystical religion. The non-mystical view holds that God is somehow 'pleased' by human conduct that is in accord with His Law, and responds by acting generously. The kabbalistic view focuses on the influences of such right conduct on the vessels that mediate the transmission of energy and sustenance to the world. In this sense, human conduct is an active influence which structures the intra-divine forces that interact with the world. The *Zohar* provides a bold image in this context: 'One who fulfils the *mitsvot* of the Torah and walks in its ways, it is as if he makes Him in the upper world. The Holy One, blessed be He, says, he – as it were – makes Me' (*Zohar* 2:113a).

For Abulafia, the deepest secrets associated with the *mitsvot* are connected with his technique of combining letters. This idea is built through an important ambiguity in the Hebrew word *tseruf*. As we saw in Chapter 6 (p. 169), one meaning of this word is 'combination', and the word is thus used for the kabbalistic practice of working with the letters of Torah. However, *tseruf* also means 'purification'. This double meaning is important since it implies that the combinatory technique is the means for purifying the soul. Abulafia takes this a stage further by referring to one of the classic rabbinic passages dealing with the reasons for the *mitsvot*. In rabbinic sources, Rav is quoted as saying that the reason that God gave the *mitsvot* is to purify humankind (Midrash, *Genesis Rabba* 44:1 and elsewhere). The use of the verb *le-tsaref* (to purify) here is construed by Abulafia as a link with the kabbalistic practice of letter combination: 'The sages said that the *mitsvot* were given only in order to purify human beings, and this is precisely what they said in . . . [the Talmud] – Betsalel knew how to combine the letters by which the heaven and earth were created' (Abulafia, *Sefer Ha-Heshek* 2002 edition: 63; for more on Betsalel see Chapter 5).

Abulafia implies that Rav's teaching is considerably more subtle than appears. At face value, it suggests that performance of the *mitsvot* is purifying in the sense that it leads to a refinement of character. Taken more deeply, however, the implication is that adherence to the ways of Torah is a preliminary to mastering the mystical practice of *tseruf* (the meditative combination of letters), which in turn is the path to revealing the secret meanings of the *mitsvot*. Through the mystical practice of letter combination the human intellect is united with the Active Intellect, completing the 'circle of prophecy', as mentioned above. Purification is achieved through mystical union with God. In this sense, the system of *mitsvot* is equivalent to the Tabernacle constructed by Betsalel: the system constitutes an organic whole capable of uniting heaven and earth.

Chapter 8

Kabbalah Today

[The idea of the golem, the artificial humanoid] is based on
a faith almost as old as the human species – namely, that
dead matter is not really dead but can be brought to life. I
am not exaggerating when I say that the golem story
appears less obsolete today than it seemed one hundred
years ago. What are the computers and robots of our time
if not golems? (Isaac Bashevis Singer)

And, I would like to add, perhaps not just the golem story!

The roots of Kabbalah may be traced to the ancient world, and
many of its insights and practices were formulated in writing during
the mediaeval period. It is legitimate, therefore, to question its
continuing value in the modern world, a world of science and a world
in which cultural aspirations reflect a distinctively twenty-first-century
globalization. Jewish tradition holds that the closer in time an
authorized text is to the revelation of God at Mount Sinai, the more
strongly it is infused with the power of that revelation. In this sense,
then, the older the source, the more valuable it is. Yet in the modern
period, the pace of discovery has led many to challenge tradition. It
would appear that we have to master something of a delicate balancing

act, through which we attempt to honour tradition whilst recognizing the substance of scientific advance and the fruits of historical scholarship. There is no doubt in my mind that Kabbalah provides a unique key to that balancing act. It offers a path to spiritual insight that is as relevant for the seeker today as it was during earlier ages, and, as I shall illustrate, it comprises a system of thought that meshes poignantly with the world of modern science.

In this chapter, I address the relevance of Kabbalah today. Just as our world of robots and computers has breathed fresh life into the idea of the golem, so developments in psychology, neuroscience and physics are revitalizing ancient kabbalistic insights. It is not simply that the kabbalistic path seems to speak to many who are searching for a meaningful approach to the spiritual challenges of our day. Of equal relevance to my theme of 'Kabbalah today' are the ways in which kabbalistic insights seem peculiarly relevant to the challenges of modern science. The spirit of Torah does not mean that we cannot look outside of the sacred books for inspiration. Indeed, I believe that the continuity of the kabbalistic tradition demands that we inquire into the nature of the mind and of the cosmos, using all our ways of knowledge, including psychology and the other sciences. And this view is certainly not foreign to Judaism: Rambam, universally acknowledged as the greatest Jewish philosopher, stated that the study of Torah would be lacking without a knowledge of science and other secular subjects. At its core, Kabbalah has always been an intellectual path, and today that means embracing and celebrating the leading edges of discovery.

OF GOLEMS AND THE IMITATION OF GOD

Mitchell Marcus (1999) relates a poignant tale concerning a connection between the folklore of the golem and three of the most influential computer scientists working on artificial intelligence (AI) at MIT in the late 1960s. The golem represents an important strand of Jewish mysticism that may be traced back at least to the time of the Talmud. The tradition holds that the adept is capable of bringing to life a creature made of clay by chanting the appropriate letter combinations as specified in the *Sefer Yetsirah*. In the context of Marcus's tale, the important theme involves the connection between the golem tradition and the challenge to imbue an artificial device with intelligence. Although the quest for AI is not 'religious' in the normal sense of the word, there is a poignant parallel between the quest of kabbalists to imitate God's pinnacle of creation – the creation of man – and that of computer scientists attempting to bring machines 'to life'.

In one of the most influential of the stories about the golem, Rabbi Judah Loew (the *Maharal* of Prague, c.1525–1609) is said to have created a golem in order to protect the Jewish community of Prague from a pogrom. The golem performed its duties well for some time, but on one Shabbat a disaster occurred. Prior to Shabbat, the Maharal would regularly return the golem to its inanimate status, on account of the prohibition against work on Shabbat. On this particular Shabbat, he was delayed and, as Shabbat was about to commence, the golem began to run amuck. It is related that the Maharal was summoned and, on discovering what was happening, immediately returned the golem to its dust, and never brought it back to life again.

With this background, let me cite Marcus's story in his own words. Marcus was told the following whilst a graduate student at MIT's AI laboratory in the 1970s. The story concerns Joel Moses, Gerry Sussman and Marvin Minsky, all of them Jewish, and all influential pioneers in the development of AI. Joel had been relating to others at the lab an event that had happened at his *bar mitzvah*:

> . . . his grandfather called him aside and told him that he, the grandfather, was a descendant of the Maharal of Prague, the creator of the Golem, and therefore that he,

Joel Moses, was also a descendant of the Maharal. His grandfather then told him that the Golem had not been returned to dust, as in the standard story, that the Maharal had actually put the Golem into a state of suspended animation. The Golem could be brought back to life by an incantation if the need were to arise, and it was the grandfather's duty to pass on that incantation to his grandson now that he was bar mitzvah. It would be Joel Moses's duty to pass on the incantation to his grandsons once they reached the age of religious maturity.

Not surprisingly, most of those present heard this tale with more than a little amazement. However, Sussman then began to speak. To the utter amazement of those assembled, he too said that at his bar mitzvah, he had been called aside by his grandfather and was told that he was a descendant of the Maharal of Prague. He too was told that the Golem was in a state of suspended animation in the attic of the synagogue in Prague, and that there was an incantation to awaken it if the need arose, and it was his duty to pass this incantation on to his grandsons.

With those present looking on in complete amazement, Sussman and Moses each wrote down the incantation that he had been told, and each passed the slip of paper to the other. Evidently the two incantations were the same. At just this point, Marvin Minsky, one of the fathers of artificial intelligence and the head of the group, walked out of his office to see his graduate students looking completely astounded. He asked what had happened, and was told what had just taken place. Marvin, a complete rationalist, just scoffed. He said, 'You believe this? Look, right after my bar mitzvah, I was told the same thing by my grandfather. But you think I believed it?' Minsky, evidently, not only did not

believe the story, but had forgotten the incantation, so we
do not know whether his version was also the same.

'Curiouser and curiouser. . .,' I am tempted to say! Even if we
dismiss the uncanny aspects of the above story, we are left with a sense
of the continuity between the skills of the AI scientist and those that a
kabbalist immersed in the secret understandings of creation might
bring to the golem ritual. For both, there is a need to engage with the
inner codes that seemingly underpin the outer product. The kabbalist
intones the letter combinations that are identified with the creative
workings of God's mind, and the AI scientist programmes the machine
with the symbolic codes that have the potential to generate
intelligence from silicon.

The talmudic source for the golem tradition appears in a
discussion of magical practices and their status as permitted or
proscribed behaviour:

> Rava said: If the righteous wished, they could create a
> world, for it is written, 'Your iniquities have divided you
> from your God' (*Isaiah* 59:2). Rava created a man and sent
> him to Rav Zeira. The Rabbi spoke to him but he did not
> reply. He [Rav Zeira] said: You are from the fellow scholars
> [possibly, magicians]. Return to your dust! Rav Hanina and
> Rav Oshaya spent every Sabbath eve busy with the *Sefer
> Yetsirah*. A three-year-old calf was created by them and
> they ate it. (Talmud *Sanhedrin* 65b)

The latter act, that of creating a calf, is specifically described as
permitted behaviour, and it is clearly implied that the creation of an
artificial man is permitted also. Indeed, the mastery of creation
entailed in the production of a golem is viewed as the ultimate act of
imitating God – a goal promoted throughout Judaism. As Idel puts it,

through a ritual which appears to be designed specifically to recapitulate God's creation of man, the mystic aspires to 'attain the experience of the creative moment of God' (Idel 1990: xxvii).

The talmudic passage contains an allusion to the role of language in the procedure for producing a golem. The Aramaic original, translated as 'Rava created a man', is *Rava bara gavra*, which involves an almost mantra-like set of permutations on the letters of *bara*, Hebrew for 'created'. In their various permutations, the three Hebrew letters *alef*, *bet* and *resh* not only generate Rava's name and the verb, 'to create,' but also the Hebrew *eiver*, meaning 'limb'. The phrase *Rava bara gavra* hints at the permuting of letters that constitutes part of the ritual for creating a golem. The kabbalists drew on these talmudic verbal connections, believing that the pinnacle of human creativity was the generation of a complete set of 'limbs' (by which was meant all constituent parts of the body), as in the golem.

As we have seen, the *Sefer Yetsirah* details the esoteric work of combining the Hebrew letters. In addition to indicating the techniques to be used, the *Sefer Yetsirah* provides key associations for each letter. One set of associations concerns each letter's relation to a specific 'limb' of the body. Thus, for example, according to one version of the text, *bet* corresponds to the mouth, *gimel* to the right eye, *dalet* to the left eye, and so on. The golem ritual entails working with these letter-limb connections. As Kaplan writes, 'by chanting the appropriate letter arrays . . . the initiate could form a very real image of a human being, limb by limb' (Kaplan 1990: 127).

A detailed discussion of the ritual for producing a golem is found in the Rokeach's commentary on the *Sefer Yetsirah*. He writes of one who would make a golem:

> It is incumbent upon him to take virgin soil from a place in the mountains where no one has plowed. And he shall knead the dust with living water, and he shall make a body

[golem] and shall begin to permutate the alphabets of 221 gates, each limb separately, each limb with the corresponding letter mentioned in *Sefer Yetzirah*. . . . And always, the letter of the [divine] name with them. (Cited in Idel 1990: 56)

He goes on to detail the elaborate arrays of letter-vowel combinations that would be chanted in combination with the letters of God's name.

We thus find two phases in the golem ritual. The first clearly draws on the symbolism of sexual polarity, the male principle of 'living water' (e.g. spring water) being mixed with the female principle, 'virgin soil'. The second phase draws on the traditions of Hebrew language mysticism discussed in earlier chapters. The two phases parallel the two stages in God's formation of the first human: 'And the Lord God formed Adam [of] dust from the ground, and He breathed into his nostrils the soul of life . . .' (*Genesis* 2:7). The mystic first imitates God by moulding the golem from the dust of the ground. God's second act, that of breathing into man the soul of life, is replaced by the linguistic alchemy through which the golem is imbued with an animating principle.

How do we approach this magical tradition of the golem today? To dismiss it as one of the more 'fanciful' chapters in Kabbalah would be to fail to recognize its relation to the essential features of the kabbalistic worldview. In the last chapter we saw that an indicator of success in the use of prophetic techniques is the vision of a human form appearing in front of the mystic. Whilst this differs from the golem in that the human form seen in the prophetic state is oneself, the emphasis on the primacy of the human form is common to both traditions. In general, the practice of *re-membering* the limbs of the human form is central to Kabbalah in view of the principle of correspondence, which sees the human as pivotal between 'lower' and 'higher' realities. I use the term 're-membering' deliberately. A psychological interpretation of the golem ritual would emphasize its relation to the self. The 'limbs', or 'members' that comprise the self are psychologically dismembered in order to be *re-membered* in the image of God. (For more detail of this psychological interpretation, see Lancaster 1997b.)

The resonances between the golem ritual and the archetypal basis of the creation of man serve to enable the mystic to forge a higher, more inclusive self. The self is no longer constrained by the finite world of personal meanings, but is expanded to embrace the infinite Otherness of God. The link with memory ('re-membering') is critical, for there are good reasons for thinking that the seeming continuity of 'I', which is central to our experience of self, is actually a product of memory. The golem ritual unties the knots that structure the continuity of 'I' in habitual ways, and re-binds the threads of self at a higher level. (Details of the relevant psychological evidence will be found in Lancaster 2004; I intend to examine the links between Kabbalah and the nature of mind, as revealed by psychology and neuroscience, in a future book.)

It will be clear from preceding chapters that the linguistic elements of the golem ritual draw on a view of language that goes to the heart of Kabbalah. The Hebrew letters are viewed as the agents of creation, and any process of self recreation must draw on the power of the letters. This kabbalistic emphasis on the role of language reinforces the psychological perspective introduced above, since language is a major determinant of self. Our sense of self is constructed as a narrative. In a very real sense, we are the person that we tell ourselves that we are. Of course, much of this self-narrative takes place below the surface of consciousness. Any transformation of self is therefore dependent on practices that penetrate into the unconscious. Kabbalistic practices that delve into the inner nature of language touch deep aspects of the unconscious process. Both Freud, the pioneer of psychoanalysis, and Jacques Lacan, who further developed the principles of psychoanalysis in the later twentieth century, held that the unconscious is essentially structured in terms of language. Kabbalistic linguistic practices have the potential to, firstly, deconstruct the unconscious basis of personality and, secondly, to reconstruct it in ways more connected to the inner nature of God. This reconstruction process depends on the ways in which the letters of the divine Name are introduced into the esoteric language practices. To the kabbalist, the letters of the Name are not simply symbolic of God, but effectively capture His presence. We may conclude that a deep connection is thus forged between the mystic's mind and the omnipresence of the divine Mind.

This psychological interpretation of kabbalistic language mysticism is not restricted to the golem tradition. It applies also to the general approach to language mysticism as epitomized, for example, in Abulafia's writings. Abulafia emphasizes two phases in the linguistic practice. The first we may characterize as *deconstructive* and the second, as *reconstructive*. Words must first be atomized, broken down to their 'prime material state', as he calls it. Only then can the mystic begin to establish new connections and bring the letters of God's Name into the practice. In one of his images, the mystic has firstly to untie the knots that bind him to time and space, and only then may he cleave to God. Psychologically, the knots are the structures of personality, and 'untying' them means entering into an undifferentiated state of consciousness. This open state of consciousness is a necessary transitional phase for any form of transformation, just as a seed must burst its shell before it can begin to grow. The reconstructive phase builds new connections in language, equating to a new structuring of self. As indicated already, the introduction of the letters of God's Name ideally brings the infinitude of God's essence into the new self. Essentially, it is the *scale* of self that is changed by these kabbalistic practices.

The Hebrew word *golem* appears only once in the Bible. The Psalmist writes, 'You [God] covered me in my mother's womb . . . My substance was not concealed from You when I was made in secret and wrought in the depths of the earth. Your eyes saw my *golem* and in

Your book all of them were written' (*Psalm* 139:13-16). This is a literal translation of the Hebrew. The reference for the phrase 'all of them' is unclear. In the context of the *golem* tradition, the phrase would seem to imply 'all of the parts of my embryonic form'. The whole of this Psalm seems to be exploring the darkness of the inner workings of creation. Two key verses precede the above extract: 'I say, surely the darkness will cover me, yet the night will be light about me; Even darkness is not dark for you; but the night shines like the day; darkness is as light.' Just as the seed has to penetrate the darkness of the earth in order to grow, so the transformation of self encouraged in the kabbalistic path requires a journey to the darkness of one's core being. With this in mind, it is interesting to speculate about possible parallels between the golem ritual and the emphasis on re-experiencing one's birth, as promoted in certain strands of transpersonal therapy.

Aside from any psychological parallels, the golem ritual and therapeutic 'rebirthing' may trigger similar questions concerning the boundary between the real and the imagined. Just because an individual believes that they have truly reconnected with phenomena associated with their birth, it does not necessarily follow that there is a genuine link with sensory and other qualities present at the time of birth. Therapeutic growth does not depend on the experience being 'real' in that sense. Similarly, in the case of the golem, the potential for a mystical experience of this humanoid creature to bring about psycho-spiritual growth does not necessarily depend on the golem being literally 'real'. In this context, it is worth noting that many of the early accounts of the golem do not emphasize the externalization and automaton-like qualities that occur in later accounts. As I have discussed in detail elsewhere (Lancaster 1997a), the form that the golem took in historical accounts was influenced by changing worldviews, the rise of science and the effects of Christian-inspired anti-Semitism. It is possible that the earliest accounts viewed the golem as a focus for a mystical state of consciousness rather than as a 'real' creature.

Whatever we may conclude about the reality of the golem, there can be no doubting the psychological power generated by the idea of the creation of artificial life. Indeed, throughout history this archetypal theme has endured. Prominent examples include Frankenstein's creature and, more recently, Hollywood icons such as the Terminator. The power in the image of inanimate matter coming to life certainly reaches back into early childhood, when soft toys become alive and imaginary companions take on substantive qualities. Again, the psychological value of exploring the childhood roots of these fantasies has been extensively studied in the therapeutic literature.

In terms of the themes set out in the *Sefer Yetsirah*, it is not only the golem image that has endured. As illustrated in Figure 8.1, many aspects of our modern world can be traced to the imaginative conceptions of this text. This figure proposes that there are essentially three tracks through which the approach of the *Sefer Yetsirah* has coursed through to the modern world. The *computational* track is based in the *Sefer Yetsirah*'s model of the rotating wheel that serves to permute elements of a code, and eventuates in our day in the challenges of computer science. The Spanish Christian mystic, Ramon Lull, seems to have been influenced by the *Sefer Yetsirah* in his attempts to devise divinatory devices using letters in turning wheels. I have also included on this track Pascal and Leibniz, who were both fascinated by the possibilities of computing machines. The *hermeneutic* track draws on the *Sefer Yetsirah*'s vision of language and the interpretation of meanings through associations and linguistic codes. As should be evident from earlier chapters, any number of kabbalists could be situated on this track. My inclusion of Abulafia reflects the extent to which he epitomizes this approach. The presence of Freud on this track reflects the connections between Abulafia's structured associative methods and Freud's more open 'free association', the method which he used to penetrate into the deep meanings in his patients' psyches. The relationships between psychoanalysis and kabbalistic language mysticism serve to illustrate the debt owed by the therapeutic world to the Jewish pioneers of language

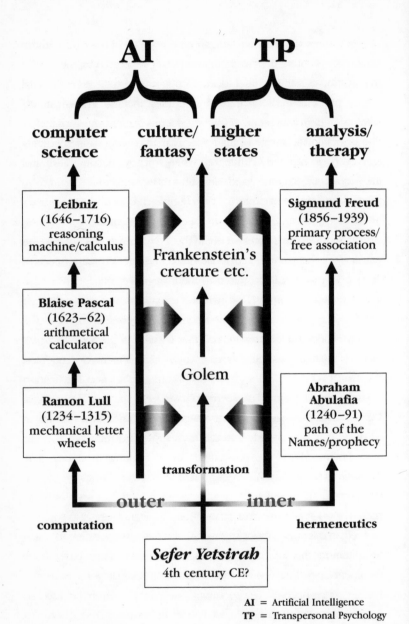

Fig. 8.1. Some historical developments from the language mysticism of the *Sefer Yetsirah*

mysticism. Finally, the *transformational* track emphasizes the potential for achieving a higher state of being through the use of practices enunciated in the *Sefer Yetsirah*. I have used the golem to exemplify this track since the power to bring animation to the inanimate epitomizes transformation. This track eventuates in the countless fantasy images that populate our movies and computer games. The predominance of fantasies of transformation should not obscure the fact that the mystical interest in achieving genuine self-transformation is very much still alive in our day.

As the figure indicates, the two disciplines of artificial intelligence and transpersonal psychology are the modern heirs to the worldview of the *Sefer Yetsirah*. In its search to produce intelligent computers and ever more sophisticated means of connecting the globe, AI is having a profound impact on contemporary culture. It is no exaggeration to suggest that the kabbalistic dream of *tikkun olam* (healing the world) – making the world whole – is being significantly advanced at the material level by the revolution in IT. The discipline of transpersonal psychology brings together the therapeutic and the spiritual quests for transformation. In its mission to forge non-sectarian paths of spiritual growth for today, transpersonal psychology draws inspiration from the world's great mystical traditions, as well as from the insights of the pioneers of therapeutic psychology.

MIRRORING THE MIND

> The Holy One, blessed be He . . . made this world corresponding to the world above, and everything which is above has its counterpart here below, and everything here below has its counterpart in the sea; and yet all constitute a unity'. (*Zohar* 2:20a)

With these words, the *Zohar* expresses the central tenet of Kabbalah: that the world is built on correspondences. The 'lower' realm is reflective of the principles upon which the 'higher' realm operates. This principle applies to all aspects of reality, including the mind and brain. The human mind is reflective of the 'divine Mind' and the human brain functions in ways that correspond to the 'brains' of the higher conformations in the *sefirotic* system – those of *Arikh Anpin* and *Zeir Anpin* (see Chapter 3, p. 91).

To what extent does research into the functioning of the brain support this kabbalistic principle? In addressing this question, I shall briefly consider recent research into the neuroscience of consciousness. It is beyond the scope of this book to explain the relevant research in depth. My interest here is simply to demonstrate the continuing relevance of kabbalistic insights in this branch of science (see Lancaster 2004 for considerably more detail on the subject). It appears that two features of brain functioning are critical for consciousness. The first is that of *phase synchrony* in neural systems, or as I shall call it here, *resonance*. The essential feature of the code used by the brain to enable its neurones to unite in functionally important ways depends on the resonance established amongst the oscillatory responses of the neurones. This 'brain code' provides the framework through which consciousness attaches to such cognitive processes as perception, emotion, thought and memory. The second feature currently favoured in neuroscience to 'explain' the brain's role in consciousness is that of *recurrent processing*. This refers to *re-entrant* activity in neural systems. So-called 'feed-forward' neural pathways extend 'upward' from the sense organs through a hierarchy of brain-processing regions, by means of which ever-more complex features of the sensory input are analysed. However, the system is far from being 'one-way'. The 'higher' regions in the hierarchy send neurones back down to intersect with the 'upward' stream. These are the re-entrant pathways. The re-entrant pathways, then, flow backwards from 'higher' brain regions, that is, those associated with memory and other cognitive functions, to 'lower', more sensory, regions. Research has shown that it is only when the re-entrant pathways become active that consciousness arises. These two features of brain processing are connected: recurrent processing depends on resonance of neuronal systems.

The principle of correspondence underpins any consideration of possible kabbalistic significance in relation to these features of brain processing, for the principle asserts that the dynamics of the world of the *sefirot* should be reflected in the ways in which the microcosm of the human brain operates. As I shall indicate, both of the above neurophysiological features are indeed in accordance with key kabbalistic teachings. It would appear, therefore, that the credibility of kabbalistic texts is enhanced through a consideration of these recent developments in neuroscience.

What are these key kabbalistic teachings? The first is that of 'unification'. The major task allotted to humankind in the kabbalistic scheme is that of restoring harmony in the *sefirotic* realm, which may be achieved through the practice of unification. 'This is the mystery of unification. One . . . must unify the Name of the Holy One, blessed be He, unifying the limbs and upper and lower levels, to integrate the whole and to raise all to the place where the knot is bound' (*Zohar* 2:216a). The 'place of the knot' is a reference to the brain, since the knot of the head *tefillin* is placed at the back of the head and is said to relate to the brain. The essential concept here is that of unifying diverse parts of the *sefirotic* system, which corresponds to what we now understand of the logic through which the brain operates.

More generally, the importance of resonance is detected by the *Zohar* in the first word of Genesis, *bereshit* (In the beginning). Noting that this word is an anagram of *shir ta'ev* (a song of desire), the *Zohar* suggests that the whole of creation is a resonant song, mirrored and expanded by that of the angels in the heavenly hierarchy (*Zohar Hadash, Bereshit*, 5d). (In transliteration this anagram may be clearer. The Hebrew for 'In the beginning' is *Br'shyt* and 'a song of desire' is *shyr t'b*).

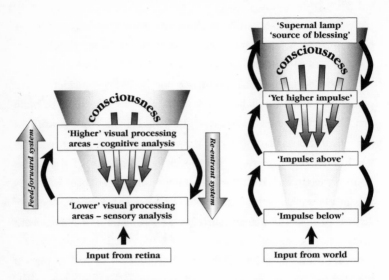

Fig. 8.2. Parallels between brain systems for visual consciousness and the *Zohar*'s view of 'lower' and 'higher' impulses

We may perhaps think of phase synchrony in neural systems as merely one level of this grandiose scheme. It would constitute a particular expression of a more universal role for resonance in bringing about alignment, or unification, within systems. From this perspective, phase synchrony amongst brain neurones should not be viewed as the *cause* of consciousness, but rather as the code by means of which the brain is able to engage with the consciousness that pervades the whole of creation. The seeming unity of phenomenal consciousness is but a reflection of the unity of the whole, that is, of God.

The second key kabbalistic teaching is that the 'impulse from below brings forth an impulse from above'. This teaching is a crucial extension of the overall principle of correspondence. Not only does the 'below' correspond to the 'above' in a structural sense, but, when it is in proper alignment, the 'below' activates the 'above', thereby bringing about a flow of the supernal influx:

> Come and see. Through the impulse from below is awakened an impulse above, and through the impulse from above there is awakened a yet higher impulse, until the impulse reaches the place where the lamp is to be lit and it is lit . . . and all the worlds receive blessing from it. (*Zohar* I:244a)

It seems evident to me that the greatest of the 'blessings' we receive from the 'place where the lamp is to be lit' is consciousness. With this assumption, the teaching of the *Zohar* bears a strong relation to the neuroscientific view of recurrent processing. As far as the brain is concerned, as illustrated in Figure 8.2, activity in 'lower' areas triggers activity in 'higher' areas, and consciousness arises when the higher activity impinges on the lower through the re-entrant pathway. In a manner that is consonant with kabbalistic teachings, the brain functions as a microcosm of the larger scheme presented in the *Zohar*. From a scientific perspective, the question of the cause of consciousness is intractable. There is no unequivocal evidence to assert that it is actually generated by the brain itself. Clearly, the brain is critical for the processes through which consciousness enters into thoughts and other cognitive activity, but it does not necessarily follow that the brain is solely responsible for consciousness itself. In Kabbalah and all other traditions of theistic mysticism, the essence of consciousness is viewed as a blessing from God.

I noted above that the two features of resonance and recurrent processing are linked in brain function. Recurrent processing depends on the brain code of resonance in order to ensure that higher-order activity is linked to matching lower-order activity. In the same way, the *Zohar* links the idea of unification with its view of the generation of the higher impulse. This is symbolically conveyed in the following cryptic passage:

> Whenever all the limbs dwell together in a single bond, and
> they enjoy pleasure and desire from the head, above and
> below, and from this pleasure and desire they all empty into
> him [Joseph], then he becomes a flowing river going out of
> the real Eden. This is more than 'Eden', for it is the supernal
> Hokhmah . . . Then all is included in the blessings and all is
> one. (Zohar 1:247b)

The passage concerns the blessings that were bestowed on Joseph (*Genesis* 49:22-6). We saw in Chapter 5 that Joseph depicts the *sefirah* of *Yesod*, which is identified with the male organ. The passage envisions the act of intercourse (the 'single bond') through which the powers of the various parts of the body flow through the penis. The *Zohar*'s primary interest in the above passage concerns the unification of the *sefirot*. The point that is of interest in the context of my theme in this section is the allusion to the 'Real Eden', namely, the supernal *Hokhmah*. The *Zohar* is referring here to the 'impulse from above', and, if the complex imagery is decoded, we can see that the trigger for the arising of the higher impulse is unification through the binding of the *sefirot*.

In this section I have presented some provocative parallels between key kabbalistic themes and our understanding of brain function. It is important to be clear as to what these parallels imply. I am certainly not suggesting that the kabbalists of the past had access to the kinds of data generated by modern neuroscientific methods. But what is worth considering is that there is some fundamental truth in the notion that reality is built on the basis of correspondences, that the brain functions in ways that recapitulate the dynamic principles that are found on the macrocosmic scale. Kabbalah can be a worthy guide to those macrocosmic principles and is therefore a valuable adjunct to modern science.

THE DIMENSIONS OF ALL

What, then, is real? Physics is the branch of science that comes closest to addressing this ultimate question. Anyone who has attempted to grapple with modern physics, especially quantum mechanics, will know that the world of the senses that constitutes our view of reality is but a surface to a much more complex world at the micro-level. Many have remarked on the rapport between mysticism and modern physics. Mystics assert that consensual reality is but a mask to deeper forces and structures. This view relates to the assertion in quantum mechanics that the logic of our everyday world differs from that of the micro-particles, or strings, which constitute the fundamental basis of that everyday world. The world revealed by modern physics is one in which particles may go backwards in time, may seemingly be in two places at once, and are able to move from one place to another without passing through the space between them. Like other traditions of mysticism, Kabbalah is not uncomfortable with these phenomena; they are not out of place with the secret world revealed at the deepest level of the Torah.

Any approach to what is real must recognize the importance of *levels* of reality. In psychological terms, the conscious level is underpinned by that of the unconscious. To deny the reality of the conscious mind would be absurd, for without it we would have nothing. Nevertheless, the conscious mind is merely a surface to the inner world of the unconscious. Reality as described by modern physics presents us with a similar dilemma: the solidity of the table leg against which I stub my toe is no less real for my understanding that it is comprised of particles or strings which behave in ways that seem to bear little resemblance to the behaviour of table legs! The real mystery lies in understanding how one level relates to the other. It is unclear how the paradoxical realm of the quantum level, in which causation and time seem to run counter to our experience of everyday reality, translates into the order of objects and events that we daily encounter. Science has yet to provide adequate answers.

The notion of levels in the scheme of things is a major tenet of Kabbalah. There are *four worlds* (Chapter 4, p. 120ff), each of which is a realm in the created hierarchy of levels. The principle of correspondence, enshrined in the maxim 'as above so below', addresses the relationship between levels. And the *sefirotic* tree lays out the pattern through which one level unfolds into another. At the heart of all these conceptions of levels lies the kabbalistic understanding of the Torah. The secret level of the Torah has its own logic, in terms of codes and the symbolism of the *sefirot*, which is far removed from the narrative logic at the surface level. For the kabbalist, the interesting aspects of the Torah are not the stories it narrates, but the secrets revealed by the deeper logic at its core. This deeper logic transcends time and the normal causative chain of meaning. 'There is no before or after in Torah,' states a central rabbinic maxim, and meanings are commonly extracted by following bizarre and codified links across disparate sections of the text.

It is arguable that the true meaning of the assertion that the Torah *is* reality could not have been fully appreciated in any other age than ours. Of course, kabbalists would have known that the physical world mirrors the Torah in that both are comprised of levels, but it is only in our day that there has been independent confirmation of this insight. There is a profound concordance between the physicist exploring a level of reality ruled by its distinctive and bizarre logic and yet, at the same time, living by the everyday logic of our shared world, and the kabbalist exploring the codified depths of the Torah, whilst living a life structured by the surface level of the Torah. This concordance extends to psychology, for, again, there is independent confirmation that two levels of 'mental reality' – the conscious and the unconscious – operate according to distinctive rules of logic.

And what of the fundamental building blocks of physical reality? Current theorizing holds that these are strings that vibrate in distinctive ways. The same strings underlie everything, but whether they build quarks or photons, electrons or neutrons, depends on the form of the vibration. Perhaps this is the deeper meaning of the 'song of desire' discerned by the *Zohar* in the first word of the Torah. If a string 'desires' to be a quark it sings a specific tune; if its desire is to be something else, it changes its tune! String theory has taken centre-stage in modern physics because it appears to be able to unify the various different theories that arose in physics during the twentieth century. Prior to the development of string theory, it had proved impossible to find a formulation that would relate quantum theory to Einstein's theory of gravity, even though both were irrefutable. String theory has overcome this incompatibility. In order to achieve the synthesis that string theory brings to physical theories, it proved necessary to revisit our understanding of *dimensions*. In addition to the standard three dimensions of space and one of time, string theory posits another six dimensions. The additional six dimensions are thought to be 'compacted' to such tiny scales that we are unaware of them. They are, nevertheless, real, for if they were not, quantum theory could not co-exist with the theory of gravity.

It is tempting to speculate on the concordance between the number of dimensions of reality posited by current thinking in physics and the number of the sefirot. String theory posits ten dimensions which seems to accord with the kabbalistic assertion that there are ten sefirot – understood as the dimensions of reality. A recent advance on string theory, 'M-theory', posits a total of eleven dimensions that somehow appear as ten. In terms of the sefirot, maybe the ambiguity over the inclusion of da'at should somehow be incorporated into the debate between string theorists and M-Theorists...!

I would not want to build a justification of the Tree of Life on the basis of the latest theory in physics – after all, that theory may be 'here today and gone tomorrow'. Moreover, the meaning of 'dimension' needs some careful analysis, for the kabbalistic understanding is not the same as that in modern physics. Nevertheless, the concordance is poignant, for the *sefirot* are viewed as the dimensions of reality. In Chapter 3 (p. 77ff), I discussed the *Sefer Yetsirah*'s description of the *sefirot* in precisely these terms. As noted there, the kabbalistic vision posits a moral dimension at the core of reality, which is clearly not to be found in the world as depicted by physics (although it is arguable that for many physicists the notion of 'beauty' constitutes a component in the laws of the universe). At the level of *number*, however, the two systems – Kabbalah and string theory – are in accord: the number of dimensions is ten.

Ultimately, the fundamental reality of the world of the *sefirot* is nothing other than that of number; the *sefirot* are ten numbers. This is the essence of Kabbalah. Behind our world of meanings lies an immutable realm of numbers, and the notion that there are ten dimensions to all things is the core statement of Kabbalah. All is encompassed in the Tree of the *sefirot*:

> 'I, Y-H-V-H, make All, I alone stretch forth the heavens, from Me the earth is spread out' (*Isaiah* 44:24). I am the one who has planted this Tree for the whole world to enjoy. I spread out the All in it, and I called its name 'All'. For All depends upon it and All goes forth from it and All need it. Into it they gaze, and for it they long, and from it burst forth souls. (*Bahir* 14)

Again, things we now take for granted have given additional impetus to this vision at the heart of Kabbalah: that an inner world of number determines reality. I stare at my computer screen as I write, seeing the words and pondering the extent to which they adequately convey the meaning I wish to share; yet I know that the screen is merely a convenient formulation of the more inward world of numbers on which the computer operates. A computer game can draw you into a whole world of fantasy, yet, again, the 'real' operation entails nothing beyond numbers.

The numbers are the closest we can come to the 'Real'. For Kabbalah, the *sefirot* are the articulation of *En Sof*. This is why they are described as '*sefirot* of nothingness'. Kabbalah is the path through which we may enter into that sensual play with the ten that enables us to know our root in the All. Through Kabbalah we may join the dance of nothingness in order to realize who we truly are.

Glossary

The Bahir (*Sefer ha-Bahir*). Kabbalistic text attributed to Rabbi Nehunia ben ha-Kahana, who lived in the first century CE. First documented evidence for its existence is in twelfth-century Provence. Includes discussion of God's Names, Midrashim on the Hebrew letters, astrological material, and an exposition of the ten *sefirot*.

Betsalel. Master craftsman and builder of the *Mishkan*. His name means 'In the shadow of God'.

'Cutting the shoots'. Phrase used to refer to the heresy of denying the connection of the *sefirot* with *En Sof*. Cutting the *sefirot* off from the infinite root that nourishes them. This idolatrous heresy views the *sefirot* as powers independent of the transcendent Essence of God.

En Sof. 'Without end'. Term used for the unknowable, transcendent Essence of God.

Halakhah. The system of Jewish law. The term refers to all the details of practice, from daily observances to matters of criminal or civil law.

Hasidism. A popular movement based around mystical themes, which developed in eighteenth-century Eastern Europe. A Hasid is a person recognized for performing deeds of loving kindness, or *Hesed*.

Hebrew Bible. The 'Old Testament'. The term 'Hebrew Bible' is preferred, since Judaism does not recognize that there has been a New Testament.

Kavannah. 'Concentration'. The term refers to practices used in prayer and/or meditation to focus the mind on kabbalistic themes.

Land of Israel. Israel has always been sacred to Jews, and Jews have always lived there. The name 'Israel' is generally used of the modern state. The 'Land of Israel' is a term used to refer to this biblically specified region prior to the establishment of the modern State.

Midrash (sing.), Midrashim (pl.). Rabbinic writings which explore diverse meanings of Scripture, largely based on subtleties, or ambiguities, in the Hebrew text.

Mishkan. 'Tabernacle'. A transportable Temple which God commanded to be constructed in the wilderness, during the journey of the Children of Israel from Mount Sinai to the Land of Israel ('Canaan', the Promised Land). See *Exodus* 25ff.

Mishnah. The first written form of the oral tradition. It was redacted by Rabbi Judah ha-Nasi in the beginning of the third century CE.

Mitsvah (sing.), *mitsvot* (pl.). A command. Term used for the commands ordained in the Torah which define the system of *Halakhah*. More generally, a *mitsvah* is a good deed.

Names of God. The Names of God depict specific forms in which He has made Himself accessible. In this book, the essential four-letter Name (often translated 'Lord') is written Y-H-V-H.

Oral tradition. There are two versions of the Torah: the Written and the Oral (see below). The Oral Tradition refers to the elucidations of the Torah's meaning that were initially passed on by word of mouth only. Kabbalah is understood to be part of the Oral tradition.

Rabbis; Rabbinic Judaism. The term 'rabbi' means 'teacher', but came to be used specifically of one who is ordained. The term 'Rabbis' is used of the teachers in the formative period of post-biblical Judaism (from the second century BCE to the early Middle Ages). 'Rabbinic Judaism' is the form of Judaism that they forged, equating to 'Orthodox Judaism'.

Sefer Yetsirah. Core text of Jewish mysticism, dating from the third to the sixth century CE. Deals mainly with the mystical understanding of the Hebrew letters.

Sefirah (sing.), *sefirot* (pl.). The *sefirot* are the emanations of God. They constitute the central symbols of Kabbalah. They depict the immanence of God and define the reciprocal relationship between God and man.

Shekhinah. The 'indwelling' of God in the world. A feminine emanation of God which is the focus of the mystic's initial encounter with the Godhead.

Shema. The central declaration of Jewish faith in the Unity of God. Repeated daily in the Morning and Evening Services.

Shulhan Arukh. A code of Jewish law, written by the kabbalist Rabbi Josef Karo in the sixteenth century.

Talmud. The primary work of Rabbinic Judaism. The Talmud records the discussions of the Rabbis on elucidating the Torah and its laws. It comprises the Mishnah and the Gemara (which elaborates on the core ideas recorded in the Mishnah). There are two versions of the Talmud: the Babylonian and the Jerusalem. References in this book are to the Babylonian Talmud. The Babylonian Talmud was completed in the fifth century CE.

The Temple. The Temple in Jerusalem was the successor to the *Mishkan* as the focus for the Divine Service. King Solomon completed building the first Temple in *c*.950 BCE. This Temple was destroyed by the Babylonian king Nebuchadnezzar, in 587 BCE. A second Temple was built by returning exiles and completed in 515 BCE. This was rebuilt under Herod's rule in the first century BCE, and finally destroyed by the Roman general Titus in 70 CE.

Tikkun. 'Correction' or 'healing'. Term used in Kabbalah for the human task of correcting the imperfections in creation. *Tikkun olam* means 'healing the world'.

Torah. The revealed word of God and focus of all Jewish life. It comprises two forms: the Written Torah and the Oral Torah. The Written consists of the first five books of the Bible. The Oral includes all the traditions for elucidating the meaning of the written text.

Tree of Life. Term used for the system of ten *sefirot* and the 32 paths that interconnect them (see *Proverbs* 3:18).

Tsadik. A 'righteous' individual. The connotations of the term include uprightness, integrity and the ability to uphold a close relationship with God.

The *Zohar* (*Sefer ha-Zohar*). The primary text of Kabbalah. Attributed to the second-century Rabbi Shimon bar Yohai. First documented evidence for its existence is in thirteenth-century Spain. Elaborates on the *sefirot* and especially the symbolic expressions of the dynamic interactions between the *sefirot* in the Torah and in Jewish ritual practices.

Bibliography

Abulafia, A. (1999, 2001, 2002). From *Complete Works of Abulafia*.
   Editor A. Gross. Tel Aviv: Aharon Barzoni & Son

The *Bahir*.

   Abrams, D. (1994). *The Book Bahir: An Edition Based on the Earliest*
      Manuscripts (in Hebrew). Los Angeles, CA: Cherub Press

   Kaplan, A. (1979). The *Bahir*. York Beach, ME: Samuel Weiser, Inc.

Blumenthal, D.R. (1982). *Understanding Jewish Mysticism*. Vol 2, *The*
   Philosophic-Mystical Tradition and the Hasidic Revival. New
   York: Ktav

Idel, M. (1988a). *Kabbalah: New Perspectives*. New Haven, CT: Yale
   University Press

— (1988b). *The Mystical Experience in Abraham Abulafia*. Translated
   by J. Chipman. Albany, NY: State University of New York Press

— (1988c). *Studies in Ecstatic Kabbalah*. Albany, NY: State University
   of New York Press

— (1989). Language, Torah, and Hermeneutics in Abraham Abulafia.
   Translated by M. Kallus. Albany, NY: State University of New York
   Press

— (1990). *Golem: Jewish Magical and Mystical Traditions on the*
   Artificial Anthropoid. Albany, NY: State University of New York Press

— (1992). Reification of language in Jewish mysticism. In S.T. Katz (ed.), *Mysticism and Language*. Oxford: Oxford University Press

— (1995). *Hasidism: Between Ecstasy and Magic*. Albany, NY: State University of New York Press

— (2002). *Absorbing Perfections: Kabbalah and Interpretation*. New Haven, CT: Yale University Press

Kaplan, A. (1978). *Meditation and the Bible*. York Beach, ME: Samuel Weiser, Inc.

— (1982). *Meditation and Kabbalah*. York Beach, ME: Samuel Weiser, Inc.

— (1990). Sefer Yetzirah: The Book of Creation. York Beach, ME: Samuel Weiser, Inc.

Kramer, S.Z. (1995). Jewish meditation: healing ourselves and our relationships. In E. Hoffman (ed.), *Opening Inner Gates: New Paths in Kabbalah and Psychology*. Boston and London: Shambhala

Lancaster, B.L. (1991). *Mind, Brain and Human Potential: The Quest for an Understanding of Self*. Shaftesbury, Dorset and Rockport, MA: Element

— (1993). *The Elements of Judaism*. Shaftesbury, Dorset and Rockport, MA: Element; Brisbane: Jacaranda Wiley

— (1997a). The golem as a transpersonal image: 1. a marker of cultural change. *Transpersonal Psychology Review* 1 (3), 5–11

— (1997b). The golem as a transpersonal image: 2. psychological features in the mediaeval golem ritual. *Transpersonal Psychology Review* 1 (4), 23–30

— (2004). *Approaches to Consciousness: The Marriage of Science and Mysticism*. Basingstoke: Palgrave Macmillan

Magid, S. (2002). Origin and overcoming the beginning: Zimzum as a trope of reading in post-Lurianic Kabbala. In A. Cohen and S. Magid (eds.), *Beginning Again: Toward a Hermeneutic of Jewish Texts*. New York: Seven Bridges Press

Marcus, M.P. (1999). Computer science, the informational and Jewish mysticism. *Technology in Society* 21, 363–71

Matt, D. (1995). Ayin: the concept of nothingness in Jewish mysticism.

In L. Fine (ed.), *Essential Papers on Kabbalah*. New York: New York University Press

Scholem, G. (1946). *Major Trends in Jewish Mysticism*. New York: Schocken Books

— (1965). *On the Kabbalah and Its Symbolism*. Translated by R. Manheim. New York: Schocken Books

The *Sefer Yetsirah*.

Gruenwald, I. (1971). A preliminary critical edition of *Sefer Yezira* (in Hebrew). *Israel Oriental Studies* 1, 132–77

Kaplan, A. (1990). *Sefer Yetzirah: The Book of Creation*. York Beach, ME: Samuel Weiser, Inc.

The Talmud. Various English versions are available, e.g. the Schottenstein Edition, published by Mesorah Publications

Talmud Bavli (in Hebrew). Standard edition, 18 vols. Vilna: Re'em, 1908

Tarnas, R. (1991). *The Passion of the Western Mind: Understanding the Ideas That Have Shaped Our World View*. London: Pimlico

Tishby, I. (1949/1989). *The Wisdom of the* Zohar*: An Anthology of Texts*. 3 vols. Translated by D. Goldstein. Oxford: Oxford University Press

Weinstein, A. (1994). Sha'are Orah: *Gates of Light of Rabbi Joseph, the Son of Abraham Gikatilla*. London: HarperCollins

Wolfson, E.R. (1994). *Through a Speculum That Shines: Vision and Imagination in Medieval Jewish Mysticism*. Princeton, NJ: Princeton University Press

— (1995a). *Circle in the Square: Studies in the Use of Gender in Kabbalistic Symbolism*. Albany, NY: State University of New York Press

— (1995b). *Along the Path: Studies in Kabbalistic Myth, Symbolism, and Hermeneutics*. Albany, NY: State University of New York Press

— (2000). *Abraham Abulafia – Kabbalist and Prophet: Hermeneutics, Theosophy, and Theurgy*. Los Angeles, CA: Cherub Press

The *Zohar*. No satisfactory English edition is available. The edition translated by Matt (2004) is recommended, but is not yet complete. An excellent overview of the teachings of the *Zohar*, including selected translations, is given in Tishby (1949/1989)

Margoliot, R. (1978a). *Zohar* (in Hebrew). 6th edn, 3 vols. Jerusalem: Mosad ha-Rav Kook

— (1978b). *Zohar Hadash*. 2nd edn. Jerusalem: Mosad ha-Rav Kook

Matt, D.C. (2004). The *Zohar*. Pritzker edition. Vols. 1 and 2. Stanford, CA: Stanford University Press

INDEX